Nazi Film Melodrama

Nazi Film Melodrama

LAURA HEINS

University of Illinois Press

URBANA, CHICAGO, AND SPRINGFIELD

Library of Congress Cataloging-in-Publication Data
Heins, Laura.
Nazi film melodrama / Laura Heins.
pages   cm
Includes bibliographical references and index.
ISBN 978-0-252-03774-0 (hardcover : alk. paper) —
ISBN 978-0-252-07935-1 (pbk. : alk. paper) —
ISBN 978-0-252-09502-3 (e-book)
1. National socialism and motion pictures. 2. Motion pictures—
Germany—History. 3. Melodrama in motion pictures. I. Title.
PN1995.9.N36H45   2013
791.4302'8092243—dc23   2012045134

Contents

Acknowledgments

.

I deeply appreciate all the support I have received over the years in completing this project. I am indebted to Brigitte Peucker, from whose teaching my idea for this book first arose, for her feedback on my writing and for her valuable professional assistance and advice. I am grateful to Katie Trumpener for reading my work and giving me much needed encouragement at a crucial stage in this project. My gratitude also goes to Lutz Koepnick and Marc Silberman, who provided very useful commentary on my manuscript, and to Katerina Clark for reading an earlier version of my text. I give my thanks to Lorna Martens for her mentorship, and to Johannes Evelein, Hector Amaya, Jeffrey Grossman, Volker Kaiser, and Andrea Press for their professional support. I would also like to acknowledge Gertrud Koch, who enabled me to spend a year at the Freie Universität Berlin, as well as Noa Steimatsky for first inspiring my interest in melodrama. I am grateful to Daniel Nasset at the University of Illinois Press for his support of this project and his always helpful and efficient editorial work.

I was fortunate to receive a generous grant from the Deutscher Akademischer Austauschdienst to visit the FU Berlin and to access rare materials in Germany. The University of Virginia granted me a sabbatical from teaching that allowed me to complete this book. Thanks to Wolfgang Theis at the Deutsche Kinemathek for his friendly assistance in locating images for the manuscript. I would also like to thank Ms. Klawitter, Ms. Okrug, and all of the other archivists who assisted me during multiple visits to the Bundesarchiv, as well as the staff of the media archive at the FU Berlin.

For so much personal support over the years, I give special thanks to my family: Joel Heins, Geraldine Gail, Margaret Parks, and Michael Ehresman.

For their friendship, I thank Dan Easton, Elizabeth Floyd, Christina Gebhard, Kate Holland, Irina Kuznetsova, Patrick Macias, and Mary Katharine Tramontana. For both her friendship and her advice on this project, I am especially grateful to Masha Salazkina. For his affection and encouragement as I was completing this book, I give warm thanks to Daniel Halbheer.

Nazi Film Melodrama

Introduction

Melodrama in the Nazi Cinema: The Domestic War

The Nazi film industry, although the weapon of a regime founded on brutal militarism, produced at least ten times more domestic and romance melodramas than war films. Cinema was highly instrumentalized in the Third Reich, yet at first glance the chosen forms for the transmission of Nazi ideology may not always appear logical. How can the intense focus on the private sphere, intimate relations, female protagonists, and love in the cinema of a masculine, genocidal, imperialist state be explained? Why would the Nazis invest so heavily in a genre that, as Laura Mulvey has stated, "revolves so openly around sexuality and emotion" if the ultimate goal was to form a disciplined subject whose individual desires were completely sublimated and subjugated to the needs of the state?[1]

The most immediate answer is surely the fact that ideological work on the private, individual needs of the citizens of the Third Reich was crucial to the functioning of the Nazi system as a whole. Viewed within a totalizing model of this system, it seems evident that the emotional framework of the individual had to be continually readjusted for the fascist machine to operate; as Herbert Marcuse argued while observing Nazi Germany from exile in 1942: "In National Socialist Germany, all men are the mere appendices of the instruments of production, destruction and communication, and although these human appendices work with a high degree of initiative . . . their individual performances are entirely adjusted to the operation of the machine . . . Morale has become a part of technology."[2] The Nazis' minister of propaganda, Joseph Goebbels, attempted to engineer the film melodrama as a technology of morale as well as morality. Postwar historians and theorists have recognized, of course, that the Third Reich was not always a smoothly

functioning totalitarian system and that its morale machine sometimes mal-
functioned or began to move in unintended directions.

For these reasons, this study focuses primarily on the systematic intentions built into the Nazi melodrama while also revealing its malfunctions.
Throughout we will see that sexuality and emotion were particular obsessions
of the leaders of Nazi culture, highly problematic issues that required continual readjusting and maintenance on the screens of Third Reich cinemas.
Among the tasks of film melodrama in the Nazi state, I propose, were the
following: the management of spectator desire through a planned deployment
of the erotic, the creation of discourses of "liberation" to sell images of the
Reich nationally and abroad, and the weakening of nineteenth-century codes
of morality in favor of revised gender and familial relations to support the
future functioning of an imperialist order. As I aim to show, Nazism made
appeals to antibourgeois sentiment and attempted to initiate a reorganiza-
tion of private life while suggesting that domestic concerns must submit to
expansionist aspirations. But some elements of tradition stood in the way
of German fascism's version of modernization, and challenges surrounding
sexuality continually reappeared. The "domestic war" in the title of this in-
troduction thus refers both to the mediation between civilian life and front
warfare and to the struggle over domesticity within German fascist culture,
battles that left their marks in melodramatic films.

When considering the affinity of the melodramatic mode to propagandistic
rhetoric, the Third Reich film industry's interest in melodrama does appear
to be a logical choice. Melodrama, in its most classic form, is a binary mode
in which narratives and characters alternate between action and pathos, between vengeance and the submission to fate. Like propaganda, melodrama
describes conflict in a polemical manner, avoiding elaboration of the low-
contrast shades of facts and details. Melodrama's engagement of basic emotions and its condensation of social and economic difference into personal
conflict allow for an effective emotional appeal to the spectator. Film melodrama was thus a crucial instrument for adjusting the internal functions of
Third Reich audiences. Stories of private life work on normative systems, and
melodrama can therefore be used to diffuse emotionally charged morals that
act as models for living and contribute to action in the public sphere. As Peter
Brooks has argued, melodrama becomes particularly relevant at historical
junctures in which marked ideological conflicts must be resolved, and it does
so by defining a system of values that achieves a quasi-religious significance:
the "moral occult."[3] It is a particularly utopian mode with a fervent belief in
justice, and this sense of moral right can be defined according to a dominant
system's historically specific needs. Melodrama is especially useful at times

when traditional religious forms are to be replaced with revolutionary values. Among other uses, the Nazis employed the melodramatic weapon in their attempts to usurp the popular authority of Catholicism.

Most importantly, perhaps, classic melodramatic structures also engage elemental drives and anxieties, which account in large part for the enduring effectiveness of the mode. Pam Cook has pointed out that melodrama provides social critique through "sexualised class conflict."[4] The spectator is thus involved in ideological battles that are rewritten in libidinal terms. In personalizing class conflict, classic melodrama eroticized socioeconomic difference in the paradigmatic form of a bourgeois or lower-class girl threatened with rape by an aristocrat. According to John Cawelti, the conventions of the classic melodrama solidified around 1790, the typical pattern being a love triangle with a "virtuous young lady of some lower or ambiguous status," a villain with a higher status, and a "worthy and innocent young man . . . himself enmeshed in status difficulties."[5] Two narrative resolutions were possible: either the heroine was married to the young man once his true parentage and wealthy inheritance were rediscovered, producing in the spectator a sense of cathartic satisfaction over her union with the newly elevated hero and the suggested reconciliation of class tensions, or she succumbed to the villain and died, resulting in a tragic feeling of injustice arising from "the degradation and death of the fallen heroine" that called for real-world redress.[6] In the production of its intense affects, the classic melodrama made use of a deeply hypocritical morality, one that was later mirrored by German fascism's own perverse system: at the same time that it condemned unsanctioned sexuality, it offered to the spectator the imagination of rape and eroticized death as one of its central attractions.

Even if most of their film melodramas diverged from this conventional narrative structure, the Nazis knew how to make efficient propagandistic use of the most clichéd melodramatic devices. The most notorious example of a Nazi propaganda film, *Jud Süss* (*Jew Süss,* 1940), cast a Jewish figure as the aristocratic villain, superimposing virulent racism onto the unresolved complexes of class and gender difference derived from both eighteenth-century bourgeois tragedy and nineteenth-century sensational melodrama. In the most climactic—and by many accounts most memorable—scene of the film, the wealthy Jewish financier Süss forces the middle-class Dorothea into his bed. This scene drew on a potent reserve of erotic fantasy and social anxiety in its characterization of the Jew as a sexual and financial predator, and it reportedly had an intense effect upon contemporary audiences, eliciting outbursts of anti-Semitic hatred not only among Nazi spectators but abroad as well.[7] While it certainly drew on the anti-Semitic sentiment already deeply entrenched in Germany and in countries occupied by the Nazis during the war, it was *Jud Süss*'s strategic manipulation of erotic appeals more than its bare racist ideology that accounted for its effectiveness. By contrast, the other anti-Semitic film of the same year, the pseudo-documentary *Der ewige Jude* (*The Eternal Jew,* 1940), offered faked statistics and stark images of animal slaughter instead of rape fantasies embedded in a melodramatic narrative and failed to elicit widespread spectator interest.[8]

The case of *Jud Süss* points not only to the affinities between fascism and melodrama, but also, conversely, to the limitations of film melodrama as an instrument for ideological control. As Linda Schulte-Sasse has shown, the management of spectator desire was not absolute in *Jud Süss,* and the sexualization of the Jew in the film attractively eroticized the character for many viewers.[9] Furthermore, resolutions to melodramatic narratives are tenuous by nature, since melodrama attempts to negotiate ideological contradictions that are not reconcilable in simple terms. Schulte-Sasse has suggested that melodramatic conventions worked against the seamless transmission of Nazi ideology in Third Reich films: "many films thrive on a melodrama not necessarily accommodated to Nazi totalism, which . . . involves an exorcism of the private sphere. In other words, it could be that what works as film competes with the working of indoctrination—even if all films have ideology as their by-product."[10] Thus, generic convention at times prevented a perfect welding together of Nazi cinema's multiple aims of propaganda, commercial success, and artistic aspiration. As Schulte-Sasse hints here as well, domesticity and the individual's emotional life were challenging categories for the Nazis, since their promotion was politically undesirable yet cinematically indispensable. The Nazi melodrama was thus charged with exorcising the private sphere by means of a focus on precisely that sphere.

Another problem with melodrama is that it is a somewhat risky mode for the expression of repressive ideologies, since it conventionally takes the viewpoint of the victim. This may function effectively when the Germans are represented as victims of a foreign aggressor, as in Veit Harlan's hyperbolic war film *Kolberg* (1945). However, Nazi films in a melodramatic register are more often set in the private realm of romantic relations, in which a German lover or family member must be cast in the role of antagonist. As many scholars have emphasized, the domestic melodrama has often functioned to reveal the contradictions of bourgeois ideology, specifically those posed by patriarchy.[11] As I intend to show, Nazi romance and domestic melodramas did critique patriarchal relations, but they did so in order to explore more corporatized forms of social organization rather than to support any genuinely emancipatory concept of feminine subjectivity.

As a result of its complex relationship to ideology, melodrama has been a particularly fascinating film form for theorists and historians of various national cinemas. Since it so clearly deals with social contradictions, it potentially allows for the expression of system-contrary critique. When defined as a female-centered genre, melodrama gives voice to women's concerns in a manner that may undermine patriarchal or fascist designs. Marcia Landy has suggested that film melodramas in Fascist Italy provided more instances of covert ideological critique than more realist works by means of their dualistic structures, or as she says, by "dramatizing the contradictions of immediate life under fascism."[12] Pam Cook, when writing about classical Hollywood melodrama, has argued that the genre is by nature ideologically fissured, specifically at the point of sexuality: "in order to appeal to a female spectator, melodrama must first posit the possibility of female desire, and a female point-of-view, thus posing problems for itself which it can scarcely contain."[13] As a result, melodramas often indulge in moments of stylistic excess that some theorists may interpret as instances of ideologically subversive distanciation effects, since such excess functions to place the spectator at a distance from the overt ideology of the films' narratives and to undermine conservative narrative closures.[14]

Third Reich melodramas, like their classical Hollywood and Italian Fascist counterparts, attempted to negotiate multiple ideological contradictions and to address the conflicting demands of spectators, resulting in filmic texts that are sometimes fractured and stylistically excessive. Stylistic excess and the management of spectator emotion were constant problems for the Nazis, and some melodramatic film projects did threaten to evade the minister of propaganda's total oversight. However, even when stylistic excess does point symptomatically to the complex ideological work of Nazi films, the melodramatic mode of much of Nazi cinema ultimately does not negate its propagandistic effects. Unlike Landy's understanding of the melodrama in Fascist Italy, I do not view the Nazi melodrama as essentially subversive. Indeed, as I intend to demonstrate, it is precisely those moments in Nazi films that have sometimes appeared covertly oppositional to film historians that are central to certain Nazi ideological strategies—namely, the moments in which Third Reich melodramas offer eroticized images with liberatory or antibourgeois overtones.

At this point it is important to note that definitions of what exactly constitutes melodrama and which works should be placed in this once maligned category vary widely. By some accounts melodrama is a mode rather than a genre, a form that narratives of any genre or medium may take.[15] Peter Brooks, for one, has defined it as a mode marked by a hyperbolic style and a concern for ethical imperatives, a mode that was implemented as much in the novels of Henry James as in the films of D. W. Griffith.[16] In postwar scholarship the association of melodrama with women's spectatorship has been enduring and had led to a continual collapsing of melodrama into the "woman's film," thereby viewing melodrama as a genre marked by conventions of narrative, setting, and spectator address.[17] As other scholars insist, however, the melodramatic mode applies as much to the "male" genres of Western and crime film as to genres that are conventionally addressed to female spectators.[18]

In selecting films for closer analysis in this study, I chose to concentrate on the areas where the woman's film and the melodramatic mode overlap, with some consideration of the "male dynastic" melodrama as well. Rather than examining the melodramatic elements in all of Nazi cinema, I focus on films that are principally concerned with romantic and familial relations, even when these are set against a backdrop of the public spheres of work and warfare. I proceed from a definition of melodrama that centers on the following basic traits: a preoccupation with sexuality and emotion, a focus on protagonists who are called upon to make dualistic choices about romance or parenting, a concern for the conflict between individual desire and social norms, a mood of pathos underlined by an expressive use of music and mise-en-scène, and a strong appeal to the identificatory and empathetic responses of the spectator.[19] Following this understanding of melodrama, I view it in this study more as a genre or complex of genres than as a mode. In further dividing Nazi melodrama into the subgenres of romance melodrama (chapter 2), domestic melodrama (chapter 3), and home front melodrama (chapter 4), I explore the particular ideological negotiations at work in each category.

Another key concept that is used throughout this book and that should be clarified here is "German fascism," a term I have chosen to use alongside the term "Nazism" because it supports both the comparative nature of this study and my stress on the negotiation of cultural modernity in Third Reich film melodramas. Although the term has not been frequently used in film studies scholarship since the 1980s because of its resonances with Marxist criticism, it has been given new relevance in recent historiography of twentieth-century Europe. Historians who have returned to the consideration of Nazism as a variety of generic fascism have similarly emphasized that Nazism was a revolutionary-utopian movement that claimed as its mission a radical cultural renewal in order to rescue Europe from the decay supposedly precipitated by late nineteenth-century bourgeois society. As historian Roger Griffin has repeatedly argued, Nazism did not advocate the conservation of traditional forms of life, but was rather a hypermodern movement that sought to blend archaic or mythic elements with the technocratic organization of a future-oriented and imperialist society. In this respect German fascism shared much with other forms of fascism, all of which claimed to provide an alternative model of modernity to that offered by Western democratic liberalism and Soviet communism.[20] This understanding of German fascism, as Griffin has also emphasized, does not seek to relativize the crimes of Germans during the Third Reich or to downplay the Hitler regime's peculiarly extreme racism, but rather to highlight the supranational implications of Nazism. Such a perspective, I propose, is particularly relevant to a study of Third Reich cinema, an industry with pan-European aspirations, and to a focus on sexuality and family politics in Nazi culture, since these were particularly problematic aspects of German fascism's project of alternative modernization.[21] Furthermore, the historian upon whose work this study most relies, Dagmar Herzog, has similarly made use of the term "German fascism" in her revised account of sexuality in the Third Reich.[22]

Early scholarship on the cinema of the Third Reich elaborated its explicit propaganda functions, concentrating on the most notorious films that aimed to legitimate racism and glorify war, militarism, and the *Führerprinzip*. Such studies drew portraits of Nazi cinema as an institution of mass manipulation and indoctrination, with a form that was clearly different from other national cinemas.[23] Most work on films of the Third Reich conducted since the 1990s, however, has taken a more nuanced approach and has examined indoctrination and popular entertainment as inseparable elements, highlighting the previously neglected question of spectator pleasure. Recent scholarship has repeatedly shown that Nazi cinema shared much with Hollywood and thus with the classical cinema of virtually all Western, industrialized countries of the first half of the twentieth century.[24] The search for a definition of Nazi cinema's specificity now requires that it be viewed in relation to others rather than as a historically, geographically, and ideologically isolated phenomenon. Leaning on this recognition, a recent strand of scholarship on Nazi cinema has been concerned with the study of stardom and fan culture, particularly the study of female stars.[25] Such studies have succeeded in defining how even highly ambiguous and cosmopolitan images of femininity were recruited to serve Nazi ideological and aesthetic programs, though they sometimes inadvertently undermined propagandists' intentions as well.

Regardless of these trends, few books have tried to undertake direct comparative analyses of Nazi films with their Hollywood generic counterparts; thus the specifically fascist nature of Nazi films remains an open question, and one that I propose should not yet be closed.[26] A central goal of this book is to distill the differences between melodrama in the Nazi cinema and in Hollywood. The Nazis, of course, were not particularly inventive, and their adaptation of already well-established patterns to their own political needs does make up the major part of Nazi cinema's specificity. Yet I do proceed from the assumption that significant specificities may be located on the level of form as well in narrative. However, when I describe formal and ideological differences between Nazi melodramas and classical Hollywood melodramas at various points throughout this book, it should be understood that I am not arguing for a transhistorical concept of a fascist aesthetic common to the cinemas of all fascist countries in all time periods, and visible *only* in the cinemas of fascist countries. As Susan Sontag noted in her seminal article on fascist aesthetics, the formal patterns that characterize Leni Riefenstahl's films can likewise be found in Hollywood and in Soviet cinema.[27] Furthermore, as I show in chapter 1, the negative reception of Italian Fascist melodramas in the Third Reich undermines the notion of a universal fascist aesthetic, even if the regime's insistence on the superiority of the German cinema over the Italian was largely motivated by its desire to dominate the European market. Nonetheless, there were ideological similarities between the German and Italian varieties of fascism, particularly in their parallel visions of an alternative modernity, yet the means of expressing fascist propensities were not always identical.

My account of Nazi melodrama throughout the individual chapters in this book highlights several stylistic and thematic trends that were both relatively consistent over the twelve years of the Third Reich and distinct from comparable Hollywood melodramas. Following a comparison of the generic status, spectatorship discourses, and aesthetics of melodrama in Nazi cinema and Hollywood in the first chapter, I present side-by-side analyses in chapters 1 and 4 of Hollywood films that were contemporaneous with German productions and that are thematically similar. In doing so I attempt to locate the moments in which the German films exceed or elude the patterns visible in the Hollywood films. In chapters 2 and 3 I take a larger look at Nazi melodramas but refer throughout to the conventions for these genres that were established by the classical Hollywood cinema. As we will see, the formal structure of Nazi melodrama was an impoverished facsimile of classical Hollywood style, but with a generally more restrained use of those stylistic markers that constitute melodramatic hyperbole, except for a few notably excessive films that are also discussed in chapters 2 and 3.[28] More substantial differences between Nazi and Hollywood melodramas are revealed in their ideological scaffoldings, particularly in their visions of domesticity. From the very beginning of the Third Reich, film melodramas depicted modernized attitudes toward gender roles and sexual morality, although the fascist modernity presented in such films was one that supposedly had been cleansed of all "decadent" cultural elements such as feminism.

Film scholars who have written about Nazi melodramas have often struggled to explain the ideological ambiguities apparent in many Nazi films with female central protagonists, and a few scholars have raised the possibility of subtly oppositional intent on the part of melodramatic directors.[29] Helmut Käutner, for example, has been cited by scholars as the central representative of a Third Reich "aesthetic opposition" (an interpretation that my own discussion of a Käutner film in chapter 3 argues against).[30] More often, however, scholars of Third Reich cinema have posited that melodramas that appear to undermine nuclear family relations by inviting identification with protagonists who escape traditional gender and familial roles are structured in a highly duplicitous manner as spectatorial traps. Some have explained ambiguities in individual film texts with an "inoculation" model similar to that of Roland Barthes and Fredric Jameson.[31] As Barthes wrote in *Mythologies*: "One immunizes the contents of the collective imagination by means of a small inoculation of acknowledged evil; one thus protects it against the risk of a generalized subversion."[32] Following either the inoculation metaphor or the concept of distraction or enchantment, scholars have typically argued that Nazi melodramas allowed for a limited amount of ideological contradiction via a parallel reality of wish fulfillment in order to ultimately indoctrinate against individualized desire and to more effectively fulfill apparent Nazi goals.[33] Key in this view is the assumption that the ultimate aim of Nazi melodrama was to reinforce the status quo of patriarchal family structures.

Unlike in most past approaches to the topic of melodrama in the Third Reich, I suggest that there is something else underlying the discrepancies between the Nazis' public pronouncements regarding private life in the Third Reich and the design of their films. Many moments of seeming contradiction in Nazi melodramas were actually indicative of tendencies within Nazism itself. Thus, filmic ambiguities should not be considered small acts of directorial sabotage. What appear to be spaces of freedom, moments of subversion, or ideological inconsistencies in films of the Third Reich were not just limited concessions to the enemy intended to make the fascist attack all the more effective by containing subversive tendencies from within, but were often instances of the Nazi attack itself. And cultural tendencies publicly pronounced as detrimental by the Nazi leadership were sometimes privately cultivated as desirable, giving rise to the seemingly contradictory economy of desire that was evident in Nazi melodramas.

Contrary to what has been surmised by many film scholars, Nazi cinema did not generally aim to reinforce the status quo of the nuclear family and argue for a return to pre-twentieth-century gender roles. Instead, the discourse of liberation in Nazi melodramas, film writing, and popular media supported an image of the Nazi state as dynamic and revolutionary, in which a repressive bourgeois past was supposedly being overcome through the stimulated "performance" of the fascist individual. Nazi cinema certainly owed a debt to eighteenth- and nineteenth-century bourgeois culture, and as Linda Schulte-Sasse has shown, Nazi culture defined itself in opposition to pre-Enlightenment aristocratic values in many historical films.[34] As we will see in chapters 2 and 3, however, Nazi cinema also continually argued against bourgeois morality, promising intensified forms of experience outside the confines of the home and presenting a quasi-Nietzschean challenge to middle-class mores and Christian sexual codes. The melodrama, the genre of domesticity, was used by the Nazis in a genre-contradictory manner in order to challenge the private sphere. The antibourgeois undercurrent of many Nazi melodramas exceeds the critique of the family that is evident in most contemporaneous Hollywood films. As is elaborated in chapter 4, the Hollywood wartime melodrama in particular was more invested in the maintenance of nuclear family values than was the Nazi equivalent.

While diverging from the "inoculation" model of ideological engineering, I also stress a different approach to the issue of spectator address than has been most often offered in scholarship of Nazi cinema. Recognizing an increased attention to Hollywood's transnational influence, recent studies have shown that Nazi cinema's attractions were common to all popular cinema.[35] Films of the Third Reich appealed to basic drives, including utopian wishes for harmony and fantasies of freedom and personal fulfillment. However, most scholars have argued that Nazi cinema was fundamentally repressive of erotic drives. Sontag's emphasis on sexual repression in her description of fascist aesthetics has been very influential in this regard. Leni Riefenstahl's films, Sontag wrote, evidence a "utopian aesthetics" that "implies an ideal eroticism; sexuality converted into the magnetism of leaders and the joy of followers. The fascist ideal is to transform sexual energy into a 'spiritual' force, for the benefit of the community ... a heroic repression of the sexual impulse."[36] In accordance with Sontag's analysis of Riefenstahl's style, there has been a widespread conception that Nazi feature films are likewise based upon the repression of spectator desire and are thus deeply prudish. However, historians and film scholars have recently taken a closer look at the discrepancy between official Nazi rhetoric and the often hypocritical practices of both policy and image making and have determined that this view has been erroneous.[37] As historian Dagmar Herzog has asserted, "the Nazis also used sexuality to consolidate their appeal ... We simply cannot understand why Nazism was attractive to so many people if we focus only on its sexually repressive aspects."[38] Goebbels consciously recruited erotic and material pleasures to propagandistic effects, doing so through appeals to an ideal of liberation rather than repression—even if these appeals were ultimately intended to increase spectator allegiance to an imperialist system and voluntary individual participation in the Nazi projects of mass warfare, enslavement, and genocide. Thus, following Dagmar Herzog's reevaluation of sex under German fascism, I steer away from the repression hypothesis when looking at the treatment of sexuality in Nazi melodramas. I would also like to emphasize, in opposition to Michel Foucault's assertion in his own rewriting of the history of sexuality in the West, that the "Hitlerite politics of sex" were not in fact an "insignificant practice."[39]

These politics were not universally effective, as I argue, but not because of any desexualization in Nazi cinema. On the contrary, the management of spectator desire sometimes failed because of what was perceived as an excessive eroticization of Nazi culture. Nazi cinema was measurably successful, in foreign markets as well as domestically, but skirmishes over the content and form of Nazi melodramas repeatedly broke out in the Reich. Nazi films sold visions of modern life, designed for the tastes of Berlin audiences, which were often too modern for many rural and religious spectators. Drawing upon the available evidence of the leadership's designs for and spectator responses to Nazi films, this study reveals the particularities of Nazi melodrama, as well as the historically specific points of negotiation between Nazi cinematic strategy and the sometimes unintentional effects and resistances in the field of spectatorship.

With this analysis it is not my intention to further contribute to the sinister fascination with fascism and dangerous re-eroticization of Nazism in postmodern culture that Susan Sontag very correctly criticized. Like many scholars before me, I would like to emphasize that spectators in the Third Reich were encouraged to conceptualize a murderous political system and a vicious imperialistic war in personally desirable terms. Furthermore, I would like to make it clear at the outset that this study is not intended as an argument in defense of Christian sexual morality and should not be understood as a conservative critique of Nazi cinema. My objective here is not to implicate progressive attempts at restructuring familial and sexual relations, but rather the opposite. I do not intend to argue that Nazism was in any way revolutionary or empowering, only that it sometimes advertised itself as such; this study thus highlights the false revolutionary rhetoric of Nazism, its spurious appeals to liberation. Like many right-wing movements today, German fascism's relationship to sex and the private sphere was deeply hypocritical.[40] As we will see, even when Third Reich films (in opposition to much official Nazi rhetoric) promoted women's work and female higher education, a selectively permissive attitude regarding sexuality, a reorientation of gender imagery toward the androgynous, and nontraditional family structures including single motherhood, they did not support female emancipation. It is only because these aspects of cultural modernization were most expedient in times of imperialist expansion that they found their way into the film melodrama of German fascism. Nazism's attack on bourgeois morality did not aim at the genuine liberation of women (or men), but placed all in the service of a more efficient and deadly war machine.

1. An Aesthetics of Aggression: German Fascist vs. Classical Hollywood Melodrama

Melodrama, as Linda Williams asserts, is the "fundamental mode of popular American moving pictures."[1] According to this account, almost all Hollywood films can be considered melodramatic, including "male genres" such as Westerns, war films, film noir, and action films. Melodrama, of course, can also be considered the fundamental mode of fascist film. Nazi cinema, like Italian Fascist cinema, tended toward simplification and dualistic perspectives. The Nazi propaganda minister disapproved of film scripts in which conflicts were not clearly and simply drawn. Characters in Third Reich film projects had to represent primary social functions and be immediately legible types rather than complex individuals. Film, according to Goebbels, should not speak to the intellect, and melodrama's concentrated affects were well suited to elaborating clear moral choices and embodying these in characters of limited complexity. One of the telling ways that Goebbels expressed his disapproval of films was to dismiss them as "literature," which implied a deemphasizing of emotional effect in favor of a more ambiguous portrait of character psychology.[2]

Despite the disdain that virtually all fascists displayed toward femininity, the melodrama as a genre was no less privileged in Nazi cinema than it was in Hollywood of the classical era. In both cinemas, films now considered "women's pictures" were often accorded the highest budgets and the greatest recognition by film reviewers and audiences. However, romance and domestic melodramas were not viewed by Nazi filmmakers and party leaders as being primarily for female audiences; the concept of gendered spectatorship, and particularly of gendered genres, was less developed in Germany in the 1930s and '40s than in the United States at the same time. Consequently, melodramatic affect was not viewed by the Nazis as thoroughly tainted by effeminacy.

This does not mean that their relationship to the genre was entirely non-conflicted. On the one hand, melodrama was granted a privileged status in the Third Reich; on the other, there were constant efforts to contain the risks inherent in melodramatic excess. Goebbels was vigilant about not allowing melodrama to go too far, for fear that the very same narrative and formal devices that produced desirable spectator effects could, when exaggerated, become alienation devices that could interrupt the process of ideological interpellation by making the spectator aware of the workings of the filmic text. Pathos, while necessary, could easily be overdosed. Goebbels felt that the American film melodrama delivered exactly the right dose, while the Italian Fascist melodrama failed to conform to an ideal Nazi aesthetics. The Third Reich melodrama was thus to be largely modeled after Hollywood examples.

However, there were a few significant stylistic distinctions between German melodrama of the period and its American counterpart. Hollywood cinema's greater emphasis on the communicative codes of mise-en-scène, dynamic editing, and camera movement was countered in Nazi cinema with a greater stress on bodily displays and a theatrical acting style that subordinated the intimacy of the face in close-up to the authority of the actor's voice and scripted dialogue. As we will see in a comparative analysis of a characteristic Nazi melodrama, *Der Postmeister* (1940), with the Hollywood film *Anna Karenina* (1935) at the end of this chapter, subtle formal and narrative differences in the Nazi melodrama encouraged a more aggressive form of voyeurism than was common in the Hollywood melodrama, in accordance with the Nazis' recruiting of romance to support imperial expansion in the east. Instead of the masochistic aesthetic of many Hollywood melodramas, therefore, the Nazi melodrama distinguished itself by its formally encoded appeals to spectatorial sadism and by the masculinity of its pathos.

Film Genre, Gender, and Spectatorship in the Third Reich

According to Thomas Schatz, the melodrama, the comedy, and the musical are "genres of integration," and war, action, and crime films are "genres of order."[3] Whereas the latter allows for a violent removal of adversaries or threats to the social system, the former tends toward their reeducation and a more subtle reestablishment of harmony. Surprisingly, perhaps, the Nazis generally found cinematic integration more useful than order—or at least more popular. Overall, the feature film production of the Third Reich was composed of approximately 76 percent of the first category (genres of integration) and 17 percent of the second (genres of order), and about 30 percent of all films produced in the Third Reich were melodramas.[4] Almost all films of the Third Reich fulfilled some kind of propagandistic or ideological function, but some were more recognizable to contemporary audiences as explicitly political films, and the number of these was (arguably) quite small.[5]

Likewise, there is much evidence that melodramas were not recognized as such at the time. The term "melodrama" was rarely used in the Third Reich; instead, terms like "dramatic fate" or "tragedy" were sometimes employed in descriptions of films in a melodramatic register. However, the avoidance of the term "melodrama" did not so much indicate an inferior status of the mode as an underdeveloped concept of cinematic genres during the Third Reich; the Nazis made extensive use of melodramatic conventions without attempting to theorize a genre taxonomy or hierarchy. In contemporary film reviews, general descriptions were given in the form of plot synopses, but there was usually no attempt to categorize films in generic types. The Reich Film Archive did make use of categories when compiling a catalogue of films from 1933 to 1942, but these were remarkably vague; melodramas were described by terms such as "dramatic narrative film," "serious entertainment film," or "historical narrative film."[6] The lack of genre theory led to an inability to adequately describe differences in narrative type and emotional register among individual films. This suggests that the production of films in the Third Reich followed a somewhat random pattern rather than a carefully planned proportion of films according to intended audience. It was not until after the war that a systematic genre categorization of films from the Third Reich was attempted.[7]

Following postwar classifications, it is evident that the distribution of melodramatic subgenres in the Third Reich differed from classical Hollywood cinema. The maternal melodrama and the family melodrama, both core subgenres for American cinema of the 1930s through the 1950s, were far less significant in terms of production numbers for Nazi cinema than the love story, the subgenre that made up the majority of Third Reich melodramatic production.[8] The *Heimatfilm,* a romance or family melodrama that celebrates rural life, is specific to the German cinema and has no genuine Hollywood equivalent (though it was a less significant subgenre in the Third Reich than in the postwar era of Konrad Adenauer.[9]) Likewise, several Hollywood melodramatic subgenres were missing in the cinema of the Third Reich, and these absences reveal some distinctions between the Nazi uses of melodrama and those of American cinema. The American "medical discourse" melodrama— in which a woman afflicted with physical or mental illness becomes the object of study and the erotic interest of a male doctor who attempts to unravel her mystery and cure her—was virtually impossible to copy in the Third Reich, since the Nazis had more interest in eliminating than curing the sick; the film that stands perhaps closest to Hollywood melodramas like *Dark Victory* (1939) and *Now, Voyager* (1942) is the notorious euthanasia film *Ich klage an* (*I Accuse,* 1941). The "medical discourse" film, as Mary Ann Doane has outlined it, was a result of the explosion of interest in psychoanalysis in America during the 1940s.[10] No comparable interest in solving the riddles of feminine desire and its repression could be found in Germany at the same time. Freud was banned by the Nazis, and German exiles, who had explored psychoanalysis in Weimar films, took the subject to Hollywood.

There was also no genuine equivalent of gothic melodramas such as *Rebecca* (1940), *Suspicion* (1941), and *Gaslight* (1944) in the cinema of the Third Reich.[11] According to Tania Modleski, such films expressed a paranoid consciousness and spoke to the fantasies of women who suffered from the nuclear family structures that were romanticized in the majority of classical Hollywood features. Modleski connects the renewed popularity of gothic melodramas in 1940s Hollywood to women's wartime experiences, chiefly to a fear of what would happen when men returned from war and reassumed their positions as head (or tyrant) of the household and workplace.[12] In Germany such paranoid visions were rarely so openly expressed. Furthermore, as we will see in the next chapters, the image of the nuclear family was generally less stable in the Reich than in the United States, and there was ultimately less risk that German men would return from the war, particularly after 1942. The absence of the gothic melodrama also coincided with an extreme scarcity of the mode of horror in the cinema of the Third Reich.[13] The Nazis had little tolerance for the uncanny, and even the fantastic was repudiated in favor of an unambiguous classicism. Hitler disapproved of all forms of the gothic as tainted with religiosity; as Goebbels wrote: "The Führer is a man who is completely antiquity-oriented. He hates Christianity . . . What a difference there is between a gloomy cathedral and a bright, free antique temple. He wants clarity, brightness, beauty. That is also the ideal of our time. In this respect, the Führer is a totally modern man."[14] Even the Third Reich film melodrama was expected to convey an impression of transparency, in concert with fascist modernity's revival of the imperial style of antiquity. Accordingly, even melodramas were supposed to conform to Nazi cinema's compulsory optimism and to avoid too much "effeminate" gloom and rumination by stressing the heroic value of sacrifice.

It is a common assumption today that family melodramas and romance films address themselves primarily to female spectators, while crime and action films are "male" genres. The gendering of narrative types has led to a hierarchy of genres along male/female lines: while the "male" action genre has taken its privileged position as the big-budget blockbuster and is thus the very prototype of postclassical Hollywood cinema, romance films are relegated to a special-interest ghetto. Similarly, the gender divisions and their accompanying quality labels are still in force in popular thinking about classical Hollywood cinema: while film noir has been elevated to the status of art, 1930s and '40s romances remain low-culture kitsch. Scholarship of the last forty years has certainly done much work to rescue melodrama from its earlier critical dismissal as trivial, and the label "woman's film" has become a productive critical category.[15] For most cinemagoers, though, it remains a derogatory designation.

However, this genre hierarchy is a relatively recent invention, as Stephen Neale has shown. According to his study of film reviews in industry journals of the 1930s to 1950s, the classical Hollywood melodrama was by no means considered an inferior form by producers or critics, and the term "melodrama" was not employed in a negative or derogatory sense, as it often is in contemporary film reviews. According to Neale, melodrama was also not identified exclusively or even primarily with female spectators: the prison drama *The Big House* (1930), for example, was called a "virile realist melodrama" by the contemporary reviewer.[16] Even maternal melodramas were not seen as trivial, B-list productions at the time of their original release; rather, films such as *Stella Dallas* (1937) were considered "prestige projects" by their producers.[17]

Similarly, melodrama was not considered a trivial or inferior form in the Third Reich either but was actually privileged in many respects. Indeed, some of the highest production budgets were invested in love stories starring Zarah Leander. As Felix Moeller has pointed out, melodramas had the deepest effect on Goebbels personally.[18] The language Goebbels used to describe his reactions to films suggests that he saw melodramas as producing the most intense and most politically desirable spectator effects. Goebbels often wrote that he was "moved" (*ergriffen*), "swept away" (*mitgerissen*), or "spellbound" (*hingerissen*) by a film, all words that connote a violently imposed emotion, a forcefully "moving" experience that only the melodramatic mode is capable of producing.[19] Likewise, Third Reich film reviewers sometimes praised films by calling them "distressing" (*erschütternd*),[20] and this positive valuing of the experience of shock or distress suggests a sensationalism that is at the heart of melodrama. Although he was not particularly articulate or consistent in his judgments, Goebbels's comments on film suggest that, for him, melodrama also had the highest aesthetic potential. In his March 1933 "Kaiserhof" speech, Goebbels praised the 1927 Greta Garbo melodrama *Anna Karenina* (alternatively titled *Love*) for delivering purely cinematic art and proving that film is not a debased "surrogate of theater," and he proposed the Hollywood production as a model for Third Reich filmmakers to copy.[21]

The fact that Goebbels was particularly moved by Garbo melodramas proves that, according to his thinking, films with female main protagonists did not preclude male spectator identifications. Like classical Hollywood producers and critics who could describe a film as a "virile melodrama," the Nazis also did not think of melodrama as a form for women only. In fact, there is little evidence that they generally thought of genres as gendered, even if they did feel that male and female spectatorship were somehow different. Some films were certainly planned with female spectators in mind, but they were rarely advertised openly as "women's films." On the contrary, melodramas were marketed to both genders, and some love stories were apparently more warmly received by male than by female viewers. Veit Harlan's *Immensee* (1943) is a well-known example of a romance melodrama that was very popular with male viewers, especially soldiers, although this sentimental tale features a female protagonist caught in a love triangle with two men and it celebrates feminine self-sacrifice. Kristina Söderbaum, the film's star, referred to *Immensee* as a film that "gave male spectators the most," and she added that it appealed to adolescent males in particular.[22] Correspondingly, Astrid Pohl's study on melodrama in the Third Reich has identified a whole sub-genre of "men's melodramas."[23] Third Reich crime films, on the other hand, often feature female main protagonists, and the crime film was by no means considered an exclusively male genre as it often was in Hollywood. Even war films were apparently supposed to appeal to female spectators. Battle- and war-related historical films were shown to girls during the compulsory film screenings of the League of German Girls (Bund Deutscher Mädel, or BDM), as well as to boys in the Hitler Youth (Hitlerjugend, or HJ).[24]

In general, Nazi cinema aimed to be universal and to appeal to spectators of both sexes and all regions of the Reich, yet spectators did not always react to films as the propaganda minister intended. The issue of spectator response became even more crucial after 1939, since, as Goebbels said, cinema and the good moods it manufactured were "decisive to the outcome of the war."[25] Starting in October 1939, the Security Service (the Sicherheitsdienst, or SD) of the Schutzstaffel (SS) provided Goebbels and other leaders with reports on the opinions and morale of the civilian populace. Many of the spies were placed in cinema seats; an important section of these reports concerned reactions to newsreel and feature films. The SD noted the differing reactions of men and women as well as regional variances in responses. Based on these reports, Goebbels recognized that the reception of films was not uniform and that spectator response could not be entirely planned, but this fact often took him by surprise. As late as 1942, for example, he noted in regard to an SD report: "I get word from various cities that the film *Die Entlassung* [*The Dismissal*, 1942] is not enjoying the sort of success in certain sectors of the population that we expected from it. It is a typical men's film, and because it doesn't represent any real women's conflicts, it is generally being rejected by women . . . when one measures it by a higher standard, it doesn't seem to completely fulfill the hopes that we initially had for it."[26] Although Goebbels does speak here about "men's film," suggesting some awareness of gender differences in spectatorship, he also reveals his previous expectation that one film could successfully speak to all viewers. His comments furthermore reveal his somewhat limited grasp on audience film preferences. The leaders of the Nazi regime were clearly preoccupied with the effectiveness of their propaganda efforts, but there was little empirical audience research conducted during the Third Reich, in contrast to the United States. Hollywood studio heads were regularly informed about audience opinions through Gallup polls and preview screening interviews, and they would alter films accordingly. Because of the general Nazi hostility toward "democratic" methods of opinion polling, the SD reports were more anecdotal than systematic.[27]

Consequently, few reliable statistics exist on the percentage of female spectators in Third Reich cinema audiences, and information about their preferences is sparse. One survey was conducted in 1944 in an attempt to discover which films were preferred by young German audiences, and included responses by 1,260 girls and 686 boys who were members of the BDM and HJ. The survey's author, A. U. [Anneliese Ursula] Sander, listed the film titles most popular among the youth in aggregate and did not distinguish between titles preferred by girls and those favored by boys. She did, however, find that girls under eighteen went to the cinema far less frequently than boys: while only 14 percent of girls went to the cinema regularly (fifty times per year or more), 38 percent of boys went an average of once per week.[28] After age eighteen, Sander added, girls began to go to the cinema more frequently. Sander's study says little about female viewing preferences in general, but it does suggest that the notion of a widespread feminine *Kinosucht* (cinema addiction), which had given high culture proponents so much concern during the Wilhelmine and Weimar eras, was largely fiction. Sander's study coincides with the findings of Emilie Altenloh's 1914 survey of German cinema spectators, which stated that women overall went to the cinema less frequently than men.[29] Against Siegfried Kracauer's conception of the "little shopgirls" who made up the cinema masses, Altenloh's statistics showed that it was primarily the little shop and office boys, the young men of the petit bourgeois class, who were addicted to film and who also went to see melodramas.[30] Supporting these conclusions were a few studies conducted during the Third Reich that, although limited in scope, showed that women were often too overburdened with their double duties of paid work and housework to attend films frequently; rural women and middle-age women in particular went to the cinema less often than their male counterparts.[31] Thus, the notion of cinema audiences as being predominantly female, a claim that was often made by American commentators in the 1930s and 1940s and repeated by a few Nazi journalists, was not entirely correct.

Journalists and academics in the Third Reich shared some views of female spectatorship with American researchers, though their ideas of gendered spectatorship were less clearly defined. In a 1938 article in the *Film-Kurier,* Walter Panofsky, a professor at the Institute for Film Studies at the University of Munich, referenced both American surveys of film audiences and a small survey of German female spectators and concluded: "Generally, it could be said that female viewers demand the dream world of film much more often than men. Particularly the comments gathered in medium and small theaters proved that the episodic representation of a housewife cleaning her apartment—thus a representation of her daily work—was often rejected by means of appropriate statements ('But I see that every day!')."[32] Panofsky contrasted this female rejection of representations of quotidian realities with the enthusiastic reactions of male railway employees to a film set in their own work world, the crime film *Gleisdreieck* (*Rail Triangle,* 1937). He therefore suggested that men were more open to realism, but women primarily sought escapism through a mise-en-scène of artifice. This was also the dominant opinion of the time among American producers and critics, though the American commentators tended to stress the consumerist motivations behind female spectator pleasure more heavily. In a 1939 book, for example, American critic Margaret F. Thorp wrote about female spectators in a characteristically contemptuous tone:

> What the adult American female chiefly asks of the movies is the opportunity to escape by reverie from an existence which she finds insufficiently interesting. Better ways of enriching her life, society has not yet taught her . . . The adult female goes to the movies as she reads luxury advertising, so that she may be familiar with the ultimate in Fisher bodies and sable coats . . . Beauty, luxury, and love, those are to her the desirata of life and, being either overworked or indolent, her idea of bliss is to attain them practically without effort.[33]

While similarly condescending opinions could no doubt be found among German film producers, the view of female spectatorship was less consistent in the Third Reich. As Sabine Hake has shown, the Nazis generally dismissed women, but at the same time they were often seen as ideal spectators: "Identified with an unhealthy emotionalism and a lack of critical detachment, they personified the failures in the balancing act between fantasy and reality. On the other hand, women were often chosen to embody the audience in its purest, most desirable form."[34]

Critical detachment was not what was desired from spectators in the Third Reich, and emotionalism was by no means considered entirely unwelcome. Five months after Hitler took power, the ideologically conformist film journal *Der Film* ran an article on the question of female spectatorship and emotional response titled "She Cries in the Cinema." The article cited letters to the editor about the concerns of a man whose wife appeared to have excessive reactions to films (though the wording suggests that the letters may have been written by the editorial staff themselves, who in any case supported the opinions presented in them). A typical letter, from a Dr. K. in Rostock, read: "If you look at it completely objectively, you should be happy that you have such a strongly emotional, and therefore truly feminine wife. The ability to experience film and theater action in a lively, concentrated manner is absolutely commendable . . . Men have and need feelings too, and the manly man is even superior to the feminine woman when it comes to the depth and persistence of his emotional life . . . In some circumstances, tears are in no way shameful, even for the male hero."[35] In this characteristic example, tears and intense identification were valued as appropriate spectator responses. The Nazi leadership also viewed emotionalism as advantageous. Hitler, as is well known, thought of the masses as essentially feminine and thus easily manipulable, as did Mussolini.[36] However, not only the masses but also "the people"—a much more positively connoted category for the Nazis—were described by Hitler as feminized: "The people [*das Volk*] is in its vast majority so feminine in its inclinations and opinions that it is emotional sensation rather than sober reflection that determines its thoughts and actions," as he wrote in *Mein Kampf*.[37] Since the German populace was considered to be constituted by men and women of essentially irrational natures, melodrama appeared to be a particularly appropriate form for popular film art (*Volkskunst*). Melodramas, the Nazis believed, would address the people through their most common desires rather than through sober and abstract rhetoric.

Correspondingly, Pierre Cadars has suggested that melodrama's manipulation of desire and its emphasis on sacrifice and passive suffering make it uniquely suited for use by totalitarian systems, that melodrama and fascism share an intimate relationship: "the melodrama diffuses a moral of resignation to superior forces that is not so different from the politics of submission which every dictatorship assumes."[38] This suggests, however, that melodrama's emphasis on pathos over action works to neutralize critical energies rather than to manufacture active support for moral, or ideological, systems: passive resignation follows, but not necessarily a passionate attachment to "superior forces."

Thomas Schatz has also emphasized the tone of resignation inherent in melodrama. Melodrama, he says, is comedy's inverse: whereas comedy deals with the transgression of social conventions, melodrama shows resignation to them.[39] Yet melodrama is also heavily concerned with transgression, even if its protagonists almost always fail in their attempts to achieve personal freedom. Ultimately, comedy's transgressions may also be more controlled and its effects generally more reliable than that of melodrama. In terms of production numbers, the Third Reich did invest more heavily in comedy than in melodrama. Karsten Witte has described comedy's function in the Third Reich as the neutralization of critique: "The comedy's methods follow a double strategy: to first mobilize a departure from propaganda policy (by ironizing current events, for example), in order to then immobilize the critical energies created by the comic effects."[40] The Third Reich comedy, Witte added, also functioned to mobilize desirable emotions: "Through its double function of exclusion and integration, it conditions the audience for an emotional consensus with the propaganda line."[41]

This suggests that comedy serves fascist goals just as well as, or even better than, melodrama; laughter can be as tyrannical as tears, perhaps more. Both comedy and melodrama concern themselves with violations of social norms and the reestablishment of order, and both may address ideological questions. However, melodrama sides with the victim, while comedy chooses victims for ridicule. Somewhat paradoxically, comedy's absurdities and implausibilities also serve to naturalize ideologies rather than undermine them. The viewer of the comedy accepts the film as an unlikely proposition, an opposing image to the world of the real, which remains untouched by the comedy's temporary transgressions. Melodrama, on the other hand, concerns itself with dualistic structures that are posited as genuinely existing, and therefore it may open fissures for doubt that reference the world of the real.

Furthermore, the conditioning of spectator emotion is by many accounts more difficult with melodrama than with comedy, since melodrama primarily mobilizes sexual desires. This is especially true of melodramas that feature female main protagonists. As Pam Cook asserts, the ideological effects of the woman's picture are difficult to control completely: "It has to stimulate desire, then channel it through identification into the required paths. It negotiates this contradiction between female desire and its containment with difficulty, often producing an excess which threatens to deviate from the intended route."[42] Melodrama constantly borders on the excessive, and this risk is a multiple one. This can be a stylistic problem, a use of signs that is either overfamiliar or destabilizingly unfamiliar: both the cliché and the strange are forms of excess that threaten to undermine spectator identifications and send them outside of the text. Or their identifications may become too intense, producing excess emotion. Once spectator desires are mobilized, they may also attach themselves to the wrong objects. Filmmakers of the Third Reich had to be constantly concerned with negotiating these risks, and as we will see in the next section and in upcoming chapters, melodramas posed particular stylistic and ideological challenges for which there was no obvious solution in the form of a clearly defined "fascist aesthetic."

The Aesthetics of Nazi Melodrama

Third Reich films were intended to have a strong emotional effect upon spectators of both sexes, but this effect was never supposed to appear so carefully calculated that audiences would become aware of the workings of ideology. The propaganda minister, as Sabine Hake has pointed out, watched carefully over film projects to make sure that they did not have a boomerang effect: "any excess of representation might threaten the precarious balance between aesthetic and political intentions and give rise to dangerous forms of 'reading against the grain.'"[43] Melodramas proved to be particularly problematic for Goebbels, because their emotional effects sometimes led in the wrong direction. After previewing the Zarah Leander melodrama *Das Herz der Königin* (*Heart of a Queen*, 1940), Goebbels wrote that the film "should be anti-English and anti-Church and has become pro for both. Still has to be changed a lot. And that will cost us a lot of effort. I could work forever just eliminating the psychological mistakes in my area."[44] Goebbels's comments suggest that the risk of "psychological mistakes" may have been greater for melodramas than films of other genres, since subtle directorial choices in camera work, editing, and acting could turn a film in entirely the opposite direction from the script. Comedy, on the other hand, was particularly based upon dialogue in the Third Reich, and thus was presumably easier to control at the script stage.

Goebbels had particular difficulties with explicitly political films, since their melodramatic attempts to engage spectators' emotions quite often fell on the side of excess. Overbearing patriotic pathos was a recurring problem. Goebbels noted regarding Luis Trenker's *Feuerteufel* (*Fire Devil*, 1940), for example: "Horrendous patriotic rubbish. I have to cut it drastically."[45] *Über alles in der Welt* (*Above All in the World*), a film of the same year, received a similar critique: "Too naïve and primitive . . . Ritter says nationalistic things with a lack of inhibition that would make another man blush."[46] Similarly, he noted in March 1940 about the more female-oriented *Heimkehr* (*Homecoming*): "Still too consciously pathetic. Has to be substantially changed."[47] Later that year, Goebbels worked particularly hard to achieve the right psychological effect with the propaganda film *Wunschkonzert* (*Request Concert*) and wrote some of its scenes himself. Melodramatic moods were enlisted for emotional effect, but Goebbels tried to ensure that pathos would be balanced with opposing moods. Therefore, a brief, pathetic scene in which a mother mourns the death of her soldier son was balanced by longer scenes featuring buffoonish Bavarians chasing a pig. The mixed mode evidently succeeded, since *Wunschkonzert* became the most popular film of 1940.[48]

Despite Goebbels's vigilance, spectators still sometimes rejected a film as excessive after it had been approved and released.[49] Italian films created particular problems in this regard. For political reasons, productions from the Italian Cinecittà studios were shown in the Reich, and Italian directors were invited to make films in Germany as coproductions with German studios. Goebbels had disdain for most of the Italian Fascist cinema, however. He repeatedly complained that Italian films were not up to his aesthetic standards, but he could not prohibit their release or make the kind of cuts he could with German productions. About Guido Brignone's 1941 film *Vertigine* (released in Germany as *Tragödie einer Liebe*), he wrote, for example: "Then I examine an Italian film . . . that falls so far below normal artistic standards that I actually would like to ban it."[50] About *Rote Orchideen* (*Red Orchids,* 1938), Goebbels wrote: "a completely awful and pushy affair. [Nunzio] Malasomma as director. Good for nothing."[51] The description "pushy" (*aufdringlich*) indicates that this Italian film failed its negotiation between aesthetic and political intentions by presenting what were for Goebbels excessive stylistic markers or a too-blatant message.

The reception of Italian films in the Reich, both by the leadership and mass audiences, belies the notion of a "fascist aesthetic" common to the Nazi and the Italian Fascist cinemas. Based upon the available evidence, it is clear that the German public's reaction to Italian Fascist films was overwhelmingly negative. The SD reported in 1942, for example, on spectator responses to an Italian film released in Germany under the title *Vorbestraft* (*With Previous Conviction*): "Part of the audience also described this film narrative as too naïve, the dialogue too full of pathos, and the whole thing as bordering on kitsch."[52] Italian films were repeatedly described as kitsch, which suggests that their stylistic and narrative conventions differed significantly from those of German cinema of the same time, since they exceeded the types of filmic signs that Germans accepted as "realistic." The SD added: "New Italian films are often approached from the very beginning with particularly critical eyes and a certain ingrained contempt. There is a widely held opinion that the average Italian film is far inferior to the average German film . . . In the available reports, Italian film is generally described as too 'theatrical,' and the German spectator has a different concept of 'faithfulness to reality.' Again and again, a certain depth of mood and feeling is lacking, and in its place is only a 'flat sentimentality.'"[53] The Italian Fascist cinema, it seems from this report, was understood by German audiences to be more theatrical because it was more rooted in silent-era expressiveness than the cinema of the Nazi period, with a higher emphasis on gesture and facial expression in Italian films. Also crucial was that the Italian Fascist melodrama made more recourse to maternal pathos and to Catholic iconography than did the Nazi melodrama, differences that may have contributed to their rejection by Third Reich spectators as "flatly sentimental."

While Italian films were found to be excessive, threatening boomerang effects with German audiences, American films were admired for their ability to skillfully negotiate between emotional and ideological effects. Goebbels was particularly impressed with Hollywood melodramas and repeatedly noted that they were to serve as models for German filmmakers. About *Gone with the Wind,* he wrote: "Magnificent color and moving in its effect. One becomes completely sentimental while watching it. Leigh and Clark Gable act wonderfully. The mass scenes are captivatingly well done. A huge achievement of the Americans . . . We will follow this example."[54] The Americans, it seemed, were even better at directing the masses and moving them to tears than the Germans. American melodramas even induced covert feelings of inadequacy in Nazi culture producers. When *Gone with the Wind* was shown in a closed screening to a group of film journalists in 1940, some damage control was deemed necessary. The journalists were supposed to be impressed with the film, but Goebbels also feared that they would be so completely moved that an inferiority complex might result, one that would show up in the pages of the Nazi film press. This fear was expressed in the minutes of Goebbels's conference in the Propaganda Ministry on November 21, 1940:

> The Minister gives head of ministerial section Fritzsche, who will screen *Gone with the Wind* with a small number of chief editors this weekend, the following guidelines for an introductory speech. It should be said that the film is based on a book with worldwide success, that it was worked on for three years, that the costs of the film production have run up to 15 million dollars. It should

also be mentioned that the climate conditions in America facilitate the production of color films, and that the style of representation in American films
is fundamentally different from the German style. The latter concentrates on
deepening the narrative, while the Americans portray the milieu and present
numerous "gags" on the margins of the narrative. Additionally, it should be
said that Czech cameramen shot the film, while the German film [industry] is
fundamentally constrained to working with German personnel.[55]

The strength of American capital, the superiority of its émigré film techni-
cians, the popular appeal of scripts based upon American best-selling novels,
and the Californian weather were all given as excuses for the Hollywood
melodrama's finer visual quality and emotional effects. Meanwhile, Nazi
film scholars and journal editors were encouraged to assert the superiority
of German cinema, a superiority based primarily on its quality of being German. Quite often the reference to "German film art" in Nazi writing takes
on the character of incantation, as if by repeatedly speaking of it, it might
suddenly appear.

Peter von Werder was one such writer, a fervent Nazi who also fervently
wanted Nazi cinema to be exceptional. In his 1941 book *Trugbild und
Wirklichkeit im Film* (*Illusion and Reality in Film*), von Werder claimed that
a specifically German film aesthetics was in the process of being formed.
Characteristically, however, he simply listed films that he found to be exemplary but evaded any attempt to describe their specifically German or
specifically Nazi character. Instead, he invoked only a general subjective
feeling about German film's difference:

> Recent film production has finally shown that German cinema is in the midst
> of a fundamental transformation. One only has to think of films such as *Un-
> ternehmen Michael* [*The Private's Job/Operation Michael*, 1937] or *Urlaub auf
> Ehrenwort* [*Furlough on Word of Honor*, 1938], as well as *Bismarck* [1940], *Schil-
> ler* [1940] or *Ohm Krüger* [1941], *Der Postmeister* [*The Postmaster*, 1940] or
> *Operetta* [1940], or *Heimkehr* [*Homecoming*, 1941] or *Ich klage an* [*I Accuse*,
> 1941], to realize that a new film style is announcing itself here, one that we can
> feel, more and more, is our own. Such a feeling, which still cannot be captured
> in rules or principles, comes from the fact that we sense in these and similar
> films strong tendencies toward a conception of reality consistent with our era.[56]

Von Werder's claim that Nazi film had a specific "conception of reality" suggests a confusion or collapsing of film style into ideology, and most of the
films on his list are explicit propaganda features that directly satisfied his Nazi
sensibilities. As Sabine Hake has shown, Nazi film writing often transforms
the concept of realism from a formal principle to a mode of reception; ac-

cording to Nazi thinking, realism is not a particular aesthetic but, rather, whatever the receiver feels to be realistic.[57] However, von Werder's feeling about stylistic specificity was perhaps not completely incorrect. Although Nazi films by and large follow classical Hollywood models, the spectator of Nazi films is often left with the sense of an elusive but nonetheless palpable difference in cinematic style, independently even of ideological differences.

Among contemporary film scholars, Eric Rentschler has offered the most concise summary of primary differences in the style of Third Reich films from their Hollywood counterparts. While much of his description is accurate, some points require reevaluation. He writes:

> In an attempt to control the articulation of fictional worlds, only a small proportion of films was shot outdoors or on location . . . Features of the Third Reich favored carefully crafted artificial realms and showed a predilection for studio spaces, costume design, and script logic . . . Film narratives of the Nazi era generally privileged space over time, composition over editing, design over movement, sets over human shapes. Compared to Hollywood movies, most features of the Third Reich appeared slow and static. They were more prone to panoramas and tableaus than to close-ups, decidedly sparing in their physical displays (very little nudity, few stunts and action scenes). Nazi film theorists stressed the importance of kinetic images as well as galvanizing sound tracks. Music worked together with visuals to make the spectator lose touch with conceptual logic and discursive frameworks.[58]

Let us now look at each of these points more closely before moving on to a comparative close analysis of a Nazi melodrama with its classical Hollywood counterpart.

Rentschler notes that there was a greater frequency of location shooting and more movement in Hollywood than in Nazi films, and suggests that this can be attributed to a unique obsession with control over mise-en-scène in the Third Reich. Yet location shooting or the lack thereof, I would like to suggest, was more a function of genre and financial constraints. Melodrama, in both Hollywood and the Third Reich, offered few location shots, and the proportion of exterior sequences in melodramas was about the same in Nazi Germany as in Hollywood. The "predilection for studio spaces" is actually a feature of the classical style as such, a style that demands harmony, closure, and the extraction of ambiguities.[59] However, the studio spaces were larger and the sets more elaborate in Hollywood than they were in the Third Reich, with higher budgets that allowed for more camera movement and more range of camera angles. Camera movements were rarely used in films of the Third Reich for expressive effect on their own and were generally limited to small and unobtrusive pans and slight tracking shots. This was partly because producers in the Third Reich were concerned with reducing costs, especially during the war. For the 1940 melodrama *Das Herz der Königin* (*The Heart of a Queen*), for example, a low-cost trompe l'oeil set was built in which an essentially flat wall was painted to mimic the three dimensional space of a grand hall. Since the space was not actually three-dimensional, camera movements had to be avoided. The film journal *Der deutsche Film* praised German set-building ingenuity when it reported that *Das Herz der Königin* was made cheaply and entirely without camera pans.[60] According to Goebbels's plan, such technical limitations were eventually to be remedied through the conquest of new filming space beyond the borders of the Reich.

Rentschler points out that the impression of stasis in Third Reich films is also due to less dynamic editing and the favoring of fixed compositions, which may also be attributable to a differing aesthetic. Instead of the shot/ countershot constructions preferred by Hollywood, Third Reich films often make use of a two-shot construction, a more theatrical staging in which the actors move to and from the camera, alternately facing it and turning away or presenting themselves in profile during a dialogue. As a result, the camera work of Third Reich films privileges the face of the actor less than Hollywood films do but includes the body more. As Erica Carter has argued, the actor's body in Nazi cinema was called upon to carry a different ideological weight by functioning as the representative of a national "soul" and the conduit of a neo-Kantian aesthetics. Film writing of the Nazi period distinguished between German cinema's treatment of the body and Hollywood's, as Carter explains, by favoring "the performing body over the cinematic apparatus as a source of 'soul' . . . [and] regularly extoll[ing] the specific national quali-ties of cinematic practices that masked the medium's technological nature."[61] In an effort to disguise the apparatus, Nazi films tended to avoid shots that emphasize editing and reference offscreen space. Correspondingly, bodies are framed so that they are visible in Third Reich films, while faces are treated with fewer and shorter close-ups than in Hollywood films. The result is that the spectator often cannot observe the fine reactions of actors, and this lessens the sensation of intimacy and the melodramatic effect of Nazi films. Emotion was primarily conveyed through actors' voices rather than through their facial expressions or gestures; therefore "script logic" or dialogue was indeed privileged over editing and movement.

If melodrama is a "text of muteness" in which gesture and mise-en-scène speak for the inarticulate protagonist,[62] then the spoken texts of Third Reich melodramas are louder than usual. The voice has a more important role than gesture in German sound cinema. In general, actors usually say what they mean rather than having the mise-en-scène speak for them—or against them, as it does in the most interesting of Hollywood melodramas. Set design and costuming are certainly very important sign systems in Nazi melodrama, but the camera is generally not allowed to make use of the languages of décor and dress to their full expressive extent; objects, like actors, generally do not receive many close-ups. Rentschler's conclusion about the primacy of sets in Nazi cinema, therefore, is only valid for genres in which sets are by nature primary and in which the body itself is transformed into décor: the musical comedy and the revue film.

Rentschler suggests that Hollywood films of the 1930s and '40s offered more to the voyeuristic eye than films of the Third Reich, yet this point must also be qualified. Nazi cinema did have fewer stunts than Hollywood, but it had far more nudity. Actresses were filmed either partially or fully nude in numerous Nazi films, while the common mise-en-scène of dressing rooms allowed for voyeuristic looks at women removing clothing.[63] Bedroom scenes were not banned in Third Reich films, and couples were not required to sleep in separate twin beds as were Hollywood's married men and women. Likewise, Third Reich cinema had few scruples about premarital seductions, as we will see in later chapters. More sexual situations and physical displays were allowed by German censors than by Hollywood's Production Code standards, following a conscious attempt by the Nazis to assert cultural superiority through fascist body culture. As film writer Rudolf Oertel claimed in a 1941 book, Nazi cinema's "healthy" attitude toward nudity distinguished it from the hypocritical morality of "bourgeois" cinema: "The concept of nudity has lost for us that sinful overtone of a false, bourgeois world, which was sometimes full of virtue on the outside and full of corruption on the inside . . . Body culture, sports and a natural relationship of the sexes to one another have prepared the way for our healthy view of the world. We also know that a beautiful naked body seems less erotic than a refined décolleté."[64] Despite their repeated claims that German film was inherently "clean," the Nazis made extensive use of both naked and erotically costumed bodies, as the female body in particular was exploited as one of the central attractions of Third Reich cinema. Indeed, Laura Mulvey's critique of the misuse of woman's image in classical Hollywood cinema might be considered even more applicable to Nazi cinema, especially since, as we will see later in this chapter, an aggressive form of voyeurism predominated over more scopophilic displays in Nazi films.[65]

When Rentschler writes that Nazi theorists emphasized the importance of music, he suggests that the Nazis were even better at manipulating the emotions of viewers through sound tracks than were Hollywood filmmakers. However, it is not clear that this was true in practice. Nazi melodramas and musicals certainly had some effective music, as the popularity of Zarah Leander's hit songs proves. Song sequences differ from sound tracks, though, since they break the flow of the narrative and the texts of songs are often contrapuntal to the plot rather than adding up to a complete, overwhelming synthesis. And there is some evidence that Nazi melodramas actually made less effective use of sound tracks than Hollywood melodramas. Ever wary of excess, film critics in the Third Reich often wrote disapprovingly of the use of music to punctuate emotional moments in films. *Das Mädchen Irene* (*The Girl Irene,* 1936), for example, is an exceptional Third Reich melodrama, one that attempted to give music and camera work a higher degree of expressive power, and in which gesture is sometimes allowed to replace speech. The reviewer for the *Film-Kurier* commented on the film's music as follows: "the use of the orchestra in crucial scenes is occasionally a bit overbearing."[66] Goebbels's reaction to *Das Mädchen Irene* was even more damning, and he was so disgusted by the film that he cut short his private screening.[67] In contrast, many films of which he did approve had comparatively sparse sound tracks. *Der Herrscher* (*The Ruler*), Veit Harlan's propagandistic melodrama and the winner of the 1937 Nationaler Filmpreis (national film prize), included long sections in which there was no musical accompaniment, even between the many long pauses in dialogue—hardly an effective use of the sound track for emotional intoxication. The Security Service also repeatedly reported that spectators preferred more sparing sound tracks and that film music was not entirely successful in galvanizing audiences.[68]

Lighting was generally also not used to the same expressive effects in the Third Reich as in Hollywood, usually remaining comparatively inconspicuous. Nazi crime films and melodramas did make use of low-key lighting, but the lighting in Third Reich films rarely became as artistically expressive as in Hollywood film noir, following the Nazis' general disapproval of ambiguity and filmic style for style's sake. As Erica Carter has shown, there is also a crucial difference in Third Reich filmmakers' lighting of actors in that they avoided the "halo effects" of Hollywood-style lighting and placed more emphasis on the ensemble of performers than on illuminating the individual star.[69]

Indeed, the image of the small ensemble was more common than both the individual and the mass in Third Reich melodrama, despite the privileged place that the geometrically ordered mass holds in film scholars' understanding of Nazi film style. Fascist aesthetics are most commonly described as the abstracted composition of "human shapes," as the ornamental massing of bodies. According to Karsten Witte, fascist film aesthetics are characterized by the "rigorous over-designing, standardization and ultimately the corrosion of topical patterns, which all lead to a hypertrophy of the mass ornament."[70] Witte's account corresponds to Susan Sontag's description of Riefenstahl's *Triumph of the Will* as typical of fascist aesthetics, characterized by "over-populated wide shots of massed figures alternating with close-ups that isolate a single passion, a single perfect submission . . . [and] the rendering of movement in grandiose and rigid patterns."[71] However, these descriptions of fascist aesthetics apply primarily to the dramaturgy of party meetings, parades, and other street spectacles, but such aesthetics are rarely to be found in Nazi feature films. Mass scenes are not common in the cinema of the Third Reich, since few filmmakers were accorded the budget to organize large groups of extras (Veit Harlan with his literal armies of extras for the filming of *Kolberg* being the most obvious exception). Yet overall the spaces of the Nazi narrative film are tight rather than monumental, characterized more by a mediocre rigidity of style than by a grandiose rigidity of ornamental movement, and bodies are much more commonly grouped in couples than in masses.

In the following section I will extend some of these general comments on film style by comparing a characteristic melodrama from the Third Reich to a Hollywood model. Of the films that Peter von Werder listed as representatives of a specifically German film style, *Der Postmeister* presents perhaps the most opportune example for close study. Contemporary audiences reportedly felt that it was one of the best German films ever made, and it was repeatedly described in the press and among spectators as a great work of art. However, there were apparently many criticisms of the film's narrative and setting, so the film's "art" was seen by contemporary audiences as being independent of its subject matter. *Der Postmeister* seems therefore a particularly good test case in the effort to isolate a characteristic Third Reich melodramatic film style. As a Nazi recycling of the classic "fallen woman" theme, this melodrama also allows for close comparisons with Hollywood films of the same genre.

Der Postmeister was one of the most popular melodramas of the Third Reich,[72] though this may seem barely conceivable today. The film is grim in mood, claustrophobic in its scenic construction, and overbearing in its acting style. These, however, were perhaps precisely the elements that struck contemporary viewers as artistic and as characteristically German. The journal *Der Film,* in a typical review of *Der Postmeister,* called it "shining proof of German cinematic creativity."[73] Goebbels noted in his diary that the film was a "a great work of art," and he particularly praised the "outstanding portrayal of milieu."[74] As with most films designated as examples of German cinematic high art, however, there is little in the film that can be singled out as a specifically German invention. The film is set in Russia and borrowed from a foreign literary source, Alexander Pushkin's short story "The Stationmaster." The film also owes much to classical Hollywood models, which was openly admitted at the time; *Der Postmeister* was positively compared in the Nazi press to George Cukor's *Camille* (1936).[75] It is likely that the film's director, Gustav Ucicky, also looked very closely at another Greta Garbo vehicle, *Anna Karenina* (1935), following Goebbels's citation of Garbo's 1927 silent version as a model for German filmmakers to copy.[76] *Der Postmeister* particularly invites comparison to *Anna Karenina* because both are set in nineteenth-century St. Petersburg, share Russian literary sources, and are narratives of a woman's downfall through illicit sexuality into suicide.

Der Postmeister's narrative concerns a young woman who is seduced by an aristocrat, lives for a time as his mistress, and begins to suffer the social consequences of this role. The girl, Dunya (Hilde Krahl), leaves her father (Heinrich George), the postmaster of an isolated provincial outpost, and moves to St. Petersburg with her seducer, Count Minskij, on the pretense that she will marry him. Once in St. Petersburg, she attempts to separate herself from Minskij, takes a job as a seamstress, and becomes engaged to the naval officer Mitja (the conventional "worthy and innocent young man"[77]). Meanwhile, Dunya's father hears that his daughter has become a prostitute and comes to St. Petersburg in a drunken rage with the intention of murdering her. Dunya escapes, but is then filled with such tenderness for her father that she returns to Minskij and asks him to stage a fake wedding so that her father will be deceived into thinking her relationship with Minskij was legitimate. Dunya's actual fiancé, Mitja, who knows nothing about her past relationship with Minskij, happens to arrive at the fake wedding and, realizing that Dunya is not the woman he imagined her to be, calls off the engagement and loudly humiliates her. Dunya takes her father to the train station after the wedding, they have a melodramatic parting, and the postmaster returns to the provinces, still under the illusion that his daughter has married an aristocrat. Dunya then shoots herself in Minskij's apartment, but just before dying, she asks him to write to her father that she died of an illness.

A close comparison of *Der Postmeister* to *Anna Karenina* reveals some differences in film style, direction, plot, scenic construction, and, finally, in ideology. Overall, *Der Postmeister* is darker in tone than *Anna Karenina*. Whereas most scenes in *Anna Karenina* are brightly lit with halo effects around the star Garbo, much of *Der Postmeister* is filmed with low-key lighting. Differences in lighting point to differences in the imaginary of the Russian milieu in the two films: whereas *Anna Karenina* offers nostalgic, glamorous, though at times also farcical visions of the St. Petersburg upper class, the low-key German version of Russia suggests a primitive and somewhat sordid environment. Camera work in the respective films underlines this difference in the vision of Russia, and as we will see, the differing mise-en-scène had further political implications. The first sequence of *Anna Karenina* serves to characterize the milieu: men in extravagant white and gold military uniforms engage in gluttonous feasting and excessive drinking in a large and luxurious ballroom. The sequence opens with a close-up of a bowl of caviar and features an extended movement down a long table filled with candelabras and food, a background-to-foreground sweep that is a virtuoso display of camera technique. This movement, staged in the space of a two-story-high studio set, adds to the impression of lightness and luxury that pervades most of the film (even as Garbo begins suffering, she does so with dazzling lighting and the full luxury of costly costuming and décor). The large spaces of *Anna Karenina* allow for large movements of the main characters and the many extras, all of which add a lively quality to the overall impression of the film. By contrast, the initial sequences of *Der Postmeister* are shot in the cramped space of a comparatively cheap-looking studio set, the limited number of characters confined in two shots or medium close-ups. This pattern continues even after Dunya has departed her village to live in luxury in St. Petersburg. Again, this tight framing and lack of large movements not only indicates a distinct, peculiarly fascist aesthetic but also points primarily to material constraints.[78] *Der Postmeister,* which indirectly supported Hitler's campaign to conquer new "living space" in the east, testified to the lack of studio space in the Reich.

There were some similarities in the imagination of milieu, however. Naturally, neither film was shot on location, and both films imagine St. Petersburg mostly as a series of interiors. In both films, scenes are played out in the spaces of a men's sauna and in a music hall, and a comparison of these sequences shows some interesting variations. The sauna scenes of both films have similar narrative functions, though the effects of their staging are quite different. In both films, two male characters discuss the heroine while taking a steam bath. In *Anna Karenina* the discussion takes place as the two main male characters are being awkwardly flogged with branches by other corpulent men in towels. There is a brief suggestion of homoeroticism, but this impression is quickly neutralized through physical comedy, as a bucket of cold water is abruptly poured over the head of one of the characters at the end of the scene. The military men in *Anna Karenina*'s sauna are treated farcically, an effect that is heightened by the placement of the sauna sequence directly after the opening feast sequence's parody of Russian military life as elaborate, ritualized drinking and gluttony. The differing staging of the two sauna scenes, it may be noted, is actually consistent with Goebbels's claim that American films tend to retard narrative progression by means of "gags," whereas the Nazi melodrama is concerned with intensifying the forward drive of the narrative. *Der Postmeister,* unlike *Anna Karenina,* does not attempt to reroute the sexual undertones of its sauna sequence and even attempts to deepen them through dialogue while simultaneously foreshadowing upcoming plot events. Perhaps referencing Riefenstahl's sauna scene in *Olympia,* the athletic bodies of *Der Postmeister*'s military men are allowed to retain their erotic appeal; there is no effort to undercut voyeurism through comedy. The tone remains serious even when the man on the top bench of the sauna turns over to look at Mitja on the bottom and asks, in reference to Dunya, "You've fallen head over heels in love, haven't you? . . . Tell me, have you done it with her yet?"

Similar distinctions are evident in the music hall sequences of each film. In both films the ballroom party sequences serve to signify a decadent side to Russian life, and in both the presence of "gypsy" musicians and dancers connotes a milieu of loose morality. In *Anna Karenina,* however, their costuming remains firmly within Production Code standards. Their lascivious lifestyles are connoted with oversized jewelry, but their chests and shoulders are fully covered. The framing of the dancers does not in any way emphasize their bodies; one of the women is placed with her back to the camera so that little of her is visible, and the view of the other woman is blocked by the table. Rather than visual pleasure, therefore, this music hall scene is played for comic effect: while Anna's very drunk brother speaks lovingly of his wife and ineptly flirts with the dancers, a clownish violin player hangs over their heads.

The corresponding sequence in *Der Postmeister,* on the other hand, appeals to an aggressive voyeurism. The first scene set in St. Petersburg, it begins with a traveling shot along a staircase adorned with sculptures of nude female torsos, and ends on a shot of a woman sitting on a man's lap, framed with another sculpture of a naked torso just above her head. (By contrast, the sculptural décor in *Anna Karenina*'s music hall is of a geometric, nonrepresentational pattern.) Soon this woman, Mascha, is shown unbuttoning her shirt, jumping down from the balcony, and throwing off her blouse for a vigorous topless dance. Reaction shots of male audience members underline their pleasure and approval, modeling the expected response of the nondiegetic audience. The camera then moves in to offer the spectator a better view of the dancer, alternating between shots of her chest and close-ups of her exposed legs as her skirt spins open. The cutting between these alternating body fragments is quick, and the editing is synchronized with the music, creating a rhythmic and rousing effect. Curiously, the pacing of the editing

Nazi cinema's sadistic voyeurism: the dance sequence of *Der Postmeister* (1940).
Copyright Studiocanal Video

of the dance in *Der Postmeister* only has its parallel in the rapid editing of
Anna Karenina's death scene, the alternating shots of legs and breasts in
Der Postmeister corresponding to the alternating shots of train wheels and
Garbo's horrified face in *Anna Karenina*. The editing rhythm of both of these
sequences connotes a sense of intensification before release. (The death scene
in *Der Postmeister*, by contrast, is performed in a rather perfunctory manner.)
These differing points of intensification suggest what was most important to
each respective film: stimulation of an aggressive eroticism on the one hand,
and the stimulation of a melancholy mood of loss on the other. Indeed, this
relatively heavier emphasis on sexualized violence than on mourning may
be considered paradigmatic for Nazi melodrama in general.

Most spectators of *Anna Karenina* certainly came to the cinema primarily
to look at Garbo and watch her suffer beautifully. Its melancholy sentiment is
supported by camera work and framing. There are abundant, relatively long
close-ups of Garbo's face in the film as the camera lingers lovingly on her
in hazy soft focus. In contrast, there is little glamorous treatment of Hilde
Krahl in *Der Postmeister*; the camera work instead supports an undertone
of brutality throughout the film. Although there are a significant number

of medium close-ups of Krahl in the film, the camera rests on her only long enough to register reactions necessary for the progression of the narrative but not long enough for the audience to develop a strong sense of intimacy with and sympathy for her character. Lingering on Krahl would hardly have been productive, since she was in no way as auratic as Garbo and there was little subtlety of feeling to be read on her face. In the scenes in which she must mimic separation trauma from her father on a train platform, shouting is substituted for tender camera work and more subtle acting registers, which is consistent with the Nazi melodrama's tendency to place greater emphasis on the voice than on gesture, framing, or editing. Krahl, who was born in Croatia, had a hard, dialect-tinged delivery and a voice that actually suggested an inability to suffer.

Hence, acting style is perhaps one of the most noticeable differences between films of the Third Reich and their Hollywood counterparts, and the variations in actor types likewise suggests variations in audience identification patterns. Except for the two Swedish stars Zarah Leander and Kristina Söderbaum, most of the actresses of the Third Reich were not particularly good at portraying melodramatic suffering. Other actresses often used in Third Reich woman's films—Hilde Krahl, Marianne Hoppe, Brigitte Horney, and Ilse Werner—were better at interpreting hardworking and optimistic characters with boyish allure, and this is generally the preferred type in cinema of the Third Reich. Their appeal is quite comprehensible; identifying with such characters provided women in the Third Reich with "illusions of female autonomy" and the illusion that fascism was modern in a liberating sense.[79] Male actor types of the Third Reich, on the other hand, are less comprehensible in their appeal. The star of *Der Postmeister,* Heinrich George, was, along with Emil Jannings, one of the most influential actors of the Third Reich. It is a peculiarity of Nazi cinema that these two could elicit audience admiration, since they do not have parallels in Hollywood films of the same time period. Hollywood cinema had little use for excessively corpulent men who sweated profusely, panted, growled, and screamed, except perhaps as parodic figures. In their Third Reich films, both Heinrich George and Emil Jannings specialized in portraying fathers and husbands, their violent rages alternating with sentimentality. A postwar star study describes Heinrich George's style thus: "So this colossal giant with the booming voice that demanded obedience stomped through his great roles. Even when his face turned red and clouds of rage gathered around his powerful forehead, one still sensed that there was a soft core in this stocky primal phenomenon. His vital feelings simply had to pass through him and out of him."[80] Many Third Reich spectators presumably identified in some fundamental way with this release of violent feelings. Whereas the patriarchal figure in *Anna Karenina,* Anna's husband, Karenin, plays his role with cool, soft-voiced detachment, *Der Postmeister* offers a characteristically German despot who screams and demands obedience. The spectator was apparently supposed to take pleasure in searching for the soft center among his powerful rage.

Characteristically also, it is to this figure that the spectator is asked to attach his or her sympathies. Whereas the central identificatory figure in *Anna Karenina* is clearly Garbo's Anna, the main protagonist of *Der Postmeister* is actually George's father figure, with the titles of the two films announcing these respective orientations. The identification patterns are set up mainly through dialogue, but also through camera cues. The scene in which the postmaster comes to kill his daughter is an example of how *Der Postmeister* attempts to position the spectator on his side and manages to justify his murderous anger. The murder-planning scene is staged in Dunya's tenement room, which she shares with her friend and coworker in the dress factory, Elisawetha. The postmaster waits for Dunya while she is on a date with the soldier Mitja (and thus is in effect made innocent through association with the military, though we are asked to sympathize with the father's intentions nonetheless). The postmaster is sitting on Dunya's bed as Elisawetha enters the room, and as she sees him, she shrinks away from him in fear. He forces her down on the bed next to him, and the emphasis on his strength suggests the potential of rape. At the end of the sequence, there is a shot of Elisawetha, who, despite the threat of physical violence to which she has just been subjected, watches the tyrannical patriarch tenderly as he exits the tenement, adding, "I think he is an unhappy man. I think one should pray for him." Later in the film, another character observes the postmaster and remarks, "He is really a magnificent man!" The father is thus framed by dialogue that suggests to us the correct interpretation of his character: a splendid dictator. Most importantly, however, the spectator is asked to identify primarily with his suffering, and not with that of the suicidal woman.

Two train station sequences further underline the difference in identification structures in *Der Postmeister* and *Anna Karenina.* In the German film, a final parting between Dunya and her father takes place on the nighttime train platform, and the scene is supposed to express the pathos of separation. There is a conventional shot: the train pulls away, wrenching the two lovers apart (the father being Dunya's most significant lover in this film). Somewhat contrary to expectation, however, the camera is placed inside the train so that we see Dunya on the platform in disappearing perspective. There is no corresponding reverse shot of the father pulling away in the train. The camera is thus placed in the physical position of the father, and the spectator watches the woman disappear from the male point of view. In *Anna Karenina* the nighttime train station platform sequence is Anna's suicide scene. Here she is alone, without diegetic male spectators. The camera takes her position, alternating between the shots of her face and the wheels of the train, so these close-ups of the wheels are presented as her vision, with which the spectator is invited to identify. In *Der Postmeister,* on the other hand, there are no point-of-view shots from Dunya's perspective in the suicide sequence. Rather, the sound of the pistol shot is edited over a shot of Minskij, thus the spectator is asked to react to Dunya's surprise death as he does.

Notably, although both *Der Postmeister* and *Anna Karenina* are generically woman's films, the plotting in both cases allows the main female protagonist to be framed by male speech. In both films the protagonist's fiancé/lover (Mitja/Vronsky) is presented on screen first, and the dialogue in these scenes introduces the woman before she appears. In both films also, the man has the final word. The final scenes of both *Der Postmeister* and *Anna Karenina* are constructed as epilogues and follow the suicide sequences. In both cases the woman's lover expresses his regret at her suicide and asks whether he might have been somehow responsible for her death. (Thus, both serve the melodramatic convention of the final recognition of virtue, in the tear-jerking tense of the "too late.") Both films also costume the lover in military uniform and direct him to deliver this recognition speech to a comrade who is also in uniform. In *Anna Karenina,* however, a close-up of the lover Vronsky gives way to a camera movement screen right to a close-up of a portrait of Anna. The camera rests on this image before fading out, the final shot returning us to female subjectivity. Somewhat inappropriately for the historical setting, this portrait is a contemporary photograph rather than a painting, which would have placed her image in the past rather than the present. The photograph comforts the spectator with the sense of the ever present and suggests that Anna's vision persists, that she still has lively eyes that can witness her vindication and can still look back, even though the narrative has required her to die. No such final image of Dunya is offered in *Der Postmeister*: the final shot in this film is of Mitja's carriage disappearing into a snowy landscape that is empty except for a few dead trees, an image that marks the extinction of the woman's vision. This differing final vision is a further indication of the way in which identification structures in *Der Postmeister* side with the male protagonist, whereas they are clearly on the side of the female protagonist in *Anna Karenina.* Although *Der Postmeister* has been classified generically as a *Frauen- und Sittendrama* (women's and moral drama) in a postwar lexicon,[81] it is a woman's film hijacked by male subjectivity.

This apparently did not go unnoticed by female spectators at the time. For example, an SD report from April 1940, when the film was released, noted: "The members of the Frauenschaft in Augsburg regret that, in this hit film, the woman is once again represented from the negative side."[82] This wording suggests that the NS-Frauenschaft (National Socialist Women's League) primarily objected to the "negative" representations of Masha and Dunya as sexual and somewhat calculating individuals. If this is true, then the discomfort caused by the film's construction of point of view and spectator identification was almost certainly expressed in the more localizable terms of character representation. In any case, women realized that the film was not on their side, at least not on a side with which they identified themselves. Interestingly, the public reportedly also responded negatively to the film's narrative, particularly its resolution in suicide. The SD commented:

> The film is generally being praised as a great artistic achievement and is considered one of the best German films ever. But reports about the public reception of the film also express a much more critical view in regard to the film's content . . . [Viewers] feel that it is pointless now that we are at war to allow Slavic material into German films again, especially since this film narrative ends in a passive and suffering inactivity that stands in crass opposition to the heroic contemporary experience of the German people.[83]

Thus, audiences felt that melodramatic suffering did not conform to the historical moment, to the thrills of the Blitzkrieg. The public apparently wanted less self-sacrifice and more celebratory optimism. The other hit of 1940, *Wunschkonzert,* apparently better fulfilled the public's momentary generic needs by mixing battle with musical comedy.[84]

Most spectators could not foresee how *Der Postmeister* corresponded to historical circumstances, and they could not anticipate the film's propagandistic value. Eight months after the conclusion of the Hitler-Stalin pact, and fourteen months before the invasion of the Soviet Union, the film served to draw (or redraw) Russia onto the mental maps of German spectators. *Der Postmeister* was presented as a quasi-documentary vision of the Russian landscape and an explanation of the Russian soul. The reviewer for the *Film-Kurier,* for example, wrote that the film was such a "realistic" portrait of Russia because it was a Viennese production: "Here they know the Slavic mentality better than anywhere else. So what first makes a strong impression in the new film is the authentic-looking atmosphere of the Russian milieu and its convincing Slavic essence . . . When the screen fades in on the troika as it drives through the godforsaken, snowy solitude and stops in front of a deserted straw-covered postal cottage, then there is Russian atmosphere.

Then one feels the endless expanses of the landscape in which souls become melancholy and humble."[85] Heinrich George, acting out this Nazi notion of the "Slavic essence," played his postmaster as a semi-illiterate, childish, but touchingly violent character. The extras in the film, representatives of the Russian proletariat and peasantry, were costumed in rags and unruly wigs and directed by Ucicky to play their characters as hunched-over, shuffling idiots. The Russians would be easy to conquer, the film suggested, since they were all essentially melancholic and full of humility. (Mitja and his fellow army officers were somewhat problematically presented as having stiff-standing Prussian natures, but the film was set, of course, under the Czarist monarchy. In the arrogant German imagination, the contemporary Bolsheviks no longer possessed such attractive uniforms or evidenced any militarist discipline that could compete with their own.)

As for the German aesthetic imagination, the artistry of the film was defined in reviews mainly as a series of great and realistic performances by the actors. *Der Film* commented that it was the acting in particular that proved Ucicky's directorial talent and added: "The postmaster Heinrich George was a grandiose example of highest acting perfection with his portrayal of farmer's humility and boundless fatherly love, with his touching humanity, in anger, rage, desperation and happiness, in boasting vanity and naïve anxiety . . . The artistically perfect film, masterful and brilliant in its acting and staging, deeply impressed the audience."[86] It is doubtful, however, that all of the spectators of *Der Postmeister* went to the film primarily to experience great German art, or were simply lured to the cinema by the star allure of Heinrich George. Certainly, no small percentage of cinemagoers were tempted by suggestions of mastery of another kind.

The topless dance sequence follows shortly after scenes in the postmaster's dark house, in which he pulls Dunya onto his lap and expresses his love for his daughter, whom he calls his "feast for the eyes" (*Augenweide*). This "boundless fatherly love" is clearly incestuous; the kisses and other physical contact between the two step over the boundary of what is usual between father and adult daughter. *Anna Karenina*, for its part, offers us a very tender scene of a mother putting her son to bed and certainly does not lack appeals to incestuous desire. But the German equivalent of this family romance is much more suspect. As is typical for Nazi melodramas, the mother is missing from *Der Postmeister*; Dunya's other parent has been killed off before the film plot even begins. Thus, whereas the Hollywood melodrama engages oedipal or even pre-oedipal desire for the maternal, the Nazi melodrama supports the father's aggressive phallic power by extinguishing the maternal entirely. Gaylyn Studlar has argued that the "masochistic aesthetic" characteristic of

Hollywood's masochistic maternalism: *Anna Karenina* (1935). Courtesy the Kobal Collection at Art Resource, New York

the Hollywood melodramas of Josef von Sternberg appeals to the spectator's desire for the pre-oedipal mother, and thus for a union with a femininity imagined as all-powerful and lacking nothing.[87] In contrast, *Der Postmeister* appeals more to sadistic voyeurism and the pleasures of masculine mastery.

Shortly after the father-daughter scene in *Der Postmeister,* the paternalistic aristocrat Minskij enters the house, fixes Dunya with a desirous look, praises her figure, and then grabs her from behind, forcing a kiss as she struggles against him. Since they are framed next to a smoldering fire and an over-boiling pot of water, the spectator is invited to accept such rape fantasies as naturally ignited passion. Much of the film was composed of rather dubious erotic attractions, and this was clearly a conscious strategy. Posters for *Der Postmeister* show that the topless dance sequence was advertised as a main attraction of the film. The advertisement in the May 1940 issue of *Der deutsche Film* shows photos of Heinrich George and Hilde Krahl in the foreground and the topless dancer in the background, just above their heads. The breasts of the dancer are airbrushed into hazy indistinctness; spectators had to buy a ticket to see the rest of the striptease. Reviewers understood that the topless dance sequence was an essential part of *Der Postmeister*'s appeal, and, accordingly, they did not neglect it in their praise of the film's art. The reviewer for *Der Film* praised the "brilliantly masterful scene," which showed "Mascha in Petersburg, suddenly and wildly flying with her bare chest in whirling dance lust."[88] The official Nazi Party film journal, *Der deutsche Film*, also praised the topless sequence, while adding an ideological justification for it: the dancer Margit Symo presented the audience with a "bursting dance from far-off Asia," as the reviewer wrote.[89]

Thus, in a characteristically duplicitous manner, the exposing of Symo's body was explained as a supposedly realistic document of cultural difference, described in terms of the "Asian" nature of Russian culture, and the voyeuristic gaze was employed for propagandistic purposes. *Der Postmeister* put St. Petersburg on the mental map of viewers as a place where women tear off their clothes and dance wildly, an image that no doubt served the upcoming military campaign against the Soviet Union. The dance scene is also a typical example of Nazi cinema's strategic use of eroticism. As we well know, Hollywood cinema—and classical narrative cinema as such—also relies on the spectacle of the female body to create the sensation of pleasure in the (male) spectator.[90] However, the spectacles of *Der Postmeister* are intensified beyond that which is conventional for comparative American films of the same era, and its very palpable sense of sexual violence exceeds the boundaries of what was allowed—or desired—of Hollywood melodramas.

Of course, sexual violence, as David Rodowick has noted, is central to the melodrama as a narrative form. But in Hollywood melodramas this violence is usually suppressed, "regulated only by an economy of masochism which often gives the narratives a suicidal thrust."[91] In *Der Postmeister* this conventional violence is more released than suppressed; although the film, like *Anna Karenina*, ends in suicide, its economy is ultimately more sadistic than masochistic. This distinction, I propose, holds true for most Nazi melodramas in comparison to their Hollywood counterparts. Both *Anna Karenina* and *Der Postmeister*, on a manifest level, offer similar ideological messages. Both films provide images of Russian "decadence" (i.e., the propensity to drunkenness or "indecent" behavior) and thereby in some fashion serve the anticommunist politics of both the United States and Nazi Germany. Following the convention of "fallen woman" melodramas, they are also warnings about what could happen to women who choose to step outside the boundaries of accepted behavior and seek their own experiences independently of male authority. But *Anna Karenina* and *Der Postmeister* address different spectatorial subjects and engage different desires, inviting female identifications on the one hand and male pleasures on the other. Both films make use of melodrama's traditional sympathy for the victim. *Der Postmeister,* however, manages to reroute this conventional sympathy and convince its spectator that it is not the dead woman but rather the man with murderous intentions who is actually the victim. In this way it is truly a great example of Nazi style.

Conclusion

The goal of this chapter has been to delineate the generic and aesthetic differences between film melodrama in Third Reich and classical Hollywood cinema, and to a lesser extent, between German and Italian Fascist film. These subtle distinctions, as will be elaborated further in upcoming chapters, corresponded to the distinct political goals and the practical constraints of German fascism. Melodrama was as central to Nazi cinema as it was to American cinema of the same era, though there were variances in the types of subgenres produced: maternal and family melodrama were less significant for Nazi cinema than for classical Hollywood, as were Hollywood melodramatic subgenres that specialized in the exploration of psychic instability. Despite the centrality of melodrama (and comedy) in the popular cinema of the Third Reich and the regime's keen concern with the reception of films by audiences, the Nazis lacked clearly articulated genre and spectatorship theories and a strong concept of genres as gendered. Because emotional response was expected of all viewers in the Third Reich, melodrama was privileged as a highly effective mode and was not considered to be exclusively or even primarily for female spectators. The Nazi view of female spectatorship was similar to the American view in the common belief that women sought escapism more often than men, though American critics stressed the consumerist element in female spectator pleasure more openly than the Nazis. As we will see in chapter 4, this difference had important implications for spectator address in wartime home front films. In comparison to American critics and film producers, Nazi officials had a less systematic understanding of film spectatorship, particularly of gender differences in film-viewing preferences. Even melodramas were primarily designed with male spectator pleasures in mind.

Despite being a privileged mode, melodrama posed problems for the Nazi minister of propaganda, as it proved difficult to control spectator responses to the pathos and hyperbolic style of melodramatic films. This was particularly true of imported Italian films, which reportedly were received skeptically by Third Reich audiences because of their excessively melodramatic style, and which therefore shed doubt on the existence of a transnational fascist film aesthetic. Although Goebbels dismissed most Italian Fascist films, he recommended that Nazi filmmakers study Hollywood melodramas for lessons on how to blend ideological effectiveness with aesthetic quality. Nazi film-makers derivatively emulated Hollywood films, but there did remain some slight stylistic differences between Nazi melodramas and their American counterparts, including a more theatrical acting style, less dynamic camera movements and editing, a greater emphasis on voice and dialogue than on facial expression and mise-en-scène, a more restrained use of music to punc-tuate emotional moments, and more overtly voyeuristic physical displays. Of these differences, only the last one was likely a consciously calculated formal strategy rather than the effect of limited material resources, limited skill on the part of Third Reich filmmakers, and apprehension regarding stylistic excess on the part of the propaganda minister. As my comparative analysis between *Der Postmeister* and its American model, *Anna Karenina*, has aimed to demonstrate, Nazi melodrama was structured to appeal to a more intense form of sadistic voyeurism than classical Hollywood melodrama. The next chapter examines in greater detail how romance melodramas elicited erotic investment in the aggressive, expansionist designs of the Reich.

2. The Nazi Modernization of Sex: Romance Melodrama

According to a statistical analysis of the titles of films produced during the Third Reich, *Frau(en)* and *Liebe* were the most common nouns used in naming products of the Nazi cinema.[1] "Women" and "love" were the terms deemed most effective for drawing audiences to the theaters, and presumably they were also considered the most effective for the drawing out of nationalist energies and the erasing of internal conflicts. The erotic drive can be considered the main motor of German fascist cinema, the very basis of spectator pleasure, narrative construction, and the creation of meaning. In this it was entirely consistent with the interests of classical Hollywood. As Mary Ann Doane has pointed out, film narrative and film meaning in American cinema also depend on romance: "the couple is a constant figure of Hollywood's rhetoric and some kind of heterosexual pact constitutes its privileged mode of closure."[2] The cinema of the Third Reich, following Hollywood, placed the heterosexual couple at the rhetorical and narrative center of almost all of its films.

Romance, one could say, formed the very basis of Third Reich cinema, the scaffolding onto which all other genres built their specific architecture; comedies, musicals, and even war and crime films were built upon the core of coupling, their generic patterns inserted over the basic structure of romantic relations. Not all romance was melodramatic, of course. Romance was more often taken lightly in Nazi cinema than seriously; in fact, the majority of films with "*Frau*" (woman) or "*Liebe*" (love) in their titles were comedies.[3] But the focus and ideological task of each romantic mode varied. Whereas romantic relations in comedy were most often the vehicle for elaborating problems of the social order, such as class conflicts, the romance melodrama took coupling seriously and privileged it over other thematic concerns, investing its energies into the production and management of sexual desire.

The romance melodrama, although somewhat less extensive than the romantic comedy in terms of production numbers, was nonetheless a privileged genre in the Third Reich, receiving far more screen time than war films. The Nazis' cinematic obsession with the mechanics of desire was surprisingly central for a society that specialized in technologies of death. Far more feature film footage was used for defining sex roles and suggesting sex acts than for defining concepts of national character, generating hatred of enemies, or fabricating notions of race—ideological tasks that were more commonly left to the press and cinema's paratextual discourses.[4] Whereas the Nazis needed little internal negotiation to carry out their genocidal "final solution" to racist paranoia, gender and sexuality were issues that film melodrama had to continually readdress. As Goebbels stated in 1937, "The issue of women's rights [die Frauenfrage] is our most difficult problem."[5]

For the fascist man the problem lay in the question of how to maximize women's productivity and reproductivity while minimizing the costs arising from her own demands for fulfillment and recognition. Evidently, even if the vast majority of Nazi film narratives circled around sexual concerns, romance films still had military implications. Women were to be made serviceable for the Nazi regime's massive project of imperial expansion, and the cinema helped to articulate what role they would play in an expanding Reich and ultimately in colonial territories abroad. The shifting borders of the regime's dominion over both foreign and domestic populations necessitated recalibrations in its gender ideology. One of the most problematic issues concerned women's participation in paid labor, which was considered undesirable at the beginning of the regime due to high unemployment rates but ultimately became indispensable as the Reich moved closer to war. Love stories in Nazi cinema often took up the issue of women's place in the public sphere and addressed the issue of the relative values of professional and private life. Contrary to common assumption, most Nazi romance films did not advocate a return to traditional feminine roles or oppose the Weimar era's advances into sexual modernity. Instead, Nazi romance melodramas often supported a turn away from domesticity while arguing for the maintenance of hierarchical structures and self-sacrificial positions in the workplace. This was true of prewar as well as wartime films.

Nazi romance melodramas also spoke to men and aimed to condition male desire as well. As noted in the last chapter, melodramatic spectatorship in the Third Reich was not assumed to be primarily female. The melodramatic love story appealed to male viewers via lead actresses and supporting dancers who were explicitly selected for their erotic charms. As the present chapter shows, the choice of male romantic heroes followed a primarily racial-eugenic logic, while the choice of romantic heroines supported Nazi cinema's imperial ambitions. These ambitions included the annexation of new audiences abroad. The sexual content of Nazi films was calculated to exceed that of Hollywood in an attempt to make Nazi rule appear more attractive to German, occupied, and neutral audiences. The romance melodrama supported an image of Nazi culture as revolutionary; rather than forcing a return to tradition, Nazi love stories often promised to liberate spectators from the constraints of nineteenth- and early twentieth-century sexual mores, which were denounced in Nazi media under the heading of "bourgeois morality." Contrary to the assumptions of scholars who have argued that the Nazis attempted to desexualize the cinema, historical evidence shows that Goebbels and his subordinates explicitly recruited the erotic attractions of female performers in order to suppress political critique.[6] Yet the "woman question" continually threatened to interfere with the propaganda minister's instrumentalization of the female body. Nazi cinema's deployment of the erotic sometimes backfired, resulting in excessive film texts and resistant spectators. There is evidence that some female spectators declined to embrace the Nazi vision of romance—a fascist love that was, at its heart, the romance of war.

The Functions of Romance: Gender Coding and Imperialism

In the classic melodramatic structure elaborated by nineteenth-century theater and early twentieth-century silent cinema, conflicts are simplified in dualistic forms and embodied as a clash of characters who represent either preferred forms of identification or prohibited desires. In the most simplified melodramatic form, excessive desire is located in the villain, and it threatens a heroine who is innocent and thus without illegitimate desire. Film melodrama of the 1930s and 1940s, however, alters this model; instead of a struggle of innocents against villains, conflicts of desire are generally internal, based in an overabundance within the heroine herself. Her desires are multiple and mutually exclusive and thus impossible within the economy of the classical film narrative, or they are forbidden by some generally accepted moral code. The melodramatic narrative thus attempts either to limit her desire and focus it on one object or to purge her of illicit desires. In this way such narratives may serve a pedagogical or ideological function by warning of the consequences of illicit acts or by training desire to attach itself to the "correct" object.

Romance can thus be recruited for political service; even if it does not name an external enemy, as does the most original form of the melodrama, it can form desire in ideologically useful ways. On the most primary level, romance melodrama serves to define erotic objects. Usually it does so by a process of elimination of excess desire—of desire for what is politically or socially undesirable, usually embodied in personal or sexual terms by conflicting characters. Alternatively, the elimination of excess desire follows a pedagogical process of surrender and self-correction. In Molly Haskell's taxonomy of the classical Hollywood woman's film, love stories are generally either "choice" films, in which the female protagonist must choose between potential lovers, or "competition" narratives, in which she must struggle against a rival. Or they are "sacrifice" films, in which a choice has to be made between love and another life goal, usually work.[7]

Nazi romance melodramas largely conform to this scheme as well. The triangle was one of the most common shapes for romance narratives in the Third Reich. In innumerable melodramas and comedies, a woman finds herself in competition with another for the affections of a man, or she must choose between potential mates. The choice of mates was often also a choice between marital fidelity or infidelity. The ideological advantages of such a narrative pattern are clear: through the eventual elimination of one of the participants in the triangle, romance films could demonstrate preferred forms of identification while reinforcing the traits and values connoted by the "successful" partners. Likewise, "sacrifice" narratives provided lessons in accommodation to social norms. However, the forms of identification promoted by Nazi melodramas and the desires they elicited did not always conform to the most familiar fascist pronouncements about the restoration of woman to her "natural" position as housewife and mother.

Romances instruct audiences in partner choice, an issue that was of no small concern to a state obsessed with eugenics. As Reichsfilmintendant (Reich General Director of Film) Fritz Hippler asserted, the Nazis were very aware of how cinema conditioned male desire in particular: "the right woman, chosen for her external appearance as well as her internal qualities and characteristics, if used repeatedly and successfully in the cinema, can unconsciously but significantly influence the general level of taste and the ideal of beauty in a great number of men to very advantageous results."[8] It may not be immediately clear how the actresses who were cast the most often in Third Reich films were advantageous to the racist Nazi state. As has often been noted before, the feminine beauty ideal offered by stars of Third Reich films was not always consistent with the racial ideal promoted elsewhere in Nazi media.[9] While the press repeatedly insisted on the inbred superiority of blondes and asserted that German-ness itself was synonymous with beauty, some of the most privileged stars of the Third Reich were dark-haired foreign-born women, such as Hitler's favorite actress, Lil Dagover, and Goebbels's favorite mistress, Lida Baarova. Blood-and-soil ideologues praised the purity of the farm woman and railed against the urban, androgynous styling of both genders in the Weimar cinema, yet most Nazi female film stars were clearly cosmopolitan in origin as well.[10] And although other forms of visual culture in the Third Reich sometimes idealized maternal and hyper-feminine figures in retrograde imitations of nineteenth-century styles, in the cinema such thoroughly domestic types were generally considered unappealing.

Indeed, the chaste, housewifely model of femininity was rarely romanticized in Nazi cinema, a fact that was long overlooked by film scholars who took the blood-and-soil Nazis at their word.[11] Romantic heroines were generally energetic and boyish in the manner of Marianne Hoppe, Brigitte Horney, and Ilse Werner, the latter of whom a postwar star study described as "the German pin-up girl" and who influenced the tastes of the World War II generation by being "energetic, quick-witted and independent."[12] Other lead actresses of romance melodramas, such as Zarah Leander and Olga Tschechowa, exuded an air of worldly sophistication that made them unsuitable for roles as contented, provincial German wives. However, the choice of actresses in the Third Reich was not made primarily according to the values of middle-class domesticity or the perverse logic of racial engineering. The cinema supported an image of Nazism as a modern, revolutionary movement, and its star system had psychological occupation in mind. The foreign and masculinized female faces of Nazi cinema promoted the imperialistic aims of both the militarist state and of the film industry itself. Goebbels justified the continuing reliance on foreign-born stars by pointing to the coming extension of the German film industry's empire: "We have to expand our [actress] types, since we will have to provide films to many more peoples after the war," he wrote in 1941.[13]

Likewise, the Nazi trade press was often concerned with the international success of German cinema and asserted that film actresses had to give a new face to the new state. In a 1937 article titled "Stop 'Gretchen'!" the editors of the *Film-Kurier* suggested that romance films had long given German femininity a bad reputation abroad and had failed to correct the enduring image of women in Germany as passive, suffering housewives. However, the *Film-Kurier* suggested that Nazi culture had actually begun to change this image. The German actresses and dancers who had taken part in the 1937 "German Art Week" in Paris had given the French another impression, the editors claimed, citing the commentary of French journalists who "realized, with no small amount of surprise, that these German girls were anything but 'Gretchen-like,' but rather appeared as slender, athletic Amazons and as beautiful, lively, attractive beings."[14] German cinema, the editors of *Film-Kurier* insisted, should export an image of German women as erotic and dynamic rather than prudish and homebound: "In this respect, German film, which constantly travels beyond the German borders into foreign countries, can clear up misunderstandings . . . German cinema must also help to overcome the stereotypes with which the German woman and the German girl are still frequently viewed abroad. Our young femininity no longer represents the Gretchen of yesteryear, who was marked by a 'sour respectability,' a 'conceited humorlessness' and domestic skills that suffocated all life."[15] And in fact the classic melodrama of feminine innocence threatened by male Faustian drives rarely played on Third Reich screens. The typical heroine of Nazi romances was neither domestic nor entirely chaste; instead, she advertised the joys of international border crossings and the pleasures of seduction. The romantic heroine of Nazi cinema was often a privileged adventuress who did not have to possess household skills, since she had servants to perform the suffocating duties for her. Fixated on upper-class fantasies, German film romances most often narrated the love lives of star stage performers or members of the international moneyed elite, regardless of Nazi ideology's claim to represent the Germanic masses. Yet the cultivation of this type of gender imagery had a logic. The heroine of the Nazi romance melodrama was a prototype suited to the conquest of new territories, imaginable either as an imperious German mistress of newly seized *Lebensraum,* or as the attractive foreign territory itself, as the spoils of war.

The film *Man spricht über Jacqueline* (*Talking about Jacqueline,* 1937) is one such high-society romance and is about the training of an Amazon of sorts. Premiering the same year as the *Film-Kurier*'s call to end representations of passive German femininity, this mediocre melodrama was a classic competition narrative, pitting a sexually assertive tomboy heiress against her more demure and Gretchen-like younger sister. The Jacqueline of the film's title is masculine and adventurous enough to be called Jack or Jacky for short and is referred to by her male best friend as "the best guy [*Kerl*] in the world." She is described both in the dialogue and in the visual iconography of the film as untamed and even impossibly wild. Played by the dark-haired Wera Engels, she is predictably coded as more decadent than her sister, played by the blonde Sabine Peters. While Jacky jets between luxury hotels in London, Rome, and Biarritz, her sister, June, stays in one place (Paris), dutifully studying music. Despite the fact that the younger sister does show some career ambitions and leads a metropolitan existence, the design of the two characters opposes one sister as a representative of modern, independent femininity and the other of more traditional, cloistered womanhood. Jacky is costumed in manly riding boots and hunting suits and is shown eternally in motion, either on trains or on horses, while her more static sister appears in monastic black dresses with white trim around high necks. Accordingly, the primary distinction between the two characters is one of sexual knowledge. Jacky smokes lots of cigarettes and has multiple erotic adventures, but June remains a model of self-denial and sexual innocence. At the beginning of the film, Jacky also flatly rejects marriage, preferring instead to engage in short affairs of her own choosing. Somewhat surprisingly, perhaps, the film's sympathies clearly lie with her; she not only wins the romantic competition but also gets far more screen time than her less erotically appealing sister.

In this regard *Man spricht über Jacqueline* participated in a common convention of romance melodramas, which often favor initially transgressive female roles. The narrative and iconography of *Man spricht über Jacqueline* could be compared to the later Bette Davis romance *Dark Victory* (1939), which features a similarly willful horse-riding heiress. Not surprisingly, in both romance melodramas the heroines eventually fall from their high horses. The riding iconography that appears in so many Nazi and Hollywood romance melodramas makes for an appealingly gender-bending visual design, though it also suggests that unfettered female desire is akin to a wild bestiality and requires eventual reining in by a dominant trainer-lover. The romance film in virtually all classical cinema evidences a hypocritical morality in that the narrative trajectory ends in the punishment or retraining of the liberated woman, even while it simultaneously makes her freedom appear enviable.

However, unlike in *Dark Victory* and other Hollywood "medical discourse" melodramas, female sexuality is the explicitly articulated problem at the center of *Man spricht über Jacqueline,* not an invisible illness that requires diagnosis and sympathetic treatment by a paternalistic doctor husband. In many Third Reich romances it is the woman who is lusty by nature, while her male partner is restrained. Jacky's primary love interest, Michael, is a rigid middle-age divorcé taking a break from his position as an overseer of unspecified British colonies. As he soon makes clear, he tolerates no insurrection on the "dark continent" of female desire, just as he tolerates no political resistance by colonized peoples. He refuses to play along with Jacky's flirtation and is

„Man spricht über Jacqueline"

Suggestions of sexual modernity: *Man spricht über Jacqueline* (1937). Source: Deutsche Kinemathek

overtly disgusted when she takes the sexual initiative. Women, he says, are all as unreliable as his unfaithful ex-wife: "They are all the same: unbridled and uninhibited," he proclaims, later taking a horse whip into his hands and threatening to use it on Jacky to retrain her. Still, the uninhibited and some-what masculine girl is considered more desirable than her virtuous sister. At the end of the film, Jacky has been tamed via Michael's brutal masculinity and has repented her promiscuous past (but still wears transparent lingerie in postmarital hotel beds, thus transferring ownership of her stimulating sexuality to her husband). Her more properly dressed sister, briefly in the running for Michael's attentions, fails in the end to attract a mate. Evidently, the high-spirited object of sadistic discipline was considered a better match for the colonial master, since in her new position as mistress of a foreign estate, she would be more likely to turn the whip against colonized others than would a more cloistered type.

Man spricht über Jacqueline's "taming of the shrew" format was reproduced in many other Third Reich romances. Curiously, this structure can be seen as opposite to the conventional form of Anglo-American literary romances, which tend toward the domestication of the male partner through a recognition of the woman's virtue. As Tania Modleski has observed in regard to American romance novels of the eighteenth to twentieth centuries: "Like the Harlequins of the present day, the novels repeatedly insisted on the importance of the heroine's virginity . . . in novel after novel, the man is brought to acknowledge the preeminence of love and the attractions of domesticity at which he has, as a rule, previously scoffed."[16] Unlike such American literary romances or the classic American film melodramas of D. W. Griffith, Nazi film romances usually do not insist on the chastity or the domesticity of the heroine, even if they do warn against female sexual excesses.

Indeed, women in Third Reich romances are granted enough signs of autonomy and androgyny to make them appear modern and occasionally almost liberated, though ultimately they may still be subject to the authority of conventional narrative closure. Third Reich romances often end their battles of the sexes in vicious forms of capitulation of the female partner (sometimes signaled by an at least partial surrender of masculine traits). However, these films do offer female roles that were considered somewhat transgressive at the time the films were screened, since their thematization of sexuality was more than what Hays Code–era Hollywood melodramas were able to risk. The forceful reining in of such transgressions was certainly viewed by much of the audience as necessary to prevent sexual chaos, but at the same time, such liberties were what sold Nazi films in the Reich and abroad.

Clearly, what was at work in Nazi film romances such as *Man spricht über Jacqueline* was not a reestablishment of traditional roles and representations in complete opposition to the gender imagery of the Weimar Republic, but rather an extension of Weimar's sexual modernization—though with a sadistic fascist edge. Historian Dagmar Herzog has stressed that Nazism promoted an intensified liberalization of sexuality, at least for the heterosexual, non-Jewish segment of the Reich's population: "Although in countless instances, above all in its thorough racialization of sex and in its heightened homophobia, the Third Reich represented a brutal backlash against the progressivism of Weimar, Nazism brought with it not only a redefinition but also an expansion of preexisting liberalizing trends."[17] One aspect of these liberalizing tendencies was the maintenance of fluidity in gender styling.

Despite the Nazis' rabid homophobia and their mass murder of gays, female androgyny of the sort found in *Man spricht über Jacqueline* remained very much a staple of Third Reich visual culture. The ambiguous gender identity of Nazi cinema's highest-paid star, Zarah Leander, has often been noted by postwar film critics and was even acknowledged during Third Reich as well. In the advertising materials for the 1937 Leander melodrama *Zu neuen Ufern* (*To New Shores*), there was a suggestion of the star's bisexual appeal: "The secret of Zarah Leander's effect is that she touches equally on masculine, as well as feminine feelings."[18] In an effort to cultivate masculine feelings, Nazi cinema often presented women in drag costuming. Marlene Dietrich–style cross-dressing in top hat, trousers, and tailcoat was common for both film and stage revue numbers in the Third Reich, as was the manly, aristocratic horse-riding ensemble.[19] Some film narratives go even further than mannish fashion and allow women in drag to pass as men, thus blurring the borders of "essential" sex differences.[20] Such gender ambiguity, however, was not intended as covert support for lesbianism or female emancipation. Rather, manly costuming corresponded to the general masculinization and militarization of German society and to German cinema's efforts to remain at the forefront of industrial modernity.

As a result of such imagery, many contemporary viewers of Third Reich films certainly considered the gender roles presented in them to be highly modern rather than regressive.[21] The Nazis cultivated a falsified self-image as a revolutionary movement, and many contemporaries correspondingly believed that Nazi culture offered the potential for sexual revolution, both in terms of style and in sexual behavior. In 1934 Wilhelm Reich cited the following report that he had received from a former colleague in Germany, who believed that he had seen a clear change in sexual morality under the Nazis: "'The boys and girls of the Hitler Youth (H.J.) and of the League of German Girls (B.d.M.) enjoy unheard-of freedom at school and at home, which naturally manifests itself, inter alia, in sexual activity and friendships. In the past, no girl of school grade would have dared to be seen with a boyfriend picking her up after classes. Today, boys (especially H.J. boys) wait outside the school in a crowd, and everybody accepts this as a matter of course. Everybody says that B.d.M. stands for Bubi-drück-mich (I-wanna-be-hugged).'"[22] Wilhelm Reich insisted that such examples were not actually proof of a new degree of sexual freedom under the Nazis, and he emphasized that Nazism was in fact deeply reactionary in its sexual ideology. But the popular sense that Nazi culture promoted a liberation of sexual morality was widespread at the time, regardless of how repressive the rhetoric of the more extreme Nazi ideologues and the reality of gender relations in the Third Reich actually were. Many observers, both in the Reich and abroad, felt that there had been an eroticization of public life under Hitler and that morals of the masses were loosening according to a master plan. In 1942 Herbert Marcuse wrote in regard to Nazism and its self-representation in art:

Sexual life has become a matter of political training and manipulation . . . Official encouragement is expressed in the deliberate herding of boys and girls in and near the labor camps, and in the stimulating distinctness with which National Socialist artists expose the erogenous zones of the human body . . . This new National Socialist realism fulfills its political function as an instrument for sexual education and inducement. The political utilization of sex has transformed it from a sphere of protective privacy in which a recalcitrant freedom could endure to a sphere of acquiescent license.[23]

In fact, the Propaganda Ministry did view the intensified eroticization of Nazi culture as an effective political strategy. In 1937 Goebbels noted approvingly in his diary that liberalization was already taking effect: "Sex life in this gigantic city somewhat loosened. It has to be that way."[24]

The cinema of the Third Reich attempted to create and capitalize on such illusions of sexual liberation. Just like the *Film-Kurier*'s article about modern German femininity, Third Reich media often compared past moments of repressive bourgeois morality to the Hitler era's more "enlightened" sexual morals and gender roles. Goebbels, at least, felt that the Third Reich was at the forefront of a cultural revolution that showed itself in its feminine beauty ideals. Nazi women were more modern than their repressed Wilhelmine grandmothers, he noted in his diary in 1939: "We chat at the Führer's about the variability of the concept of female beauty. What was considered beautiful 40 years ago is now chunky, fat, flabby. Sports, permissiveness, gymnastics, and the battle against hypocrisy have changed humanity . . . We are racing at full speed toward a new antiquity. And in all fields, we are the pioneers of this revolution."[25] Film, of course, was Goebbels's preferred medium for beauty revolutions. Continuing the fight against nineteenth-century styles of living, Nazi cinema consciously cultivated the erotic attractions of its female stars.

Documents that remain from a state-sponsored program of training camps for future Nazi film stars (*Nachwuchsforderung*) show that actresses with a strong sex appeal were actively recruited. Prospective candidates were given screen tests and evaluated according to their physical features and their general attractiveness. The candidates' body and facial shapes were analyzed in detail, though what was sought was less an impression of ideal beauty or even racial purity than of erotic appeal. This appeal was generally synonymous with a sense of the exotic, not necessarily of the *Volk* (people). Candidates who had what the Nazis considered to be ideal facial and racial features were nonetheless rejected if they failed to excite male fantasy, as the following memo from Reichsfilmdramaturg (Chief Script Editor) Frank Maraun regarding the screen test of one candidate showed: "The shots show that

[she] has a pretty figure, nice legs and an appealing naturalness in her manner and acting. But her face seems a bit boring and expressionless. It reveals a nice but rather unimaginative ordinary person without the attractions of an individual personality. Therefore it does not appear justified to make a further attempt with [her]."[26] Nice legs were not enough for the Nazi cinema if they suggested only the banal beauty of the average German girl; what was desired on the screen were not female representations of "the people" but rather of less common and more individual, even willful, types. Despite the often-repeated rhetoric of the Nazi press and other forms of printed propaganda insisting that the form of femininity desired in the Nazi state was based on *völkisch,* racialized aesthetics and rural values, the femininity cultivated on the screen was of a distinctly wealthier and worldlier class.[27]

The Nazi leadership's rejection of what they viewed as bourgeois morality did not necessarily extend to bourgeois or aristocratic style; there was a clear discrimination against rural, proletarian, and petit bourgeois types in the Nazis' cultivation of stars. In 1941 Goebbels wrote that the selection of trainee actors and actresses who make a "petit bourgeois impression" should be avoided, because "in almost no case do they have the possibility of gaining international clout."[28] One candidate, whom Frank Maraun described as an exceptionally talented actress with an already successful stage career, was nonetheless rejected for film roles because she had a "pronounced poor-person-characteristic in her face."[29] By way of contrast, another female candidate, who was given a screen test in 1942 and whose last name indicated aristocratic origins, was chosen for star training even though she had no acting experience, because she could "probably be developed into a sophisticated type of young socialite [*Salondame*]."[30] What was worth developing in the socialite type—besides the attractions of wealth and glamour—was the image of self-aware female sexuality; the upper-class mistress of the salon consciously applied erotic charm, the appeal of which was international.

In general, Third Reich actresses who showed an ability to portray characters that clearly possessed sexual knowledge were preferred over more wholesome types, particularly for use as the heroines of romance melodramas. Sometimes eroticism could even take precedence over ideal physiognomy, and occasionally an actress was chosen specifically for her less sophisticated, rawer form of sex appeal. Maraun's assessment of the facial features of another female candidate in May 1942 is surprising in this regard: "As a result of her low hairline and her noticeably small forehead, her face has a pronounced animalistic quality. The expression around the mouth intensifies the impression of a whore. But this tendency toward whorishness in the candidate is not unappealing. One could imagine that the candidate could develop into a striking and useful type."[31] The fact that Maraun considered this actress to have a usefully "whorish" look indicates the extent to which eroticism was consciously instrumentalized by Nazi culture producers. His use of the terms *"prägnant"* (striking, or fertile) and *"einsatzfähig"* (useful, or capable of being deployed) in describing the desirability of this type of actress reveals that the female body was considered a key weapon on both domestic and international fronts. Nazi cinema, like Nazi society in general, clearly had a continuing need for prostitutes.[32] Usually they appeared as minor background figures rather than romantic leads, lending harbor bars and colonial nightclubs their fascinatingly exotic atmospheres (as in Helmut Käutner's melodrama *Grosse Freiheit Nr. 7* [*Great Freedom Nr. 7*], 1944). In lead roles the prostitute was generally promoted to the level of wealthy courtesan and given the tragic higher art status of a fallen woman, as in *Der Postmeister*.

Another of Hilde Krahl's lead roles, however, offered the reversed logic by rescuing a woman from a brothel and integrating her into Hanseatic high society. At the beginning of the 1939 romance/adventure film *Die barmherzige Lüge* (*The Merciful Lie*), Krahl's heroine Anja is coded as a prostitute, and, more remarkably, her national and ethnic origins remain somewhat uncertain throughout the film. The initial sequences are set somewhere along the Manchurian-Mongolian border, in a town that, as the introductory titles proclaim, is the starting point of dangerous expeditions into frontier regions. At the center of the mise-en-scène of this wild East outpost is a female-owned tavern and brothel (offering, as a sign indicates, "Equipment of All Kinds"). Anja, the niece of the brothel owner, is shown in her first scene on horseback, winning a race against a group of male riders. When she returns to the tavern from her riding expedition, she is propositioned by a French man who offers her furs in exchange for favors, and she brushes him off with a bored "maybe," after which a wandering camera explores the other Eurasian prostitutes' legs and chest regions. This eastern wilderness is represented as a space where everything can be either purchased or taken by force, and where individual Europeans have the right to explore unmapped territories and to colonize what they find useful.

The hidden potential of this fertile ground and its main character is revealed in the next sequence, when the viewer discovers that the wild rider Anja is also the single mother of a half-German baby. Within a few cuts the unwitting father of the child (the "explorer" Dr. Thomas Clausen) unexpectedly returns in colonial khaki, ready for another expedition into the Soviet-controlled borderlands. Determined to unite with the father, Anja watches in disappointment as he helps another woman out of his tank-like truck. This rival is the explorer's German wife, and her character is constructed

The "eroticism-filled air of colonial surroundings": *Die barmherzige Lüge* (1939).
Rights: Friedrich-Wilhelm-Murnau-Stiftung; Distributor: Transit Film GmbH

to provide an obvious contrast to the vampish Anja. Unlike Anja, the legal wife is sexually naïve and unexciting, a young blonde with the virginal name Maria, who takes care of her husband with complete devotion. In one scene she explains their marriage thus: "He needs someone to sew on his buttons, and I also transcribe his journal," to which her husband sarcastically answers, "What would I do without you?" She also inquires what the male fur hunters are doing in the tavern, failing to understand the sexual economy of this world. The contrast between the sexual knowledge of the two women is also connoted through dress: while Maria covers herself in respectable wool suits, Anja appears in a low-cut dress with a feather boa and a coquettish fan. Significantly, though, the chastely dutiful Maria is also childless, and here the viewer is perhaps supposed to infer a connection between her ignorance about the facts of prostitution and her own lack of fruitful sexuality. At this point in the narrative, we might expect the competition structure to be resolved according to the standard international convention for melodrama, whereby women of ambiguous sexual morals are punished and eliminated in order to make room for "pure" heroines and to reaffirm the status quo of marriage. However, in *Die barmherzige Lüge* it is the sexually innocent legal wife who is given a quick offscreen death, while the prostitute and premarital mother is finally recognized as the legitimate romantic partner. After Maria dies of food poisoning and Thomas disappears on an expedition, Anja travels to Germany and integrates herself into his wealthy Bremen family, masquerading as the dead Maria.

The vision of German family life portrayed in the rest of the film is typical for Nazi romances, and also typically at odds with the official Nazi ideology of large families comprised of classless members of a national community. The Germany of Third Reich romance films is populated by corporate directors, abundant servants, and few children. When Anja brings her son into the family mansion, there is a flurry of dynastic excitement, since she has succeeded in finally rescuing the imperiled family corporation by means of a male heir and future director. The supposedly valuable child, it should be noted, does not receive more screen time than is necessary to simply state its existence, since the interests of the film lie more with adult situations. This, as we will see in the next chapter, is fully consistent with Nazi cinema's ambivalent attitude toward children.

Although she is not eliminated, the sexualized heroine in *Die barmherzige Lüge* does go through a retraining process before her final integration into the couple, but this process is less brutal than in the earlier *Man spricht über Jacqueline*. While in Bremen, Anja smokes, unpacks and fondles her sequined dress nostalgically, and offers herself for casual sex to a friend of the family, but she soon surrenders these markers of her past life in order to assimilate into upper-class society for the sake of her child. The final shot of the film has Anja complacently sitting in the springtime backyard in a flowered dress, surrounded by her son and his father (presumably now her legitimate husband, though no wedding is ever shown). The transformation from fur to floral prints, from horse riding in the steppe to a chair under an oak, marks a classic taming-of-the-shrew narrative. It should be noted, however, that while a retraining process occurs here—as in most romance films that feature somewhat transgressive heroines—there is no explicit punishment. Rather, the formation of the family and the heroine's rise in class status at the end of the film is presented as a final recognition of the inherent legitimacy of the premarital mother.

Thus, although the ending of *Die barmherzige Lüge* is entirely conventional, this film is another example of how the sexual morality of Nazi melodramas often differed significantly from that of Hays Code–era Hollywood. This difference can perhaps be explained by the same political intent evident in Hilde Krahl's later starring role in *Der Postmeister*. Like the later film, *Die barmherzige Lüge* does double duty by picturing the spaces of war and suggesting the sexual possibilities of wartime conquest while setting standards for gender roles at home. The Manchurian setting of the beginning sequences of the film clearly locate it in an area of conflict related to the upcoming military campaign. If *Der Postmeister* promised erotic adventure as a main attraction awaiting the soldier/colonizer in the Soviet East, *Die barmherzige Lüge* paved the same road by providing a similar spectacle of foreign bodies that could be either taken by force or purchased with goods acquired by guns. The eastern territories pictured in *Die barmherzige Lüge* seem to offer something to female military-entrepreneurial spirit as well. Anja's aunt Vera is not only a madam but also a merchant of materiél for European expeditions, and she is described in the film's dialogue as making a highly profitable *Bombengeschäft* (literally, a "bombing business") in doing so. She is also the most powerful person in town, commanding an army of subordinates. There was thus a subtle lure written into this script, a promise of new economic possibilities in the East for Nazi women. In the German Reich, it also made clear, making large sums of money remained a hereditary male trade.

While suggesting the attractions to be found in the business of war, the film's voyages across the two spaces of foreign and domestic, East and West, also created a hybrid model of femininity that was typical for Nazi melodramas. Romances required their female leads to display both erotic appeal and public restraint, fertility and masculine energy, self-sacrifice and individualized character. Though the previously wild heroine becomes partially domesticated through insertion into urbane society, she is still clearly in possession of the skills that allowed her to survive at the borders of civilization—and is ready to unpack them again for German wartime use. The western movement of the heroine in *Die barmherzige Lüge* conformed to the *Heim-ins-Reich* (return-to-the-Reich) structure of many Nazi melodramas that featured women abroad. By first locating the heroine in foreign territory and then repatriating her into the Reich, such films fabricated an integrated national body whose aggressive arms reached across many continents. Curiously, though, the heroine of *Die barmherzige Lüge* is never explicitly identified as being of German ethnicity; thus, nationalization occurs here with a woman of ambiguous origins.

This ambiguity of origins was not at all atypical for Nazi romantic heroines, since Nazi cinema as a whole relied heavily upon the allure of the foreign in terms of both casting and setting. The contradiction between the Third Reich's racial policies and its cinematic imaginary was a thorn in the eyes of some Nazis who insisted on ideological consistency. In his 1941 treatise on the ideals and failings of Nazi film, Peter von Werder criticized what he saw as a still rampant preference for exotic types and suggested that German cinema's eroticization of foreigners and even non-Europeans was being carried out at the expense of German women. This had to be changed, von Werder insisted: "the colored woman is still not represented in film in a way which reflects our actual views. A corresponding correction of the female image as it appears in the foreign and therefore particularly pungent eroticism-filled air of colonial surroundings is practically and theoretically important: practically with regard to the colonial expectations of the Germans and theoretically with regard to the overall attitude toward the German woman."[33] Erotic fantasies of dark-skinned women, von Werder implied, were threatening the ability of German men to be both efficient administrators of colonial territories and pure breeders with German women. Films should be structured according to racial motives, he asserted: "A romantic admiration for the foreigner, especially in his most private area, is not appropriate . . . The dramaturgical objection that foreign eroticism creates a first-class attraction for the cinematic form takes second place to ideological-political considerations, as well as to the racial law of breeding."[34] Even in the Third Reich, as von Werder implies here, film producers depended upon eroticism as the main foundation of cinematic effectiveness, and fantasies of the foreign remained a primary source of spectator pleasure. Von Werder, however, clearly neglected to understand just how central such fantasies were to the Nazi imperialist (and even racist) project.[35] As we have seen in *Der Postmeister* and *Die barmherzige Lüge,* the erotic gaze onto foreign territories and bodies indeed supported the "ideological-political" aims of militaristic expansion, as did Nazi cinema's visions of femininity in general.

However, I would suggest that the standards set by actors in romance melodramas were actually more crucial for the Nazi racist logic than those of actresses. Representations of femininity were perhaps not always consistent, because they were less central to the fascist project than rigid conceptions of masculinity. The eroticized or romanticized foreigner, as von Werder suggested, was therefore primarily a female role. With the exceptions of the Dutch actors Johannes Heesters and Frits van Dongen, almost all the male stars of Third Reich romance films were German or Austrian. This fact did have a basis in the divided attitudes towards inter-ethnic reproduction: Nazi leaders often accounted for the fact that German soldiers would produce children with foreign women, particularly through prostitution or rape, which they considered natural effects of war and colonization. According to their perverse logic, this could only further the ultimate goal of the Germanization of the world. Since German men would not be expected to take responsibility for children fathered with women abroad, their foreign affairs would have no effect on the ethnic constitution of the Reich. On the other hand, German women's romances with foreign men would lead to a disastrous degeneration of "the blood" and the contamination of the "national body," according to Nazi thinking.[36] The fact that Nazi propaganda did not manage to entirely eradicate German women's attraction to foreigners, especially to non-"Aryans," was a constant source of anxiety for the authorities.[37]

Thus, Nazi cinema allowed for some foreign attractions when it came to the choice of actresses, but its choice of male romantic leads was less adventurous. Classical cinema's conventional gender divisions also influenced the choice of actors. In Germany, as in Hollywood, the actresses were the primary spectacle. The male leads of Nazi romances were so similar in their physical type that for today's viewers they may be virtually indistinguishable from each other, and their character types were also standardized. They were uncomplicated winners, as this contemporary description of the popular actor Hans Söhnker demonstrates: "He has always been given victorious roles, men who not only always get their due and attain their goal, thus remaining the hero in the sense of the old cinematic norm, but who also stand on the sunny side of life, and who, above all, must never go through any tragic transformation themselves, or make any steps toward devilish temptation."[38] The typical Nazi romantic hero was always right and was never asked to undergo character developments.[39] Male actors were often chosen according to their ability to create an impression of "manliness," which, as we have seen in *Man spricht über Jacqueline,* was often synonymous with sexual restraint. An actor who seemed too arrogantly aware of his seductive powers could be rejected as being too feminine, as proved by another of Frank Maraun's memos regarding the screen test of a male candidate for actor's training. Maraun wrote: "All in all, an unmanly appearance. Is unpleasantly self-satisfied and has the presumptuous superiority of a young hairdresser who gets girls easily, for my tastes altogether too soft . . . In sum: training does not appear worthwhile."[40] Male seducers did not often appear on Nazi screens, since sexual awareness and gender flexibility were considered female properties.

Indeed, the Nazi image of masculinity and the gender roles of German men were more determinate than that of women. Male androgyny was much less common in Third Reich media than images of female androgyny, and intimations of male homosexuality were rare in Third Reich cinema. An important reason for the greater flexibility in female representations lies in the fact that lesbianism was considered less threatening to the Nazi system than male homosexuality. Whereas gay men appeared to undermine the reproduction goals of the Third Reich, lesbians theoretically could still produce future soldiers. Furthermore, in the Weimar era there had been a greater degree of institutionalized homophobia directed toward men than toward women. While male homosexuality had been punishable by law since 1919 under Paragraph 175 of the German Criminal Code, no law officially existed on the books during the Weimar Republic or the Third Reich to punish female homosexuality. Weimar-era opponents of Nazism, we should remember, also made use of homophobia in their anti-Nazi rhetoric.[41] Nazism's association with male homosexuality in the popular imaginary had become a political liability by the early 1930s, and Nazi leaders sought to limit such associations through the murder of gay members of the paramilitary SA (Sturmabteilung), and by controlling images of masculinity in Third Reich media.

As a result, male leads in Nazi films were generally strict and efficient, lacking in the sort of character development that arose from the conflicting desires of female protagonists. The romance film's triangular choice structures confined male subjectivity into the isolation cells of either winner or loser. Much stress was placed upon the class status of male protagonists, with the winning romantic hero in Nazi melodramas almost always a man of means; there was nothing socialist about the National Socialist romantic imaginary. A favorite lead figure for Nazi melodramas before 1939 was the British aristocrat or high-level colonial administrator (as in *Man spricht über Jacqueline, Eine Frau ohne Bedeutung* (*A Woman of No Importance*, 1936), and *Das Mädchen Irene*). After the start of the war he was replaced by the figure of the *haut bourgeois* shipping executive from Bremen or Hamburg (as in the romance melodramas *Frauenliebe–Frauenleid* [*Women's Loves–Women's Sorrows,* 1937] and *Opfergang* [*Sacrifice,* 1944]). Other romance films feature business leaders with colonial connections, such as Willy Birgel's Berlin industrialist moonlighting as a pilot/adventurer in North Africa in *Verklungene Melodie* (*Dead Melody,* 1939).

Male romantic leads were commonly also medical doctors or Herr Doktors; in most instances romantic heroes represented some kind of authority figure. Although many women in Third Reich melodramas had professions, their matches were almost always higher on the professional ladder, and quite often their matches were their supervisors both at work and at home. Men in Third Reich romances were usually many years older than their female counterparts, which, as we will see in the next chapter, often gave rise to suggestions of incestuous attractions. Heroines of Nazi love stories were often barely even of legal age, and any objection to such intergenerational romances was often portrayed as outmoded bourgeois prudery. Most notably in this regard, the romances *Reifende Jugend* (*Ripening Youth,* 1933), *Arme kleine Inge* (*Poor Little Inge,* 1936), *Liebe kann lügen* (*Love Can Lie,* 1937), and *Ihr erstes Erlebnis* (*Her First Experience,* 1939) all pair teenage schoolgirls with their teachers.

Reifende Jugend was one of the first productions of the Third Reich to be highly praised in the Nazi press, and it was one of the first to address the place of girls and women in the new regime. It is particularly conflicted in its reinforcement of patriarchal structures, since it also critiques educational discrimination and pretends to present a modern and progressive perspective on gender. The film concerns a trio of girls who transfer into an elite, all-male high school in the patrician city of Lübeck so that they can study for their university entrance exams, a course of study not available to them in their gender-segregated school. Many of the all-male teachers of the school see the presence of the girls as an attack on traditional values and academic quality, a position that the film initially sets out to correct. The Latin teacher, the most sexist of the group, is caricatured as hopelessly out of date, his ideas on gender as outmoded as his Wilhelmine-style middle part and fencing scar. The boys in the school initially treat the girls with macho disdain, until the girls succeed in proving themselves against all expectations by excelling in math and science, while the hormone-driven boys begin to write love poetry and neglect their schoolwork.

Reifende Jugend stars Hertha Thiele as the main protagonist, Elfriede, and she lends a lot of the independent, intelligent vigor that she displayed in her roles in *Mädchen in Uniform* (*Girls in Uniform,* 1931) and *Kuhle Wampe, oder: Wem gehört die Welt?* (*Kuhle Wampe, or Who Owns the World?* 1932) to

Confronting sexism in the schoolgirl romance film: *Reifende Jugend* (1933).
Source: Deutsche Kinemathek

this role as well. Though the earlier film has often been cited as a classic of lesbian cinema, it was also openly admired by film journalists in the Third Reich, and consequently it was clearly a model for *Reifende Jugend* and other youth films after 1933.[42] In fact, *Reifende Jugend* replays many of the same elements as *Mädchen in Uniform,* but substitutes a heterosexual choice narrative for the Weimar film's homosexual crush. The film ultimately performs a switch by shifting the focus from the issue of girls and science education to the question of which romantic partner Elfriede will choose—either her adoring classmate Knud or her authoritarian physics teacher, Dr. Kerner. Naturally, the much older man wins the competition, becoming both the final examiner and the fiancé of the schoolgirl. Although all the girls pass their final exams with high marks, in the end it remains unclear whether they will go on to careers in medicine or simply marry. The initially progressive impulse of the film toward gender equality is thus partially defused and rerouted into romance, which is configured as a hierarchical rather than an egalitarian structure.

It was not only in schoolgirl romances that this occurred but also in many other choice narratives of Nazi cinema. In the standard choice scheme, a young and comparatively sensitive man competes for the heroine against an older authority figure who, in most cases, shows contempt for or disapproval of her. The older man almost always prevails, as if film producers feared that women might be tempted to flee the hierarchical fascist order with a young male comrade and set up a democratic community of two. A subsidiary plotline in *Man spricht über Jacqueline* provided another example of just such a training in partner choice. The young, male best friend who calls Jacky "the best guy in the world" and clearly desires her in her original form is rejected in favor of the older man who, as the heroine says, can "make what he wants out of a woman." At the end of the film, the winner, Michael, proclaims in relation to the chastised Jacky, "I tortured her because I love her." As is usual in Third Reich films, the cruel, authoritarian male is presented as the preferable choice, and brutality is presented as the very proof of love. In Nazi romances the lovers are adversaries rather than virtuous allies besieged by a villainous foe, in contrast to earlier conventions of romance.[43]

Despite their seemingly autonomous, willful characteristics, romantic heroines often proclaim in Nazi scripts that they want men who can dominate them, who are stubborn *Dickschädel* (thick heads), not tender lovers. This is perfectly consistent with international generic conventions for classical cinema, since melodramatic heroines, in both Germany and America, usually prefer men who show contempt for them. As Pam Cook stated in regard to the Hollywood romance: "the problematization of female desire in the women's picture means that her choice of the romantic hero as love object is usually masochistic, against her own best interests, and she suffers for her desire."[44] For Cook, Hollywood's problem lies in the very irreconcilability of femininity and desire, in the essential impossibility of conceptualizing feminine subjectivity within the classical representational system. Even if the heroine's choice is painful, in essence there is really no choice at all.

Labors of Love: Work Romances

In many romance films, of Hollywood as well as the Third Reich, the central conflict of interest is a woman's irreconcilable attachment to both love and work. The conventional solution to this form of triangular desire in all classical cinemas is the surrender of the latter for the former. In most Hollywood films of the 1930s and '40s, as in the majority of Third Reich films, women ended their careers in marriage. As Molly Haskell commented, female autonomy was merely a narrative ploy in American films of the era: "their mythic destiny, like that of all women, was to find love and cast off the 'veneer' of independence."[45] Casting off independence was generally equivalent to discarding the illusion of subjectivity, the claim to desire.

However, in some instances work actually appeared stronger than love. It is clear from many romance films of the Third Reich that the veneer of autonomy was still quite appealing, and the desire for recognition in the workplace remained strong among many female spectators. In the 1938 romance *Die vier Gesellen* (*The Four Companions*), the process of surrendering to a conventional female destiny appears particularly painful. The film argues that female claims to financial independence are doomed due to the ever present double standard in the economic sphere, yet it simultaneously evokes utopian desires for an egalitarian world where talent would be rewarded regardless of gender. Love, on the other hand, appears somewhat unattractive in comparison.

Die vier Gesellen stars Hans Söhnker as a professor of advertising and graphic design, and the beautifully brooding Ingrid Bergman (in her only appearance in a Third Reich film) as his art school student. At the beginning of the film, Söhnker's character lectures his soon-to-graduate class about the difficulty of making money with drawing and painting and then addresses his four female students directly, warning them about the particular futility of their career efforts. Bergman's character, Marianne, he says, suffers from "misguided feminine ambitions," so he offers her a job as his housewife instead. A subsequent scene begins to express the frustrations of a woman with ambition in an unequal world. Söhnker as the chauvinistic professor surprises her in the school kitchen as she is preparing food for the graduation party, and tells her that an apron is really the most flattering work wear for her and that cooking is the most advanced "feminine science." Bergman/Marianne responds with a furious look, leans into a loaf of bread with an enormous knife, and then drops a greasy sausage into a boiling pot of water. Not taking much notice of her castrating gesture or of her legitimate resentment, the professor details her other future job duties, such as sewing on his buttons and darning the holes in his socks, before complaining that the sandwich she has just prepared was obviously not "smeared with love." He adds that she will still have plenty of time to learn how to butter bread correctly, and then slaps her on the back and growls "*Wiedersehen!*" before exiting the room. The camera work in this scene serves to align the viewer with the female protagonist's perspective, since it reveals the rather disgusting materiality of the food that Marianne is preparing, and creates a very palpable sense of dread with regard to the daily work of a housewife. But this film does not intend to offer an escape. It is already clear at this early point in the film that this man is indeed her future husband, although the film barely maintains a discourse of love. Instead, marriage is presented in dreary economic terms, as a form of cheap labor like many others, but the rest of the narrative works on breaking down the woman's resistance to this

Foregrounding the romance of work: *Die vier Gesellen* (1938). Courtesy bpk,
Berlin/Art Resource, New York

position. The film thus reflects what Marcuse referred to as Nazism's "cynical matter-of-factness," according to which all private need was subordinated to the demands of industrial efficiency.[46]

Die vier Gesellen directly addresses gender discrimination and sexual harassment in the work world, presenting both of these as unavoidable facts of life and the result of a strained economy. After the heroine's demeaning encounter with her professor and future fiancé, she becomes determined to prove him wrong by launching her own career in advertising. A montage sequence follows with shots of Marianne searching for a job, cutting out newspaper announcements, traveling through the city, and experiencing one rejection after another—a montage that is clearly indebted to Weimar-era proletarian films like *Kuhle Wampe*. A close-up of her shoes reveals holes in their soles, directly visualizing the physical costs of feminine ambition. During one interview a lecherous company director says he might consider trying her out, with the editing of the sequence suggesting in what capacity she would be expected to work. His voice track is added to a visual montage of fragmented shots of the legs and breasts of wooden mannequins modeling lingerie, as if to suggest by analogy that female bodies are still the main unit of exchange in the business world and that they are as interchangeable as the limbs on a mannequin.

The central section of the film does manage to briefly awaken hope of escape from this oppressive sexual economy. When Marianne joins forces with the other underemployed female graduates of her design program and they launch their own advertising firm, the all-female company appears almost as a viable—though militaristically disciplined—alternative to marital life. They receive one short-lived design contract, and an ecstatic scene follows as the young women see their advertising poster hanging in the Friedrichstrasse, Berlin's main commercial street, and view the results of their work as publicly visible and validated. But once it becomes known that the firm is female-owned, the contracts do not continue, and soon they can no longer find money for food and rent. When Marianne's former professor comes to visit and renews his offer of marriage, she is already swooning from hunger, her entrepreneurial will broken. Marianne's capitulation to housewifery at the end of the film suggests the necessary failure of women's business ambitions. The only escape for the ambitious, exceptional woman, the film suggests, was in the higher sphere of fascist "fine art." Three of the four business partners end up with unplanned pregnancies or in unappealing marriages, while the fourth, the woman coded as the most masculine, remains single and finds her calling in the painting of massive, propagandistic canvases; consistent with Nazi cinema's frequent equation of the artist with the soldier, she is effectively recruited to serve the state in a warlike fashion.

In *Die vier Gesellen* paid work and marriage are considered mutually exclusive, and the film's denouement does give priority to the latter. The rest of the film, however, manages to awaken the desire for both gender equality and for same-sex community much more effectively than the desire for heterosexual love. The battle of the sexes is not resolved in a joyful embrace of romance in this film; Bergman's character agrees to marry Söhnker's because she is literally starving, and because it is the most conventional form of narrative closure. The mystique of marriage is barely maintained here, and as in so many Nazi romance melodramas, only a sense of resignation remains. As we will see in the next chapter, this is not the only Third Reich film that evidences ambivalence toward the institution of marriage.

Die vier Gesellen is also not the only film of the Third Reich that speaks to female desires for public recognition of accomplishments, even if Nazi cinema had no genuine intention of advancing an autonomous female subjectivity. *Reifende Jugend,* as we have seen, thematizes male prejudice in regard to female talents in the sciences and creates a vision of a potential world of equal access, though it derails this possibility through romance with a dominant mate. There are a few notable exceptions to the "taming of the shrew" mold. In the 1939 romance *Illusion,* a stubborn rural aristocrat demands that his successful actress fiancée give up her career to marry him, and she suffers many melodramatic torments until she finally breaks off the engagement at the end of the film and decides in favor of her audiences, a choice validated by the Nazi overvaluation of the political function of art. In several films, the work/love triangle is actually resolved in a more balanced manner. In the 1943 romantic comedy *Unser Fräulein Doktor* (*Our Miss PhD*), the heroine marries and maintains her professorial position. In *Die Großstadtmelodie* (*Melody of a Great City*), a woman's film from the same year, a photojournalist perseveres in the face of her industry's chauvinism until she finally couples with a famous photographer who encourages her work.

Most Nazi romances that address the problem of a love relationship in conflict with work do end in a surrender of career ambitions for the sake of marriage. But this can be considered as much a concession to international generic and gender standards as to specifically fascist ideologies. Most romance films in all the classical cinemas of the 1930s and 1940s ended in an implicit marital pact and a broken work contract. Molly Haskell has even proposed that this was due to market concerns in accordance with spectator preference, that the conventional endings of Hollywood films were the ones desired by female audiences themselves: "After all, most women were housewives and they didn't want to be made to feel that there was a whole world of possibilities they had forsaken through marriage or inertia; rather, they wanted confirmation of the choice they had made."[47] In an insecure world of limited options and male resistance, progressive images of successful female professionals certainly provoked more anxiety than pleasure for some female spectators.[48]

The seemingly ambiguous attitude toward women's careers in Nazi romances may point less to ideological inconsistencies in Nazi film policy and more to calculated tactics when it comes to addressing female spectators. As Claudia Koonz has asserted, the appeal of Nazism for some women was actually the promise that they would be able to return to traditional gender roles. Many German women, particularly from the lower classes, did not romanticize the work world: "While American feminists were demanding entry into paid work, poorly paid German women dreamed of escaping from it."[49] Many women voted for the Nazis in the hope that they could become housewives, but this promise for the most part went unfulfilled: "German wives and mothers who had rallied to a revival of domesticity felt cheated when Nazi policy threatened them with 'modernization' worse than the threat of New Womanhood in the Weimar Republic."[50] Both Nazi policy and Nazi imagery offered mixed messages to women, in the face of which they could easily be misled, or to which they could choose their own preferred interpretation. The Third Reich created conditions for which it pretended to be the solution, creating anxiety while promising to alleviate it in return for allegiance. Nazi propaganda promised to "restore womanhood" to a former place of esteem, a promise that appealed to women who felt maltreated by Weimar-era commodification. Nazi cinema, on the other hand, offered illusions of continuity with Weimar culture that certainly soothed those who were concerned about Nazi ideology's regressive tendencies.

For women who wished to work, Nazi cinema did offer some encouragement, since films in which a single female main protagonist does not have an identifiable occupation are in the minority.[51] Images of married professional women were less common in Nazi cinema, and in films that did feature a married woman, her main occupation was usually extramarital romance (as we will see in the next chapter). When proper housewives appeared on screen, they often did so as minor characters and negative examples. Housewives were sometimes even figures of ridicule, and working women were often contrasted favorably to women with no profession.[52]

A scene in the 1938 melodrama *Heimat* (*Homeland*), for example, actually argues for the moral superiority of the woman who can earn her own living. Although generically more a family melodrama than a romance film, it is

worth considering here. Zarah Leander stars in the role of Magda, a woman
who has made a highly successful career as a singer in America and returns
to her Prussian hometown to both pay a visit to her stern father and settle
the score with the man who many years ago made her a single mother.
Upon arrival in her otherwise stifling and hostile *Heimat,* she is invited by
an enlightened young prince to give a public performance of her music at a
royal ball. The ball guests and members of the local gentry are caricatured in
the scene as representatives of an outdated puritanical morality—a morality
that, as the film implies, had been overcome by the new morals of National
Socialism. As the review of the film in the popular magazine *Filmwelt* emphasized, Magda was to be understood as a proto-fascist fighter against the
prudish standards of Wilhelmine high society:

> In the seclusion of the upper class there were iron rules that were supposed to
> be civilized, but were often inhumane. This film, *Heimat,* freely adapted from
> Sudermann's play, tells us how a strong heart overcame such obstacles, in order
> to correct a moral code that was suffocating in ruffles and whale bones . . . In
> this way, this female fighter in the best sense of the word comes to the great
> sentence: "I believe, ladies, that every person has the right to live his own life
> as he, within the context of society, sees fit."[53]

Both this review and the film suggested that the traditionalist Wilhelmine
women in whalebone corsets were the main enforcers of a hypocritical
morality that reigned until fascism cleared the way for the more liberated
lifestyle of the working woman. All plump, older housewives, they are costumed in the Third Reich's usual way of indicating an unsympathetic and
outmoded style of femininity: with high-necked black lace gowns, Victorian
brooches, and bonnets or oversized feathered hats. Magda, on the other
hand, is costumed in a gold-trimmed, low-cut ball gown and has uncov-
ered hair. She is repeatedly framed in shots with groups of admiring men,
while the ladies are separated in their own shots or are visible in the background of the mise-en-scène, nosily inspecting Magda's provocative dress
through lorgnettes. This use of eyeglasses indicates that they have control
over vision and that women determine social manners in this supposedly
skewed society. Directing her critical look to Magda, one woman whispers
disapprovingly, "Morals are certainly loosening to an alarming degree!"
Even more, the unsightly matrons are disgusted by Magda's mobile lifestyle
and her refusal to settle into a more traditional domestic role. When one
protests that a respectable woman should have a "cozy home" (*trauliches
Heim*), Magda responds, "In my life, I have learned that it is more important
to have work, a profession."

The heroine invites audience identification through her consciously sexual provocations, and by the approving glances of the men, including the young prince who accompanies Magda on the piano as she sings a cabaret song. The matrons are so horrified by the lascivious text of her chanson that they gasp and send away their daughters and then complain indignantly to a Protestant minister who is also in attendance. But even the minister, like most of the men at the party, who are clearly impressed by Magda's talents and décolleté, defends her and sanctifies her combative will, as did the propaganda minister himself. Rather than viewing the film as a celebration of love for the provincial German homeland, Goebbels primarily embraced the film's anti-prudery message: "Milieu of the prewar era is brilliantly captured . . . The mask is pulled down on a false and hypocritical morality of honor," Goebbels wrote after viewing *Heimat*.[54] Melodramatic effect is achieved by the end of the film when Magda regains the recognition of her father, as he finally abandons his moralistic objections to her sexual history and embraces his illegitimate granddaughter. Thus, *Heimat* explicitly argued for women's work, and its construction of viewer identification supported the position of the eroticized career woman and single mother.

Nazi cinema, in fact, did more to promote female careers than Nazi society in general. A remarkable number of Third Reich films of all genres feature professionally oriented women as central protagonists. Most commonly in melodramas, as in *Heimat* and most other Zarah Leander films, the woman is an artist or performer, and her work is described as being a result of her exceptional talent. But spheres of activity other than the arts were also represented, and some films suggested that women had skills that were more commercial as well. Although *Die vier Gesellen* suggested that a female-owned business was inevitably doomed to failure, a few other films did cast women in positions as the directors of companies.[55] A surprising number of Third Reich films also featured women in traditionally male careers such as science, medicine, and law.[56] Nazi cinema was even more liberal than the Nazi legal system; at the same time that the Nazi film industry was producing seemingly progressive images of female doctors, the Nazi justice system was severely restricting women from practicing medicine,[57] reflecting the strategically mixed messages of the Third Reich in general.

In 1937 women with advanced degrees lost the right to be called "Frau Doktor,"[58] yet many films, such as *Reifende Jugend,* highlight women's education and the social status that academic titles brought.[59] Such films anticipated actual changes in the university populace during the war. By 1942 not only were female students in the majority in many German universities, but they also outnumbered men even in departments of mathematics and sciences.[60]

According to Security Service reports that tracked changes in the student population, economics and medicine were particularly popular fields of study for new female students. The Nazi leadership, while taking note of this change with some concern about women's readiness for and commitment to higher education, concluded that it would be necessary to encourage women to complete advanced degrees in order to make up for the dire lack of professors and professionals in the Reich. Academia was to become a more female sphere after the war; as one 1943 report concluded: "One hopes to fill some vacancies in the academic professions by increasing the number of female students. It will become increasingly necessary to take this route, since a not insignificant portion of male high school graduates and students who are now serving in the war will no longer be returning from the front."[61] In Germany, unlike in the United States, women were not considered to be in the work world only "for the duration." While America was plagued by the fear that women would refuse to surrender their jobs to returning soldiers and once again become housewives,[62] Germany was preparing for the eventuality that its soldiers would not return and that "housewife" would no longer be a profession widely available in the postwar period, and Nazi romance films anticipated this change.

Predictably, however, women's work was ultimately described less as a means to autonomy than as a further form of servitude to the state. As Sabine Hake has pointed out, women's ambition in the Third Reich was explained "in the context of the Protestant work ethic and its rhetoric of duty and sacrifice."[63] The *Film-Kurier* commented on the representation of a woman's career as medical researcher in the 1944 melodrama *Das Herz muss schweigen* (*The Heart Must Be Still*) in a corresponding manner: "Here . . . the sacrifice of the woman in service of science and thus for the benefit of humanity is shown. And that is not an exceptional case, since women have been engaged in many fields of scientific life, as researcher, physician, chemist. They have even sacrificed their own lives, and continue to do so, side by side with men, in service of the people."[64] The writer of this article on "women's careers on screen" thus rewrote work outside of the home as a feminine duty, and added that films representing their heroines primarily as lovers or housewives were passé, because such women were engaged only in luxuriously private, emotional concerns. The modern woman, the article suggested, could no longer allow herself to languish in the private sphere, but had a responsibility to serve science and the state, and cinema had to reflect the contemporary turn away from domesticity. Recent productions showed "how great the responsibility of film is as a proclaimer of reality, which today means that women can no longer just devote themselves to their private inclinations, but are making use of their strengths and their skills in all spheres of life."[65] Nazi melodramas such as *Das Herz muss schweigen* were thus to be employed against convention, by encouraging female sacrifice in the public sphere rather than only in the home.

It is not surprising that a film journal would promote the total mobilization of female energies in 1944, a year when the "total war" was intensified. Contrary to what we might expect, however, the cinematic promotion of women's work was not exclusively a wartime policy but actually predated it. From 1936 on, *Film-Kurier* repeatedly highlighted female careers. The journal promoted women's careers on screen in film narratives as well as off screen in film production. A 1937 article, for example, was titled "Women's Professions Created by Film" and highlighted "feminine" jobs in the film industry, such as costume designer, production assistant, and film editor, while another article published the following week underlined the importance of female film journalists and newspaper editors.[66] While promoting women's work in the film industry and elsewhere, *Film-Kurier* also called on film producers to alter their representations of female characters, which they claimed no longer reflected contemporary reality in the 1930s. Conventional romance film narratives reinforced outdated notions of female inferiority, they said: "A couple of months ago we first pointed out in the *Film-Kurier* the fact that in German films, young girls are partly represented as having inferiority complexes in relation to men, which absolutely does not reflect the attitude of the young girl of today. One can see that, in film narratives which underline their modest salaries, girls look up at wealthy men with only a humble glance . . . And that's not all—stuttering with embarrassment, they even express their worries about being so small and insignificant."[67] Quoting an editorial from the women's magazine *Koralle,* the *Film-Kurier* also subscribed to the following (limited) expression of female independence, which it described as "the general opinion of audiences" in the Third Reich: "We wish the young girls of the coming generation to know how important it is to find the man with whom one belongs and how terrible it is to be together with a man with whom one doesn't belong. They should seize for themselves the genuine self-confidence that comes from the *proud feeling of independence,* the knowledge that, when need be, they can cope with life on their own and—as it should finally be called—be *woman* enough to stand up for themselves [*ihre Frau zu stehen wissen*]."[68] But it was not the happiness of the individual woman that was truly at stake here. If cinema was successful in teaching German women not to rely on men and to come to terms with life alone, this had obvious benefits for a society that was continually preparing for industrial and imperial expansion.

One romance film that made a case for female autonomy and altered gender roles was *Eine Frau wie Du* (*A Woman Like You*), shot in the summer

Illusions of liberation for the female professional: *Eine Frau wie Du* (1939). Source: Deutsche Kinemathek

of 1939 and premiered while the Wehrmacht was trampling Poland. It is an uncommonly tender romance, one whose battle of the sexes appears more as a friendly, outdoor sport. Directed by Viktor Tourjansky, who also directed the 1941 anti-marital romance *Illusion, Eine Frau wie Du* offered exceptionally compelling images of sexual liberation and the illusion of personal freedom within the Nazi state. Its model of coupling was also somewhat different from the standard hierarchical constellations of teacher-student romances like *Reifende Jugend* and *Die vier Gesellen*. Here, the romance occurs between two lovers of relatively equal rank. Brigitte Horney stars as Dr. Maria Prätorius, a psychologist treating workers in a large factory who begins a romance with the factory's attorney, Manfred. Notably, it is the woman in this couple who owns the car, and much is made of Maria's self-reliant nature. One of her defining characteristics is her love of camping and fishing, and when she takes Manfred out for a weekend camping date, he is forced to reveal his comparative incompetence at pitching tents and baiting hooks. Despite his lack of outdoor skills, Manfred clearly proves his masculine abilities when the couple retires to the tent and he impregnates the Fräulein Doktor. This development is ultimately treated by the film not as a catastrophe but as a fortunate event, a treatment consistent with Nazi cinema's overall promotion of premarital pregnancy and single motherhood.

The central conflict of the film is that between monogamy and sexual freedom, work and pleasure. Here, somewhat unusually, it is the man who represents both freedom and pleasure, and the woman restraint and duty. While Maria spends her weekends alone engaging in outdoor sports, Manfred spends them drinking at parties and nightclubs with his friends, a collection of wealthy, glamorous young people (including a two-time divorcée), most of whom have sworn off marriage and monogamy. Manfred also dreams of escaping both work and Germany. After their camping trip there is a scene on an open, tree-lined highway where Manfred begins to sing "O sole mio" in Maria's convertible and says: "It's terrible, such a weekend! To have to go home already . . . Ah Maria, let's just keep driving, farther and farther!" She, the representative of the German fascist work ethic, laughs and answers that she has to be in the office at eight the next morning. Duty to the factory wins in the end, but the film still presents brief moments when a more liberated lifestyle appears possible for the youth of the Third Reich, a summery illusion. In a brief shot at the beginning of the film, a sign posted outside Maria's factory announces the true outdoor activities that the Reich intended for its youth: along with a swastika, the slogan "We are marching together!" is momentarily legible. With its apparent loosening of sexual standards and definitions of femininity, *Eine Frau wie Du* served to create the illusion of a progressive society—instead of one in which women worked for the advancement of a murderous military dominance.

A similar message was presented by Nazi love stories that thematized the medical profession. Unlike in Hollywood, where the romantic heroine was generally the patient/research object of the hero, the heroine of Nazi medical romances was often his employee. Such workplace romances emphasized total commitment to professional duties and, just like the teacher-student romances, reinforced authority structures at home and on the job. The 1938 romance *Die Frau am Scheidewege* (*The Woman at the Crossroads*) even suggested that a woman's duties in the hospital were more important than those in the home. The film opens in an operating room, where the director of a university clinic, Dr. Henrici, is performing his seventh operation in a row. He is observed by a crowd of male and female medical students and accompanied by his loyal assisting surgeon, Dr. Hanna Weigand (Magda Schneider). A film cut brings the camera to another room, where a male servant comments to a nurse that the chief surgeon never thinks of himself and sacrifices his own health for the sake of science, and the nurse responds admiringly that the doctor has virtually superhuman capabilities. Another cut back to the operating room follows, and the chief surgeon orders Hanna to go another round; she agrees, but then passes out from exhaustion. In a tender two shot of the sort usually reserved for lovers' discourse, he then tells her with his arms around her shoulders that her "way of assisting is exemplary," that she is "an ideal colleague," and that he "can't work without her." He then orders her to take some time off and get some rest in the interest of increased productivity, while she protests against this forced vacation under tears.

While on vacation at a seaside resort, Dr. Hanna is courted by Fred, a macho but much less disciplined graphic artist (Hans Söhnker, essentially repeating his role in *Die vier Gesellen*). A few weeks later Hanna returns to work a soon-to-be married woman, much to the professor's displeasure. He is concerned that she will quit her job to become a full-time wife, but she reassures him by saying, "God forbid! I just couldn't live without my work!" and adds that she will have to be the main breadwinner of the couple, since her fiancé does not earn much. However, once Hanna and Fred marry and move in together, he quickly becomes disgruntled by the fact that she is al-

The romance of divorce: *Die Frau am Scheidewege* (1938). Source: Deutsche Kinemathek

ways at the hospital and not at home doing housework. Instead of trying to reconcile the heroine to a housewife role, the film encourages the audience to view housework as a waste of her professional calling. When Fred ironically refers to Hanna as "the little *Hausfrau*," a reaction shot of Dr. Henrici shows a wince of disgust at this lack of respect for Hanna's surgical talents. The audience is furthermore encouraged to view Hanna's marriage as a mistake.

Indeed, *Die Frau am Scheidewege,* with the title's play on the word *Scheidung* (divorce), is in essence a melodrama of remarriage—or a romance of divorce. Its postmarital choice/competition narrative in effect argues that marital bonds that do not work should be dissolved. Modifying the standard romance film formula that educated the audience in premarital partner choice, the film's characterization elaborated all of the ways in which the heroine and her husband were an unsuitable match. While the usually unemployed Fred listens to jazz records, holds parties, and is sloppy in the house, Hanna works with utmost discipline. Hanna's sister, Elinor, a fashion designer by profession, soon moves in with the couple and begins to take over her sister's duties in the home by cleaning up after Fred and sleeping with him. But the film does not condemn this quasi-incestuous infidelity. Rather, the sister-in-law is shown as being a better match for Fred, since she has drafting skills and an attractive body that Fred can exploit to further his own career, as her figure helps to bring in business from advertising clients. On the other hand, the film rarely brings the legally married couple into the same frame together, indicating that Hanna is actually more qualified to stay at work under the authoritative eyes of her boss.

By aligning spectator identification with Hanna from the very first shot of the film through close-ups, and by provoking admiration for her dedication to the medical profession through dialogue, the film also offers an apparent argument against traditional gender roles. Hanna, it suggests, is not meant to be a domestic servant to her husband, but rather a more comradely subordinate. When Dr. Henrici reveals his love for Hanna, he does so through commanding, militaristic language. As he asks her to perform a risky experimental operation, he whispers to her passionately: "Shall we take up the battle [*den Kampf aufnehmen*]? Oh, Hanna, it's so great to work with you!" *Die Frau am Scheidewege* thus romanticizes militarily useful work, encouraging women's absolute, self-sacrificing commitment to professional duty. This level of work discipline takes on a particularly sinister note when Hanna carries out an untested and potentially lethal procedure on a human subject, foreshadowing similar practices conducted outside of the cinema.[69] After Hanna succeeds with the experiment, the professor praises her for her courage, calling her a true *Kameradin* (comrade), and in typically fascist language, lays claim to her ethically questionable scientific advances: "Comrades fight together and are victorious together!" he says. The film thus engages female spectators' desires for recognition of professional successes and gender equality in order to create a new form of servitude. *Die Frau am Scheidewege* proposed, in advance of the war, that both men and women could be self-sacrificing working and fighting machines.

The film nears its melodramatic climax as Dr. Henrici invites Hanna to dinner and fires her because he is in love with her, demanding that she divorce and remarry him if she wants to keep her job. Hanna first resolves to give up her career as her husband demands, but the following sequences insinuate just how wrong such a choice is: as Hanna languishes unhappily at home in the apartment, Fred impregnates her sister. In the series of rapidly cut, phantasmagoric shots that follow, Elinor pushes through anonymous masses at a carnival and heaves melodramatically, hearing Hanna in a voice-over saying, "I want to try to become a good wife and housewife to Fred." Countershots of a woman circling manically on a carnival swing ride suggest that this attempt at marital fidelity is entirely wrongheaded. Finally, after it is revealed to Hanna that her sister is expecting a child, the marriage is happily dissolved. The legal but unnatural union between Fred and Hanna, *Die Frau am Scheidewege* suggests, stands in the way of productive (and reproductive) efficiency. The final shot of the film ends the romance melodrama where it started: with Hanna handing Dr. Henrici instruments in the operating room, this time accompanied by triumphant music, indicating that this medical work also has romantic significance. Thus, the couples who work best together are brought together in the end, and the narrative is resolved in a manner quite useful to a militarist state: one woman becomes a reproductive artist, while the other maintains her work productivity as a doctor even after coupling. The romance between Hanna and Dr. Henrici is curiously sterile, though, as there is barely any physical contact between the two. In the final shot of the film, the passing of instruments from one antiseptically gloved hand to another substitutes for the conventional kiss—not because the film is prudish, but because the romantic pairing is essentially a labor contract.

Notably, it is the childless woman of talent who is generally the central focus of Nazi romance melodramas. The heroine of another romance from the following year, *Irrtum des Herzens* (*Error of the Heart*, 1939), shows a similar aptitude for and absolute dedication to the medical profession and also falls in love with her supervisor, again a professor and chief surgeon of a hospital. At the beginning of the film the camera briefly explores the bright modern space of a clinic decorated with Christmas trees. Professor Dr. Reimers, a middle-age divorcé, tells the adoring young nurse Angelika (Leny Marenbach) how much he appreciates her because she never loses her nerve despite being chronically overworked. The film's script is thus designed to evoke admiration for the (mostly female) hospital staff for ignoring holidays and sacrificing themselves to operate around the clock. It further dissolves any division between the private and the professional by having them reside at their workplaces. Angelika lives in a small room in the back of the hospital with another nurse, Therese, and both are constantly on call. These two are joined by the vigorously efficient and self-sacrificing chief nurse, a childless single woman who once had an affair with Reimers, the chief surgeon, and now shows a complete dedication to her work, where her maternal instincts can be applied to caring for the sick and injured. These working women are contrasted favorably to Reimer's non-employed ex-wife, whom he describes as a "dumb goose" and who enters the clinic overdressed in fur coats and makes the seemingly capricious and unreasonable demand that, for the sake of their child, he finally take a break from operating. Dr. Reimers then comes to realize his great mistake in having acquired a housewife instead of marrying one of the hardworking nurses and soon offers to marry his much younger employee Angelika. The engagement falls through when she decides in favor of a pilot who is also courting her (and is again played by the eternal winner Hans Söhnker). Finally the surgeon opts to sacrifice love altogether in favor of a total commitment to work, and the last shot of the film validates this rejection of marriage. Sitting behind an authoritative desk, the doctor hero proclaims, "Apparently, everything else besides my work was not strong enough . . . I should want to have nothing and to be nothing more than that which God intended me to be—a doctor!" A final track-in to a monumental close-up shot of his resolute face lends heroic value to this choice.

It is easy to recognize how *Irrtum des Herzens* and other work romances prepared viewers for a dissolution of the private sphere in war, even if war always remained only a subtext of the hospital or corporate setting. The nurse Angelika, we could assume, would soon be wedded to the war as a pilot's wife and caretaker of the wounded. The film thus exploits its spectators' desires for recognition of professional accomplishments to create a total identification with war-serving industries and a sentimental vision of its servants. The female workers of this romance film, as in *Die Frau am Scheidewege*, are essentially slaves to their jobs ("well-oiled machines," as the chief nurse calls them). Another similar film that concerned a hardworking professional woman unhappily in love with her supervisor, the 1940 melodrama *Das Mädchen im Vorzimmer* (*The Girl in the Front Office*), was described by the film journal *Der deutsche Film* as underscoring "such contemporary virtues

. . . as self-sacrifice for the company through renunciation of all private life, even of love."[70]

Interestingly, in a self-reflexive moment, *Irrtum des Herzens* imagined one sphere of feminine privacy: that of romance fiction. Early in the film, the other young nurse, Therese, is shown reading romance novels during her short breaks in her shared room at the hospital. Putting down her book to return to work, she excitedly relates to Angelika her romantic fantasies of owning hundreds of shoes and marrying an aristocrat who smells of English lavender instead of ether. At the end of the film, however, Therese receives a quick, businesslike marriage proposal from one of the hospital's doctors, which she promptly and dutifully accepts as though it were a job offer. The fantasy of escape from work through romance is obliquely cited by the romance film itself as just that—only a fantasy of private life.

Nazi Eroticism, Bourgeois Morality, and Excess

Romance melodramas, as we have seen so far in this chapter, designed gender roles to support the Third Reich's imperialist ambitions by inviting spectator identification and erotic investment in character types that were particularly serviceable to a militarist society. Although the main protagonists of these melodramas were usually female, romance was not considered a purely female sphere during the Third Reich. Nazi romance fiction was sold as the oil to grease the male—as well as female—libidinous machine. According to SD reports, romance novels were fashionable among adolescent boys, for whom such popular literature was an ersatz form of pornography. The Security Service reported in August 1940 that novels with titles like *Sie ward aus Liebe schuldig* (*She Was Guilty of Love*) or *Barbara im Liebesfeuer* (*Barbara in the Fire of Love*) were making the rounds among Hitler Youth troops and were avidly consumed by one group of boys before being passed on to others, and they commented that the mass influence of this form of entertainment could not be overestimated.[71] Similarly, Nazi propagandists could count on reaching a large male spectatorship with romance melodramas, another function of which was to portray Nazi Germany as the land of an alternative sexual modernity. .

Explicitly pornographic literature had been banned soon after Hitler came to power, but this did not mean that all prurient art had disappeared from the Reich. Rather, the sale of sexuality became a state monopoly. The Third Reich's repression of Weimar's freer trade in sexual imagery and services was not an attempt to reinstate a more puritanical morality. Instead, this repression was an attempt to gain full control of the market in eroticism and to deploy images of sexuality as weapons of the state. As Dagmar Herzog has emphasized, the official publication of the SS, *Das Schwarze Korps* (The Black Corps), consistently delivered pornographic representations, all the while using anti-Semitic rhetoric to disavow responsibility for its incitement of violent sexual fantasies. The journal claimed that Jews were to blame for all pornography, while the eroticism that the National Socialists advocated was a fundamentally healthy and natural expression of a revolutionary, youthful movement. *Das Schwarze Korps,* Herzog added, "aligned itself with young people's impatience with traditional bourgeois mores" by attacking what it termed "'the pathological tendency to Catholic virginalism.'"[72] As historian Annette Timm has further underlined, other Nazi media outlets made common use of rhetoric about middle-class narrow-mindedness in order to advocate a change in views about sexuality. As Timm states, there were frequent "public statements from top Nazis officials about the need to destroy notions of bourgeois sexual morality. Joseph Goebbels, for instance, viewed himself as the 'champion of progressive sexual morality' and from the first years of the regime he railed against *Bettschnüffelei* (snooping into the sexual practices of others) in the party's propaganda publications."[73]

According to the Nazi usage, "bourgeois morality" was virtually synonymous with Christian prohibitions against extramarital sexuality and the religiously motivated valuation of chastity and self-denial. Nazism, in its paradoxical rejection of the moral codes that supposedly typified the middle class, followed popular cultural trends of the late nineteenth and early twentieth centuries. However, the frequent denunciations of bourgeois hypocrisy in Nazi media were in themselves hypocritical, given that such attacks were directed toward the very same class that had most supported Hitler, the petty bourgeoisie. As sociologist Maria Ossowska pointed out in a study titled *Bourgeois Morality,* the term usually referred to stereotypical petit bourgeois attitudes rather than the practices of the upper middle classes, and it was a favorite epithet of turn-of-the century and early twentieth-century Marxists, bohemians, and (proto-)fascists alike.[74] All shared an overgeneralized portrait of bourgeois morality, defined by characteristics such as prosaicism, mediocrity, timidity, aversion to risk, and excessive concern with respectability—characteristics that overlapped with an equally generalized view of Christian or "Puritan morality," as defined by humility and, in Ossowska's words, the "hostility to every form of pleasure and pleasure-seeking."[75] It was on this latter element that the Nazis focused their critiques of bourgeois morality. Nazi propaganda appealed to members of the lower middle classes with the potential of overcoming previous social constraints through the collective experience of politics on a grand scale; it further suggested that working for the goals of Nazis imperialism would entail not only sacrifices but also intensified forms of pleasure. In their emphasis on the pleasures of transgressing mainstream moral codes, Nazi critiques of bourgeois morality differed from Marxist critiques, which tended to emphasize the self-interested material motives hidden behind bourgeois notions of virtue. Theodor Adorno's statement that "wherever we speak of bourgeois morality we think in the first instance of bourgeois work discipline" did not hold true for Marxism's right-wing opponents,[76] as we have seen in the preceding discussion of Third Reich workplace romance films. Instead, many Nazis thought first of the Christian disciplining of the drives.

The Nazi critique of bourgeois sexual morality evidently found support in Nietzsche's condemnation of Judeo-Christian morality and his predictions about a coming post-bourgeois, post-democratic era of immoralism. As Nietzsche scholar Steven Aschheim has argued, the philosopher's writings were crucial to Nazism's self-definition as a tradition-challenging movement, and Nietzsche was portrayed by Nazi theorists as having defined the main goals of the regime, among them the revaluation of the sexual drive and the aggressive instinct. Even if Nietzsche's works were very selectively read by Third Reich commentators, the philosopher was celebrated in official Nazi cultural organs because, as Aschheim stated, he "radically rejected bourgeois society, liberalism, socialism, democracy, egalitarianism, and the Christian ethos." As a consequence, Nietzsche was treated by many Nazi theorists as a thinker who was "central to the construction of the movement's promise of a thoroughly transvalued world."[77] Quoting several Third Reich commentators who drew connections between the Nietzschean and the fascist view of the body, Aschheim added: "The decadent and feminized nineteenth century was to give way to a new masculine warrior age, one that regarded Nietzsche as a pioneer of the 'German rediscovery of the body' . . . The old bourgeois ethos of security was to be rendered anachronistic by the emergence of hard personalities animated by the joy of living dangerously."[78] Nazi ideologues sought to overcome the stereotypical petit bourgeois aversion to risk and its stress on moderation by subscribing to the Nietzschean "noble morality" of the powerful against the "slave morality" of Christianity, a transvaluation that appeared to support Nazi imperialism (regardless of the fact that Nietzsche himself had refused to endorse the domination of the German empire over the rest of Europe).[79]

While battling Christian/bourgeois sexual morality, the Nazis also opposed the more progressive and egalitarian forms of sexual emancipation of the Weimar era. Shortly after taking power in 1933, the Nazis passed a law against nudism, but with this law they did not intend to force Germans to hide their bodies.[80] The main problem for the Nazis was not that Weimar-era nudists were naked, but that they formed a movement with antihierarchical tendencies. Nazism was to be the only cultural movement in Germany, and nudity became the exclusive property of the so-called *Volksgemeinschaft*. To be sure, some Nazi ideologues did advocate a more puritanical approach. While Goebbels argued in favor of more uninhibited sexual relations in his articles for official party publications, some comparatively prudish Nazis stood in opposition.[81] But social conservatives generally had less influence over the imagery disseminated to the masses in print and visual media than did the director of the Propaganda Ministry. As we have seen in *Der Postmeister,* the eroticized, exposed female body was designed by the leaders of Nazi cultural production to be the main pillar of film aesthetics and spectator pleasure.

Indeed, the exploitation of eroticism became a consciously articulated policy within the Reich Ministry for Popular Enlightenment and Propaganda (Reichsministerium für Volksaufklärung und Propaganda, or RMVP). Erotic thoughts were to replace critical thought, and fantasies of sexual liberation were to stifle expressions of discontent in the political realm. In 1939 Goebbels wrote in his diary that he was determined to eliminate all political humor in the cinema and cabaret. "The political joke will be eradicated. Absolutely and completely," he wrote with his characteristic fanatic emphasis.[82] Goebbels knew that something had to distract from the excising of political opposition, and he envisioned that nudity and sexual suggestion would fill that lack. He was determined to remain, as he wrote, "obstinate against political jokes, but even more generous with regard to eroticism . . . since playful instincts [*der Spieltrieb*] must have free rein somewhere."[83] Goebbels therefore campaigned to loosen the sexual morals of German entertainment. In 1935 he noted in his diary that film censorship had to be reworked. "We are restricting film too much," he wrote, and noted his plans to liberalize censorship codes and reduce personnel: "More freedom. Above all, the army of censors and examiners out."[84] Two days later he wrote in his diary that his instructions had been put into place, and that censors should be more forgiving when it came to the representation of sexuality: "I give the film censors guidelines. Loosen up! Don't be so moralistic. We are not from Potsdam and we don't wear any little collars."[85] The stiff collar (*Halsbörtchen*) of the old-fashioned bureaucrat signified for Goebbels a pedantic form of sexual morality that Nazism had supposedly made redundant.

Similarly, the word *Moralin* (hypocritical moralizing) was consistently evoked in the Nazi press to suggest that the Third Reich was a progressive and modern society, as opposed to some implied past in which sexuality was repressed. As we have seen in the melodrama *Heimat,* this past was generally that of Second Reich puritanism, the same cultural environment in which Nietzsche launched his attack on Christian morality. But the memory of democratic Weimar was not located far from the image of hypocritical Wilhelmine (or "Potsdam") morality for Goebbels and other Nazis involved in film production. Weimar cinema has often been considered a cinema of sexual as well as gender liberation, and many Nazi writers denounced Weimar films as degenerate. Yet there was also a strongly conservative strain in much of the popular cinema of the Weimar period, particularly after 1927, when the directorship of the UFA (Universum-Film AG) film studios came under the influence of monarchists.[86] The progressive social agendas of the women's movement and the permissiveness of alternative gay culture in 1920s Berlin did not make a strong mark on the morals of the masses or on the majority of Weimar-era popular films. According to Hans Peter Bleuel, the famed permissiveness of the Weimar period was overall an illusion, and conventional morality reigned in all but the most isolated pockets of metropolitan culture. Elsewhere, repressiveness was the rule: "The appearance of a progressive emancipation of customs, of a loosening of ancient moral statutes, was illusory. It was, despite all the legal improvements and fashionable phenomena, only a very small circle of the population that had the desire and the power to free itself from the traditional moral code."[87] The liberated sexual and gender imagery visible in the Weimar-era press, Bleuel added, was not lived out in the vast majority of Weimar homes.[88]

Similarly, Weimar cinema's reputation for being sexually emancipated is not always warranted. In most Weimar films, expressions of desire are condemned by narrative conclusions, and female sexuality must necessarily have melodramatic consequences, leading to prostitution or death. In fact, the quasi-pornographic *Aufklärungsfilme* (sexual enlightenment films), for which the Weimar cinema is generally considered to be modern and liberal, belonged to a classic melodramatic narrative type in which feminine purity is threatened by male desire. As Friedemann Beyer comments, the *Aufklärungsfilme* were sensationalist melodramas that "rarely got by without villains who defiled tender young virgins after they had seduced them into taking drugs."[89] Such films, despite their pretense to scientific objectivity and liberal views, ultimately reinforced standards of bourgeois morality by titillating audiences with the myriad dangers of sexuality.

Nazi writers exploited this hypocritical Weimar morality by continually trying to present themselves as being more sexually enlightened than the culture producers of the so-called *Systemzeit.* They attempted to distinguish themselves from the makers of Weimar-era *Aufklärungsfilme,* which they insisted were only cheap smut that revealed bourgeois prudery under their tales of prostitution. As Rudolf Oertel wrote in 1941: "We are not prudish these days. We can distinguish between morality [*Moral*] and hypocritical moralizing [*Moralin*]. Pornography under the cover of scientific enlightenment is unappetizing, and we have sharp eyes to determine whether artistic passion or greed is at work."[90] The hypocrisy of the Nazi position, with its claim to represent sexuality as a matter of "artistic passion" rather than economic desire, is clear. The Nazis, of course, did not view film purely as an art, but also as a profitable industry, despite their feigned protests to the contrary.

Eroticism in classical cinema's most concentrated form—that of woman-as-spectacle—was marketed most obviously by the revue film, which provided the most extended spectacles of exposed female bodies. The romance film's eroticism was embedded more subtly within narrative and included fetishistic close-ups of actresses and the suggestion of sexual relations. Nazi melodramas like *Der Postmeister* also effectively featured exposed extra-narrative bodies, of course. The spectacle of woman was often consciously built into the background of romance narratives in order to enhance the foregrounded relations of the main couple. The Nazi Party trade press *Der deutsche Film* specifically recommended the mise-en-scène of the nightclub or cabaret for love story scenes, since it allowed visual pleasure to coincide with the dramaturgically necessary delay of the final narrative resolution: "When 'He' flirts with another woman or 'She' flirts with another man at the bar table, then there is a dance number going on in the background . . . The happy-end dramaturgy combines here the pleasant with the practical in a perfect way: this method . . . offers the opportunity to please the ear with a hit song and please the eye with the sight of slender legs."[91] Thus, the half-naked dancers who connoted forbidden desire were exploited at the same time for the erotic effects they produced.

This was clearly a planned strategy, and often a successful one. It was this exploitation of eroticism that sold Nazi films to both domestic and foreign audiences. In comparison to Hays Code–restricted Hollywood and even the cinema of neighboring European countries, Nazi films appeared to many spectators to be risqué. The Security Service reported in April 1944 that the Catholic Church in Belgium had been agitating against Nazi films due to their thematization of premarital and extramarital sexuality:

The strongest attacks by the clergy so far have been directed against the films *Die Goldene Stadt* [*The Golden City,* 1942], *Münchhausen* [1943] and *Das Bad auf der Tenne* [*The Bath on the Threshing Floor,* 1943] . . . Sermons have very

often warned against going to these screenings. Even in larger cities, they announced from the pulpit that believers would be committing a *mortal sin* by
going to see these films . . . In most cases, people in the cities do not take the
clergy's warnings seriously, and the warnings have had the opposite effect of
contributing to an *increased level of attendance* for these films. In Antwerp, for
example, the popularity of the film *Das Bad auf der Tenne*, now in its third week,
is still not letting up. Viewers have commented that in this case, as in others, the
church unwittingly created the best propaganda for the film by trying to ban it.[92]

The "sinful" narratives of Nazi films brought Belgians to the box office, which
underlined the propagandistic, as well as economic, advantage of flouting
Christian sexual morality.[93]

In the films cited in the SD report above, sex is mainly suggested through
situation, double entendre, and fetishistic displays of bodies. Sex acts themselves were never explicitly shown in Nazi feature films but usually happen—as
in virtually all classical cinema—in ellipses. In *Die goldene Stadt* a seduction
scene ends with a shot of a couple in bed—a shot, as Stephen Lowry has noted,
that would not have been possible under classical Hollywood's censorship
codes[94]—followed by a close-up of a clock, a cut, and another close-up of a
clock, indicating the length of time that the coupling required. Although sex
acts that are more explicit are not shown, what appeared newly threatening
to contemporary representatives of bourgeois or Christian morality was how
Nazi culture appeared to dissolve the boundaries between sexual purity and sin
and encouraged the expression of elemental drives. Weimar film, in contrast,
had generally maintained the dualistic morality of the virgin and the whore,
as demonstrated by the fateful symbols used to describe acts of sexuality as
tragic defloration. In G. W. Pabst's *Diary of a Lost Girl* (1929), for example,
the melodramatic heroine's loss of virginity is indicated through ominous
symbols like the knocked-over wine glass. In contrast, the loss of virginity is
rarely even an implied topic in Nazi romance films, as melodramatic emphasis
was generally shifted away from the issue of sexual purity. Shots in Nazi films
indicating that sexual activity is taking place usually suggest that it is natural
rather than fateful. There are thus many shots of the sky or sunny, placid bodies of water inserted after a couple's kiss in the bedroom (rather than the sort
of violently rushing water in the manner of Griffith's melodrama, suggesting
that the heroine will die as a result of her loss of purity).

Obviously the Nazis had little interest in making old-fashioned melodramas that championed virginity, since this would contradict their population
policies. The Nazi attempts to increase birthrates by loosening taboos on
premarital sexuality were met with church resistance not only in Belgium but
in the Reich as well. Catholic clergymen were particularly active in agitating

against the sexualized imagery of Nazi media and attempted to fortify their parishioners against the apparent attack on Christian sexual morality, but the Nazi authorities responded harshly to such encroachments. In 1941 the SS was ordered to arrest members of the Catholic Church who had distributed pamphlets advocating virginity and celibacy.[95] The sexual morality of the Catholic Church appeared to many fervent Nazis as an intolerable form of foreign domination. Nazi film critic Peter von Werder claimed that the conventional cinematic images of women as either innocent virgins, dependent housewives, or prostitutes were all non-Aryan and anti-German in origin. Patriarchy and prostitution were Oriental inventions, he suggested, and he condemned both:

> the figure of the hetaera [is] from the ancient Orient and the deeply Eastern-influenced antique Mediterranean world, reappearing up until now in constantly altered form. On the other hand, along with the Eastern idea of the privileged position of the husband and family father, there comes a corresponding estimation of the woman as a dependent and ignorant creature, on the grounds of which a new, more uninhibited view of sensuality is not possible . . . for that reason, the reconstruction of love- and sex-life is a question of central national importance.[96]

In a Germanic soldierly state, and in a properly fascist cinema, von Werder suggested, sex would be unconstrained and men would not be considered primarily husbands and fathers. The Third Reich, he insisted, should work on liberating romantic relations from bourgeois family structures in the interests of racial and military dominance.

But the cinema of the Third Reich played with a double-edged sword here, since its project was simultaneously the provocation of desire and the attempt to make it work for the state. In order to carry out the project of liberalizing sexual relations, Nazi cinema had to encourage female spectators to participate, but it thereby risked provoking desires that could not be contained. The romance melodrama with a female main protagonist was by its very nature the most conflicted and potentially hazardous genre in this respect. By many accounts the Hollywood love story negotiated this risk by attempting to repress desire entirely. As Mary Ann Doane has stated, the main project of the Hollywood romance, and indeed all of love stories, is "the tautological demonstration of the necessity of the failure of female desire."[97] However, as she adds, there are always difficulties inherently built into this project, particularly in the case of the woman's film or romance melodrama. The love story "is one of the most vulnerable sites in a patriarchal discourse," Doane says, since "its flaw is to posit the very possibility of female desire."[98]

Even if Nazi culture attempted to reorganize patriarchy, the love story in the Third Reich was by its very generic nature a highly conflicted zone. The risks of Nazi romance were even greater than those of Hollywood, since it imagined the possibility of desire outside of the containing order of the nuclear family. Excess continually threatened romance melodrama's demonstrations of control.

Ideological ruptures, as many scholars argue, are indicated by the melodramatic mode through "hysterical" mise-en-scène or camera work. According to Pam Cook, stylistic excess is a symptom of the impossible task of balancing the representation of female desire with the containment of it; excess, in classical Hollywood cinema, is a "sign of the system threatening to break down."[99] In Nazi cinema as well the thematization of female desire sometimes coincides with signs that seem to exceed conventional signification and threaten to break apart stable narrative structures, and this melodramatic strain gives evidence of potential failures of the fascist management of desire. Indeed, one of the most stylistically excessive melodramas of the Third Reich, *Anna und Elisabeth* (*Anna and Elizabeth*, 1933) is one that reveals a problematized female desire in the form of strong homoerotic undercurrents and could be categorized as a same-sex-romance film.

Notably, *Anna und Elisabeth* starred the same pair of actresses who embodied lesbian attraction in the Weimar precursor *Mädchen in Uniform*. Dorothea Wieck plays Elisabeth, the aristocratic mistress of a rural estate, a hysteric who is bound to a wheelchair with an inexplicable paralysis until she meets Hertha Thiele's character, Anna, a boyish farmer's daughter. Superstitious locals tell Elisabeth that Anna has special powers and can heal the sick with her touch. When the pair meets, Elisabeth grabs Anna's hand and holds it on her own body until her expression turns ecstatic. Elisabeth later testifies to others, "She put her hand on me and gave me a jerk. *And what a jerk it was!*" Anna, however, does not believe that she possesses supernatural powers, and the film largely validates Anna's perspective. But Elisabeth's excessive desire for Anna is expressed in shots that also undermine narrative authority and produce a hysterical shifting of identificatory positions, leaving the spectator uncertain of the truth. Vertiginous point-of-view shots from Elisabeth's perspective allow the spectator to identify with her ecstasy and pathos while she whispers her passionate anticipation of Anna's touch. Later, when they are alone together, Elisabeth miraculously rises from her wheelchair and walks erect for the first time.

A central sequence, virtually a love scene, is so lengthy and erotically charged that the spectator is encouraged to desire the release of tension through a kiss. In one long, static close-up, Anna's head is positioned in

Female desire and excess: *Anna und Elisabeth* (1933). Source: Deutsche Kinemathek

profile above Elisabeth's as if to suggest her superior position in the relation-ship. When a cut follows, the next shot reverses this construction: Elisabeth's head is now positioned higher than Anna's, and the position is frozen into a tableau-like image of the two women on a white background, a space devoid of any social or historical context. No narrative justification is given for this rather unusual construction of shots; it appears to be merely excessive style. Covertly, these long takes with their balanced compositions do suggest some harmonious balance inherent in female homoerotic desire, and the image of the two women appears almost as a fantasy bursting forth from the uncon-textualized unconscious. As we will see in the next chapter, however, such suggestions were not actually subversive of Nazi ideology. Yet the focus on Elisabeth's desire in these sequences halts the narrative progression in such a way that the scenes become strangely extended and fetishistic, temporarily violating classical cinema's codes of transparency.

At the end of the film, Elisabeth falls off a cliff into a lake and drowns. Narratively, the film thus provides the most conventional resolution to fe-male desire and the most sadistic demonstration of its failure—death. But it also does not entirely contain the hysterical desire of its protagonist, and instead freezes in moments of narrative stasis, resting on the iconic image of this desire. Ultimately, *Anna und Elisabeth* is a romance melodrama that attempts to purge excessive desire through narrative violence, but this desire still controls the film's center and ruptures its logic from the inside. Although such ruptured narratives could still pass censorship in 1933, melodramatic excesses and avant-garde experiments were subsequently subject to stricter aesthetic control.[100]

Beyond the purely textual evidence of the difficult negotiation of female desire that "hysterical" melodramas such as *Anna und Elisabeth* provide (the 1944 domestic melodrama *Opfergang* is another example to which we will return in the next chapter), the few remaining historical documents that address spectator response in the Third Reich also prove that Nazi cinema sometimes failed to manage desire as effectively as it intended. Many women in the Third Reich, it seems, desired another form of romance than what was offered in Nazi love stories. This seems to be particularly true of more fervent Nazi women who were highly displeased with the cinema's instrumentalization of eroticism. Although A. U. Sander's 1944 study of BDM and Hitler Youth members and their opinions regarding film did not produce reliable aggregate statistics about female and male viewing preferences, it did suggest, in its quotation of interviews with individual girls, that the film production of the Third Reich did not entirely satisfy the psychic or ideological needs of female viewers. Sander quotes one BDM member who responded at length to her survey and offered a particularly interesting critique of Nazi romance films. The girl wrote:

> Which one of us working girls does not long for sun, meadows, forests, and fields? What film expresses our great love for nature? And how few films are about a deep friendship between man and girl? What film represents the love between man and woman so tenderly, that it is still emotionally appealing? Along with many really good films, we have a massive amount of entertainment films that . . . show us people in all their wretchedness, with no secure ground to their souls. These types of films show us in a blatantly obvious way things that we could guess already, but no, they also present it in word and image and sound, as if it weren't already obvious enough. Do we Germans have to be shown something so dumb, so repetitive? Not only the casualness of men in film, also that of girls—their flirtatiousness, their constant changing of clothes, their frequent application of make-up, their fickleness—are bad examples and are (unfortunately still) all too happily copied.[101]

Although this girl was probably a partisan of a more conservative wing of Nazism, the Nazi version of romance was apparently too brutal for her. According to this respondent, romance films primarily showed commodified eroticism rather than true love, failing to imagine functioning male-female relationships. No convincing myth of romance as transcendence fully succeeded in replacing the Nazi dissolution of bourgeois morality. Nazi girls, it seems, had expected fascist culture to free them from objectification and instrumentalization, but this expectation was ultimately disappointed. Sexualized violence was instead the familiar product and instrument of Nazi power, the source of the suspicious "things that we could guess already."

Conclusion

This chapter has explored how Third Reich romance melodramas attempted to form spectator desires to the benefit of Nazi imperialist aims. Nazi romance films, as I have argued, positioned Third Reich culture as a liberation from nineteenth-century sexual morality while encouraging female participation in the public sphere in preparation for a war economy. The function of romance films was to design gender role models, but these did not obviously fit the regime's racialist policies or its supposed orientation toward a classless national community. Third Reich films most often celebrated cosmopolitan and upper-class lifestyles rather than ordinary middle-class and rural virtues. Contrary to the widespread assumption that Third Reich culture was traditionalist in the sexual realm, the heroines of Nazi romance films were often single mothers and professional women and were connoted through costuming as being willful and sexually aware. Androgyny was common for women in Third Reich film, but male images were less flexible, in accordance with the overemphasis on masculinity in fascist culture. The selection of actor and actress types was calculated to appeal to audiences beyond the Reich, supporting the colonial ambitions of both Nazi cinema and the broader Nazi state. The subgenre of Nazi melodramas that I have termed "work romances"—in which a woman is paired with her teacher, supervisor, or colleague—anticipated the labor needs of an expanding regime, even before the outbreak of war in 1939. These romance melodramas supported a turn away from domesticity, advocating careers for women and sometimes ridiculing housewives, but described work outside the home as yet another form of feminine sacrifice and subordination. Although gender inequity in education and the workplace was directly thematized by some Third Reich romance films, they ultimately maintained the hierarchical structures of fascism.

The love story also fulfilled the further political functions of distraction and disavowal. Historical documents show that Goebbels encouraged the display of the female body, and erotic attractions were deliberately cultivated in order to suppress political critique. Nazi films distinguished themselves on the international market by offering sexual content that exceeded what was allowed under the Hollywood Production Code. Within the Reich, ideologues claimed that Nazi culture had overcome the repressive sexual morality of the past, including that of both the Wilhelmine and Weimar periods. Denunciations of bourgeois morality in Nazi media were partially influenced by Nietzsche's critique of petit bourgeois and Christian restraints on the aggressive sexual drive, and aided in profiling Nazism as a battle against prudery and hypocrisy. Yet the deployment of the erotic in Nazi cinema sometimes backfired, and female spectators in particular refused to embrace the Nazi version of romance. The generically determined acknowledgment of female desire occasionally led to eruptions of stylistic excess and even homoerotic undercurrents in a few Third Reich melodramas. The next chapter examines how domestic and family melodramas were used in a genre-contradictory manner to undermine nuclear family norms and to bolster an image of Nazism as cultural revolution, and also reveals further failures in the management of spectator pleasure.

3. Breaking Out of the Bourgeois Home: Domestic Melodrama

In 1943 a stenographer in Frankfurt was arrested by the SS for circulating the following satirical poem among colleagues in her office: "The one who rules in the Russian way, / His hair styled according to French fashion, / His mustache cut in the English manner, / And was himself not born in Germany, / The one who taught us the Roman salute, / Who desires many children from our women, / And cannot father any of his own, / That is Germany's leading man."[1] As this case demonstrates, Goebbels had carried out his promise to remain fanatically stubborn in eliminating all political humor. The woman's joke was a particularly threatening one for the regime, since it proved that some people in the Reich could clearly see discrepancies between the propaganda of Nazism and its practices. Germany's "leading man" Hitler was an obvious example of the hypocrisy of Nazis who pledged allegiance to the large family as the very foundation of the German nation. The most beloved screen star of the Third Reich, Hitler claimed that he could not marry and have children, because it would diminish his erotic appeal for the masses.[2] Masses of viewers sat in the cinemas and watched *Wochenschau* (*Weekly Review*) newsreels in rapt attention, scanning the surface of Hitler's face for the minutest expression that would reveal his inner emotional state, just like they had learned to read the emotions of heroes of romance melodramas. Off camera Hitler told his associates that he simply did not like the idea of marriage or family: "I am a completely non-family man with no sense of the clan spirit," he admitted.[3] Hitler was not the only one among the Nazi leadership with this attitude. Although Goebbels appeared in the public lens as the ideal husband and father of many children, he was also notoriously ambivalent about monogamous marriage. Long before indulging in scandalous affairs with actresses while at the head of the Propaganda Ministry, Goebbels had been opposed to the concept of bourgeois morality because of its demand for marital fidelity. As he noted in his diary in 1926: "Every female excites my blood. I tear around like a hungry wolf . . . And I am supposed to get married and become a good bourgeois! And then hang myself after eight days!"[4] His ambivalence about marriage, like Hitler's, left its traces on the screens of Third Reich cinemas.

Of course, most Nazi films that narrate the romances of singles do end in an engagement or some suggestion of a future marriage pact. The planned marriages at the ends of films generally serve to fix the social order after a disturbance, as the proposed solution to conflict is then sealed with the final kiss in close-up. But as we have already seen in the preceding chapter, harmonious marriage is a myth that is clearly strained in Nazi cinema. Most scholars have had difficulty explaining this strain where they have noticed it, while others have disregarded it and have taken Nazi ideologues' pro-family proclamations at their word. For example, Robert C. Reimer, drawing on the work of Boguslaw Drewniak, has claimed, "Love stories in German films of the period are more than personal love affairs. They integrate romance into the family-values rhetoric of the Third Reich. Even simple love stories . . . serve to underscore the joy of marriage and having children."[5] If love stories in Nazi cinema universally served to sell the nuclear family and the joys of domesticity to their audiences, why then, we must ask, do marriages in these films so often appear joyless, and why are children granted so little screen time? And why do Nazi melodramas invest extramarital relationships with so many suggestions of legitimacy?

We could find an answer in Roland Barthes's inoculation model and specu-late that tales of love outside of the bourgeois home only serve to exorcise subversive desires and to finally reinforce the bourgeois nuclear family model all the more.[6] To some degree this exorcism strategy certainly does apply as much to Nazi cinema as it does to the postwar striptease of Barthes's analysis, since the fear of chaos underlies both. But there is a further, contradictory process at work in Nazi cinema's erotic attractions and its visions of family life. According to Herbert Marcuse's analysis, the Nazis made political use of an ostensible liberation from traditional sexual and family constraints: "The emancipation of sexual life is definitely connected with the population policy of the Third Reich. The sexual relations are perverted into rewarded performances: controlled mating and breeding . . . The traditional taboos served to substitute another end for them by connecting sexual satisfaction with (marital) love. The National Socialist regime, in dissolving this connec-tion, replaces it with a perhaps stronger tie to a political end."[7] Similarly, Nazi films, far from universally reinforcing traditional family structures, actually profit from an undermining of sexual taboos, the ultimate goal being an increased level of efficiency of production and reproduction.

Thus, despite the repeated rhetoric of German fascism that the family was the "germ cell" or the main foundation block of the nation and the married mother of many children its most admired citizen, cinema of the Third Reich so often suggested otherwise. There is instead a sense in many Nazi films that the family represented an impediment to the building of a militarist nation rather than its solid foundation. As Klaus Theweleit asserted, the Nazis struggled to hide their true antipathies: "The politics of the family under fascism created a double-bind of profoundly destructive power. [Wilhelm] Reich and others have suggested that Nazism buttressed the family, but this is not unconditionally the case. Nazism also destroyed it . . . But public denouncements of the family remained prohibited; this was the source of the fascist double-bind."[8] Leading Nazis propagated the value of the nuclear family as a necessary matter of public strategy, but in private other plans were made. Seemingly prohibited desires actually formed the core of Nazi film melodramas; just as fascist Germany's "leading man" found the family largely unattractive, so did the imaginary of its cinema. Filmmakers in the Third Reich preferred to offer images of the dissolution of the family rather than images of harmonious familial units, and the domestic melodrama in particular reveals the highly conflicted attitude of Nazi ideology and policy regarding bourgeois morality, marriage, and motherhood.

Detours from Monogamy: Extramarital Romances

There is a curious absence of weddings in Third Reich melodramas. Couples often get engaged at the end of love stories, but Nazi filmmakers rarely invite the viewer to the weddings that supposedly take place after the lovers' tenuous embraces. Most film marriages already appear at the beginning of the narrative as a fait accompli, and often an unfortunate one. When weddings do occur in the middle of a film narrative, they usually take place somewhere in the invisible space of an ellipsis, cut out of the narrative like all banal quotidian events that have little power to produce an emotional effect. In such cases the viewer of Nazi romances must often struggle to determine whether a marriage has indeed occurred off screen or not and what the legal status of the couple on screen might be. Quite often the discourse of "happiness" is the clearest indicator; where there is marriage it is usually absent.

This is quite different from classical Hollywood melodrama, which often treats weddings with intense, fetishistic interest. The tear-jerking end to *Stella*

Dallas (1937), in which a self-sacrificial lower-class mother triumphantly watches her daughter's upper-class wedding through a window resembling a cinema screen, is a particularly memorable example of Hollywood's vision of weddings as the most concentrated image of personal and communal success. After the weddings, of course, marriages in Hollywood may become insufferable or sinister; yet even when bad marriages are shown, Hollywood films, in compliance with the Hays Code, almost always reinstate the status quo of happy marriages by the end of their narratives. Sinister spouses and disrupting adulterers are almost always arrested, killed, or reformed by the end of classical Hollywood films. According to the Production Code, all extramarital sexuality was taboo in Hollywood cinema: "Adultery and illicit sex, sometimes necessary plot material, must not be explicitly treated or justified, or presented attractively."[9] Hollywood filmmakers were admonished in all cases to defend "the sanctity of marriage and the home."[10] Nazi cinema, in contrast, had no such belief in the sacred nature of marriage and domesticity. Goebbels never wrote an explicit censorship code regarding the filmic treatment of adultery, instead capriciously applying his momentary judgments to the censoring of scripts. Particularly toward the end of the war, he considered it politically expedient to avoid the subject of adultery. Until then, unstable unions remained prime material for melodramas and comedies.

In Nazi cinema bad marriages are frequently foregrounded, even in films that are ostensibly about something else, and this proves that the status of marriage as an institution was under continual renegotiation. The problematization of marriage in the Nazi "genius" or "leader" film is particularly notable. These hagiographic biographies corresponded to the Hollywood genre of "great man" films such as *The Story of Alexander Graham Bell* (1939) or *Edison, The Man* (1940). Hollywood films, as Jeanine Basinger has emphasized, idealized the character of the "great man's" wife and thereby served to "sell women on the role of behind-the-scenes influence."[11] Nazi genius films ostensibly also served to sell women on the role of self-sacrificing spouse but did so with less conviction. As Linda Schulte-Sasse has noted in regard to *Diesel* (1942), a biography of the nineteenth-century inventor of the Diesel engine, the nod to the narrative conventions of the biopic appears particularly forced in this film. About the character of Rudolf Diesel's wife, Schulte-Sasse writes, "the film as a whole essentially dismisses her as excess baggage, as a transparent concession to family ideology."[12] The true object of the German genius's affection is not his wife, but rather technology; as Schulte-Sasse adds, Diesel's "displacement of desire onto machines" allows him to "defer endlessly a family relationship."[13] Rather than functioning as a supportive institution for the male inventor/ruler, marriage in Third Reich

Production vs. reproduction: *Das unsterbliche Herz* (1939). Courtesy bpk, Berlin/
Art Resource, New York

films is often presented instead as an impediment to industrial production.
Or technological modernity is presented as the means by which fascist men
might free themselves of the constraining demands of the bourgeois family.

A further example of a Third Reich genius film that reveals the problematic
status of marriage in Third Reich cinema is Veit Harlan's *Das unsterbliche
Herz* (*The Immortal Heart*, 1939). Advertised as a biopic about Peter Henlein,
the inventor of the pocket watch in sixteenth-century Nuremberg, the film
narrates Henlein's (Heinrich George) heroic struggle against everyone who
attempts to interfere with the development of his egg-shaped timepiece, including his wife (Kristina Söderbaum). In this case the hero's struggles inside
the home demand so much of the film's time that it could be equally classified
as a biopic or as a domestic melodrama. Curiously, the film opens with a sequence showing a ship with the name "*Stadt Nürnberg*" (City of Nuremberg)
in the middle of a heavy storm and the steadfast captain of the ship clutching
a globe in his hands. This opening serves to imply that even the land-locked
Bavarian Renaissance city was an imperialist seafaring society that required
authoritarian leadership, and that it should be seen as a direct precursor to the
modern German fascist state. The subsequent sequence introduces the main
protagonist, Henlein, in a close-up shot with a pistol, followed by dialogue in

which he speculates on an improved design for bullets, thus demonstrating that the exemplary genius's creative energies were directed toward military rather than civilian or familial pursuits. Yet the film quickly moves into the private sphere after this, and the plot soon revolves around a love triangle between the hero, his wife, and his apprentice. Characteristically, the German genius is depicted here as childless, his passion for his work allowing him to avoid the company of his wife and to remain in the homosocial environment of his workshop. The wife, who carries the archetypical temptress name Ev, attempts to seduce her own husband with the intention of conceiving a child, an effort that ultimately fails to distract the hero from his technological mission. The sexually neglected wife hesitates to act fully on her attraction to her husband's young apprentice and is shown tossing in bed alone while her husband remains in his workroom all night, scenes that effectively pit the two Nazi obsessions of production and reproduction against each other. While suggesting that familial demands interfere with imperial ambitions, the film also insinuates that Christian moral codes that require marital fidelity stand in the way of reproductivity. By the end of the film, as Henlein sits dying of heart failure after heroically sacrificing himself to design his timepiece for use on ships, he gives his blessing to his wife's relationship with his apprentice, a conclusion suggesting that looser moral codes rather than strict marital ties might have better served all of the protagonists.

The tenuous status of marriage in the cinema and the society of the Third Reich was reflected not only in individual film narratives but also in the overall distribution of film genres. Relatively few family melodramas were produced in the Third Reich; more common was the romance film featuring a post-marital love triangle, as in *Die Frau am Scheidewege* or the subplot of *Das unsterbliche Herz*. According to the Hollywood Production Code, this was a particularly perilous subject, because it threatened the "sanctity of marriage":

> The triangle, that is, love of a third party for one already married, needs careful handling. The treatment should not throw sympathy against marriage as an institution . . . In the case of impure love, the love which society has always regarded as wrong and which has been banned by divine law, the following are important: 1. Impure love must not be presented as attractive or beautiful. 2. It must not be the subject of comedy or farce, or treated as material for laughter. 3. It must not be presented in such a way as to arouse passion or morbid curiosity on the part of the audience.[14]

Although they borrowed heavily from American models, Nazi films violated each of these points of the Hollywood Production Code. Adultery was the subject of the comedy *Wenn wir alle Engel wären* (*If We All Were Angels*,

1936), which amused both Hitler and Goebbels heartily and was given the privileged rating *"staatspolitisch und künstlerisch wertvoll"* (politically and artistically valuable). Although the film involved a husband's infidelity and a wife's simultaneous flirtation with an affair, resulting in supposedly humorous moments in a divorce court, the marriage was, of course, saved in the end. However, the film was considered "politically valuable" less because of its final reinforcement of the adulterer's marriage, and more because the comic treatment of marital difficulties was considered a successful formula by a regime that required light entertainment to counterbalance the strains of life in a rapidly rearming country. As Walter Panofsky explained in a 1938 *Film-Kurier* article, the film was proof of the regime's pro-entertainment stance: "[*Wenn wir alle Engel wären*] received the designation politically and artistically valuable on the explicit grounds that it transmits two hours of genuine cheerfulness and joie de vivre to spectators in this serious and work-filled era."[15] Likewise, though in a more pathetic tone, Nazi melodramas aroused their audiences with curiosity about extramarital relations in a manner that would also not have been acceptable under the Hays Code. Particularly in Third Reich romance melodramas that featured a postmarital or extramarital love triangle, adultery generally appears more attractive than monogamous marriage.

One such extramarital melodrama is one of the most studied films of the Third Reich, *Romanze in Moll* (*Romance in a Minor Key,* 1943). The film is about a married woman's affair with another man and ends, rather conventionally, with her suicide. Since the female protagonist pays for her affair with her life, the status quo of marital fidelity is nominally reinforced. However, the film does not intend to generate sympathy for the institution of marriage. Rather, it suggests that the unfaithful wife is actually a tragic victim of an outdated moral code. The treatment of space in *Romanze in Moll* creates a sense of domestic entrapment, as the heroine is imprisoned in her small apartment and in her role as housewife. This confinement is clearly signified by the shots of a canary in a cage and by the patronizing speech of her husband, who calls her "my child." In direct contrast to the dark and confining marital domesticity, the sequences with the heroine's lover are shot outdoors in full sunlight, which suggests that the extramarital relationship is actually the more natural one. The claustrophobic shots of the married couple's cramped apartment are also designed to show marriage and the strict bourgeois morality that binds the unhappy woman to it as unbearably suffocating. The wife, Madeleine, tormented by a sense of duty to her husband and by her nineteenth-century society's insistence on marital fidelity, decides to stay with her husband rather than divorce. When her lover insists

Naturalizing extramarital relations: *Romanze in Moll* (1943). Courtesy the Kobal
Collection at Art Resource, New York

that she has a right to happiness, the film seems to question the very concept
of fidelity. *Romanze in Moll,* like *Das unsterbliche Herz,* could therefore be
viewed as a characteristically Nazi attack on what Hitler called the "moral
hypocrisy of the 19th century."[16]

Romanze in Moll has generally been treated by film scholars as an anomalous film for Nazi cinema due to its highly ambiguous position on marriage
and because of its somewhat remarkable style. The film makes use of some
darkly toned, foreboding visuals and is structured to evade the impulse to
full knowledge. It has other film noir–like effects, such as a framing flashback
narrative, use of low-key lighting, and a less than linear editing style that creates gaps in the spectator's understanding of character motivation and events.
Seemingly unmotivated close-ups give the effect of barely legible, excessive
signs. For Eric Rentschler the film was one of the few transgressive works of
Nazi cinema, a work of "aesthetic resistance" to the ruling ideology.[17] David
Bathrick similarly emphasizes *Romanze in Moll*'s lack of easy legibility as an
almost subversive trait: "In refusing to submit to a single, all-encompassing

reading, it denies the one thing which the Nazi public sphere will always ask of the desired unambiguous text."[18]

However, there is much evidence that *Romanze in Moll*, far from being oppositional, actually delivered exactly what was desired from cinema of the Third Reich. Helmut Käutner was never considered potentially oppositional, but instead was listed by the RMVP in 1942 as one of the Reich's most reliable and preferred directors.[19] Goebbels was apparently not disturbed by *Romanze in Moll*'s ambiguities, but rather praised it as an "extraordinarily effective avant-garde work."[20] Other contemporary discussions of *Romanze in Moll* actually emphasized those elements that have appeared almost subversive to postwar scholarship. The advertising materials distributed along with the film praised Käutner's direction for its realistic representation of the love affair and his refusal to condemn the infidelity of the protagonists: "The prevailing erotic mood of the film is tenderly represented by Helmut Käutner's sensitive direction. The film doesn't take sides, doesn't excuse and doesn't accuse," the anonymous reviewer wrote.[21] The taglines suggested for use by journalists and advertisers in the film's press kit emphasized that the heroine could not really be blamed for her affair and underlined the universal nature of the heroine's experience: "A woman's fate; the ancient and eternally new story of a woman who married a man she doesn't love."[22] Furthermore, the official press materials suggested that the film's ambiguities were planned in order to provoke questions about the possibilities for personal fulfillment outside of conventional family structures: "*Romanze in Moll* will become a film that, in many respects, goes beyond the bounds of the ordinary. It does not ask the question of 'guilt,' as the drama usually does, but rather asks the question of 'happiness,' which poses itself to every person at some point in life."[23]

Happiness was clearly not to be found in marital fidelity in *Romanze in Moll*. Other discussions of the film included in the studio's information packet posed the question of whether the petit bourgeois husband was actually the guilty party: "Who is to blame for the sad events?—Is Madeleine guilty because she gave in to her desire for brightness and happiness? Or is her husband to blame because his little world was enough for him and he didn't see that he was obliged to give his wife more than that paltry life that was sufficient for him?—Who would want to judge here?"[24] Similarly, the film reviewer for the journal *Das Reich* wrote about the character of the husband with a tone of disapproval in regard to his limited, confining values. In her opinion, *Romanze in Moll* contrasted two worlds: "the narrowness of the petit bourgeois man and the extravagant freedom of the artist stand in opposition to each other, and between them haunts the smiling face, the floating form of a woman who only appears to belong to the bourgeois world, but whose internal nature belongs to a free, glorious life."[25] While Madeleine's lover represented for this reviewer a life free of moral restrictions, the husband is described in the review as a "*Spießer*" (uptight bourgeois man) characterized by "somewhat slimy self-satisfaction."[26] The *Film-Kurier*'s reviewer also expressed some scorn for the figure of the "precise, small-minded, pedantic bourgeois" and praised the character of the lover as a "cavalier with the kind of daring that never lacks nobility . . . a spontaneous man who is conscious in a sympathetic way of his own irresistibility."[27] It is telling that the lover, a professional musician, is called a "cavalier" in this review, semantically transforming the artist into a military officer. While the petit bourgeois husband is trapped in his petty repetitive habits and traditions, the artist, like a soldier, is vigorous enough to create a new life for his mistress and his nation.

Although *Romanze in Moll* undoubtedly achieved a higher degree of aesthetic quality than most Nazi films, it was not at all anomalous in terms of ideological position. Indeed, many Third Reich melodramas that thematized extramarital romances treated the affairs more sympathetically than the marital relationships. *Es war eine rauschende Ballnacht* (*It Was a Gay Ballnight,* 1939), a highly popular Zarah Leander film, could be seen as a close predecessor to *Romanze in Moll*'s vision of marital life. Like *Romanze in Moll,* it tells of the illicit love of a married woman for a composer, claiming to be the real story of the great love of Peter Ilyich Tchaikovsky. Interestingly, though, it is not the "genius" Tchaikovsky who commands the camera's identificatory devices here; it is instead mainly the adulterous woman with whom the audience is asked to identify. The audience is also encouraged to view the heroine's aristocratic husband as a villain and domesticity as sinister. In a scene in which the husband confronts his wife about her affair, he is represented with the foreboding lighting and camera work that usually designates criminals or demonic characters, and his eyelids are darkened with makeup to intensify his threatening glare. Although they are supposed to be located in the same space, husband and wife are lit separately. The Leander character, Katja, is shown in flattering three-point lighting, but her husband is lit and shot from below, creating jarring shadows in his face and emphasizing his devilish goatee. Most of the cavernous dining room where the confrontation takes place is also in heavy shadow, and the gaping but completely windowless space is as anxiety-inducing as the claustrophobic mise-en-scène of *Romanze in Moll*'s marital home. In contrast, the scenes that pair the wife and her lover are performed with appealing passion, and the lover's apartment is dominated by massive windows that connote freedom. The actor playing the Tchaikovsky character is treated tenderly by the camera, with a dazzling white light directed into his eyes to emphasize their size and clarity and a top light placed over his hair to give him an angelic quality, much in contrast to the demonic husband. When Katja leaves her lover's apartment after an act of infidelity, the sound track's urgent music and crosscutting to her suspicious husband's pursuit creates an effect of anxious suspense so that the viewer is encouraged to hope that the extramarital lovers will evade capture by the sinister aristocrat. Thus, in its visual assignments of the roles of villain and hero, *Es war eine rauschende Ballnacht* actually makes use of the most conventional topoi of traditional melodrama to cast audience sympathy against the marital relationship.

Es war eine rauschende Ballnacht, like *Der Postmeister,* was visibly influenced by the Hollywood *Anna Karenina.* In particular, the image of the marital relationship in *Es war eine rauschende Ballnacht* shows strong similarities to *Anna Karenina,* although the German film's negative vision of the husband is much more exaggerated. While maternal love becomes the main impediment to a dissolution of the marriage in the Hollywood film, in the Nazi film, curiously, wealth is the sole basis of the marriage, since the married couple is both loveless and childless. Also unlike the Hollywood film, the extramarital relationship in *Es war eine rauschende Ballnacht* appears viable, although the Nazi melodrama's heroine finally decides to renounce her love so that she can stay with her wealthy husband and secretly finance her former lover's career. This choice is described as necessary due, once again, to a hypocritical nineteenth-century morality that prevented divorce and to bourgeois society's inability to recognize and properly fund musical genius. Thus, the Nazi film shifts the terms of melodramatic renunciation away from the issue of sin to the problem of creative production. While *Anna Karenina* conformed with the Hollywood Production Code by making the heroine pay for her "impure love" with death by suicide, in *Es war eine rauschende Ballnacht* it is the male lover who dies after the heroine renounces him and he exhausts himself, heroically, in work.

Clearly it is the extramarital affair in *Es war eine rauschende Ballnacht* that is uniquely invested with desire, contrary to the claims of scholars who suggest that Third Reich films featuring adulterous relationships ultimately aimed to reinforce the institution of marriage as the sole legitimate route to emotional fulfillment and societal cohesion.[28] But in this and many other Third Reich melodramas, marriage is shown to be both the ultimate form of sacrifice and a primarily economic relationship. Bourgeois marriage is the means to wealth and social status in *Es war eine rauschende Ballnacht,* but one that allows the heroine to become the patroness of her lover, and it is solely this extramarital love that offers any prospect of personal fulfillment. When the heroine renounces her lover and all personal happiness, the tragic feeling of injustice that arises in the spectator is compensated by recourse to the concept of the artistic "great work," a communal value that is supposed to transcend the individual unhappiness of marriage.

When Zarah Leander sings her hit song "Don't Cry for Love" in *Es war eine rauschende Ballnacht,* there is also another compensation offered to the female spectator for the renunciation that, as Leander's character sings, comes at the end of every love affair. The lascivious song offers to loosen the listener's attachment to monogamy: "Just don't cry for love! / He isn't the only man on the planet, there are so many in this world! / I love every man who pleases me," Leander sings, as she glares defiantly at her husband. *Es war eine rauschende Ballnacht*'s hit song is staged as a repetition of *Heimat*'s rebellion against nineteenth-century morality, since it is similarly performed as a confrontation between the Leander character and prudish female members of the ruling upper class who are scandalized by her performance. The male audience, by contrast, is once again highly appreciative. After the song a man approaches Katja, kisses her hand, and says that the world is brutal and complex, but: "As long as there are such beautiful women, it is worth living in this world." Thus, although the text of Leander's song sounds almost libertine (and for this reason, no doubt, it was later reused as a sound track for Pedro Almodóvar's irreverent 1984 anti-melodrama *What Have I Done to Deserve This?*), the song in its original context was supportive of Nazi ideology rather than subversive to it. Its intent was simultaneously to generate desire for fascist world domination through the visual pleasures of Nazi performance and to prevent heartbreak-related chastity in its spectators. The raising of the birthrate was of course the Nazis' most obsessive domestic policy after genocide, and extramarital romances such as *Es war eine rauschende Ballnacht* worked principally on loosening the law of lifelong fidelity, especially in the case of sterile marital relationships.

As noted in the last chapter, *Die Frau am Scheidewege* made a similar argument. Beyond reinforcing the fascist work ethic, the film aimed to weaken the traditional prohibition against divorce and infidelity. *Die Frau am Scheidewege* dissolved a marital relationship that lacked strong erotic attachments in favor of an extramarital affair that had produced a baby, and the rearranged relationships at the end of the film became, as the film's title suggests, an argument for individual and communal fulfillment through divorce. The closely connected film of the following year, *Irrtum des Herzens,* also argued for divorce by example. At first the head surgeon's son is bitterly opposed to his father's divorce from his mother in favor of the much younger nurse Angelika, but then he comes to see the error of his ways and agrees that his father will be much better served by having a new mate/employee. After he comes to this realization, the head nurse praises him for having finally become mature and reasonable.

Certainly not all spectators found such arguments reasonable. Family values–oriented Catholics in particular saw in Nazi culture a scandalous attack on Christian tradition. As the Security Service reported in 1941, a Catholic doctor had recently lamented the weakened status of marriage in the Third Reich in book titled *Eheglück und Gesundheit* (*Marital Happiness and Health*) in a characteristic manner: "We have to look at things today and say that, at no point in the history of the Christian world was the central core of human society, the sacred institution of marriage, as in danger of destruction as it is now in our contemporary moment."[29] In 1941 another group of Catholics distributed a brochure protesting the Nazi conception of marriage: "Marriage is a bond of lifelong fidelity and love between man and wife . . . Marriage is more than just a public institution for the production of offspring for the nation and the economy," the brochure stated.[30] And indeed it was this controversial conception of marriage as a potentially dissolvable, economically defined institution that was most often propagated by the cinema of the Third Reich.

In January 1939 the *Film-Kurier* called for the production of "divorce films." Although many films in the Third Reich had touched upon the subject, the editor wrote, few had represented the legal side of the matter or set its drama in a divorce court: "Countless films touch, in more or less explicit scenes, on the subject of unhappy, destroyed, broken marriages. Why should we shy away from showing a marriage in film as the divorce court judge sees it in his profession, which often allows him shocking insights?"[31] This call for divorce films had followed several years of wrangling among party leaders about the issues of marital fidelity and divorce. Goebbels was generally favorable to easy-access divorce and was opposed to the prosecution of adultery. The subject arose several times in 1936–1937 as the Nazi leadership debated the question of whether adultery should continue to be penalized as it had long been in the German military.[32] Goebbels fought against initiatives for the enforcement of monogamous marriage, since, as he wrote, disciplinary action against extramarital affairs would only give rise to "snooping and hypocrisy."[33] In December 1937 he noted in his diary that the discussions were still ongoing: "Further discussions about the new law. Hard fight about infidelity. Whether to punish or not. I am against it and almost everyone else is too."[34] In the end Hitler and Goebbels decided that it was indeed in the interests of the Reich's population strategy to liberalize divorce laws, and in July 1938 a reformed legal code was passed. By facilitating "guiltless" divorces, the new Nazi law loosened the bonds of marriage over the Weimar legal statutes.[35]

As historian Jill Stephenson has noted, the new divorce law fulfilled a demand for which communists and feminists had unsuccessfully campaigned during the Weimar Republic, though the Nazi goals were of course entirely different from those of the progressives. In the 1920s, Stephenson adds, "the happiness of the individual was seen as a good reason for trying to revise the law. In Nazi Germany, however, it was made clear that this policy was designed not so much to accommodate the private individual as to allow the interests of the nation to take precedence."[36] The Nazis appropriated leftist and feminist causes when they could serve their own power and population management schemes, which explains the surprising quasi-feminist discourse that occasionally appears in some Nazi films.

One extramarital romance melodrama that premiered about ten months after the institution of the new divorce law, *Umwege zum Glück* (*Detours to Happiness,* 1939), seems almost subversive on first viewing, because it explicitly considers the happiness of its female protagonists. The film, like many others about extramarital affairs, suggests that the way to contentment may lie outside of marriage—before a conventional conclusion finally brings the adulterer back to the original status quo. The film features a married, childless Prussian aristocrat named Hanna (Lil Dagover) who discovers that her composer husband is having an affair with a cabaret showgirl. She decides to file for divorce and then travels to Vienna to confront her husband's mistress. On the way there she meets a man on the train and subsequently escapes with him to the Alps for a romantic ski vacation. The mise-en-scène of these spaces, as in *Romanze in Moll,* indicates that the affair has a liberating effect. The heroine is shown outdoors in picturesque nature scenes with her lover, while the windows of the marital apartment are blocked by heavy curtains. At the end of this choice narrative, the heroine finally decides to reunite with her husband, but the detour from monogamy that she takes for the rest of the film is remarkable, not least of all due to the film's casting. Dagover had already played a married woman between two men in the films *Kreutzersonate* (*The Kreutzer Sonata,* 1937) and *Maja zwischen zwei Ehen* (*Maja between Two Marriages,* 1938), but at the time of filming *Umwege zum Glück,* she was fifty-one, and the actor playing her lover (Viktor Staal) was twenty-nine, contradicting the international conventions of romance.

Among the other surprises waiting along Hanna's detour is the scene in which she confronts the showgirl lover of her husband, a scene that supports liberalized attitudes toward coupling. The heroine's husband's mistress appears on stage to sing a song much like the one performed by Zarah Leander in *Es war eine rauschende Ballnacht.* With one hand on her hip and a feathered fan in the other, the blonde actress sings "Give Me 24 Hours of Love"

Departures from bourgeois morality: *Umwege zum Glück* (1939). Source: Bundesarchiv-Filmarchiv

in a deep voice: "It can be debated whether great love exists, / I personally don't believe in it. / . . . / You shouldn't torture me with promises, / that you never will keep. / You shouldn't talk so much about happiness, / the most important thing is that you please me today. / When we call each other on the phone later, / in four weeks, or in a year, / we will conclude with a smile / that it was all so enchanting."[37] During this song, which suggests that the only reasonable approach to romance is to view it as a short-term affair, reaction shots of Hanna indicate that she is internalizing its message and applying it to her current situation. Although the rather libertine text of the cabaret singer's performance might serve to mark her as decadent and a negative example of loose sexual morality, the camera treats her with the scopophilic fascination of an iconic figure. Instead of being fragmented into a heavily shadowed, Expressionist image of feminine threat, her face and body are brightly lit for better visual exploration by the spectator, and the mise-en-scène of the cabaret is dominated by bright white satin. After the end of the stage performance, Hanna goes backstage to confront her rival. As Hanna sits in the background of the dressing room and converses about her husband's affair, the showgirl undresses in the foreground. The camera is placed tight against the singer, and as she lifts a leg to remove her silk stockings, her robe falls open and reveals a brief view of full pubic nudity. Meanwhile, in the background, Hanna smokes a cigarette and watches the undressing showgirl with interest. The rivalry is defused as the singer assures Hanna that she has no intention of taking her husband away permanently. Hanna smiles affectionately in response to the singer's expressions of sexual independence and adds in a tone of admiration, "You know so much although you're so young . . . You are enviable." The scene, unexpectedly, intends to create a reassuring image of feminine solidarity while reinforcing the performed song's message about the necessity of emotional detachment in triangular relations.

To reinforce this message further, the film later offers another model for female autonomy. While Hanna and her lover are enjoying their idyllic fantasy of an affair in their Alpine hotel, they meet a young actress named Marianne. Surprisingly, Marianne does not enter into a competition for the attentions of Hanna's lover but serves mainly to represent the new attitudes of a new generation. Costumed in pants, Marianne is boyishly styled. While memorizing lines from Shakespeare for an audition, she rhapsodizes about leaving the mountains for the metropolis: "I just can't stand not to work. I'm going to Berlin next week . . . There you can really live and do theater!" she tells the couple. When she is asked whether she has a boyfriend, Marianne replies, "Ha, I don't have one, thank God! If you want to work, then men just get in the way!" A contrast is thereby set up between the two female characters, with Marianne representing a more modern perspective than the heroine of the film. After Hanna returns to her Berlin apartment, she meets Marianne at her acting school and admits to the younger woman that she cannot leave her husband, because her identity depends too much on her role as a wife: "You can't understand me. You are from a different generation. You have a profession, a goal that gives you a sense of security and direction. For me, ever since I got married, my love for my husband was the entire content of my life." Thus, *Umwege zum Glück* asks the audience to identify with an adulterous wife, but its minor female characters present models for living that are presented as more revolutionary. Both Marianne and the cabaret singer, the film insists, belong to a dynamic new generation that no longer believes in the myth of love but rather in polygamous relations or in the all-consuming value of work.

The end of the film relativizes this message by bringing the heroine back to her husband, but not before the husband receives a lecture on gender inequity and double standards from the fiery young Marianne. In the final scene, after Hanna's husband has been reeducated to appreciate his wife more, he offers to buy her a new hat. Hanna then embraces him and the film fades to black. Thus, while most of the length of the film questions the institution of marriage, the narrative conclusion does appear nominally to reinforce it; however, marriage is described once again as a status-based arrangement when the heroine finally chooses her wealthy husband over her middle-class lover. Although *Umwege zum Glück* might seem like a rather astounding film to have been shown on Third Reich screens, it can be understood in the context of Nazi melodrama's larger project of challenging bourgeois morality. The film suggests the possibility of a change in sexual relations for at least eighty minutes of its running time before finally conceding to convention in the final frames. The two minor female characters, while providing a model for moral change, also recruited audience desire through bodily displays. Ultimately, Hanna's young lover is released at the end of the film to find a more fertile partner. Thus, many of the film's moments that could be seen as being informed by a progressive rather than a fascist ideology actually coincided with the domestic goals of the Nazi leadership.

Although the censors at the RMVP obviously saw nothing objectionable about *Umwege zum Glück,* Third Reich audiences apparently did not embrace its extramarital fantasies. The reviewer for *Film-Kurier* wrote that the audience at the premiere laughed through most of this melodrama, an unintended spectator response. He insisted that this was quite unfortunate and tried to defend the film against its poor audience reception. The audience's rejection of the film, the reviewer wrote, should not prevent other directors from departing from convention in the future: "the film got a mixed reception during its screening yesterday, and one could easily be tempted to blame the film's underlying concept for this. That would be wrong and regrettable, since it would discourage other authors from going beyond worn-out film conventions in their descriptions of human relationships . . . the film contains so much that is valuable that it deserves the undivided sympathy of the audience."[38] The *Film-Kurier* reviewer reserved particular praise for the figure of Marianne, whom he described as a "resolute young actress, in whose mouth the script puts excellent dialogues."[39] He also praised the "fantastic scene" in the cabaret singer's dressing room and regretted that the audience did not get to see more of the showgirl later in the film.[40] The reviewer from *Der Film* ignored the negative audience response at the premiere and stated optimistically, "It is certain that this very effective material will have great success in the Reich."[41]

Aesthetically, though, *Umwege zum Glück* was obviously lacking. The audience response may have been as much a result of failed direction as of spectators' unwillingness to accept the film's "basic ideas" on changing gender relations. Much of Staal's wooden delivery of his lines produces an unintended distancing effect, which may have elicited the audience's laughter. Yet it is remarkable that this extramarital melodrama did not end in the death of the heroine but rather in a shopping trip proposal. The positive reception given to *Umwege zum Glück* in the Nazi press—but not in the cinemas—suggests that the shape of popular cinema in the Third Reich was due not only to official censorship but also to audience response. Evidently, Third Reich audiences preferred death as a narrative resolution.

Other Nazi melodramas continued to exploit the same kind of pseudo-emancipatory discourse offered by *Umwege zum Glück* but treated their heroines much more sadistically. *Die Geliebte* (*The Mistress*, 1939), which premiered two months later, also addressed the topic of extramarital sexuality, but this time the heroine was violently disposed of at the end of the film. The narrative tells of the fin-de-siècle Berlin romance between a lower-class girl and an aristocratic military officer who is engaged to another woman. The romance begins as the chief lieutenant (Willy Fritsch) saves the girl, Therese, from the waters of a lake after a pedal boat accident. Therese turns out be a perfect temporary lover for the military man; she is characterized as subordinate and self-effacing and makes no demands on the man other than to be consumed. She tells her lieutenant that she wouldn't dream of asking him to marry her: "Because you have a house with 36 rooms and because you are an officer . . . With us, it is easier. We are together, because we love each other, and then we will go our separate ways."

In addition to reinforcing class divisions, *Die Geliebte* also advertises the fringe benefits available to the military man in two sequences set in the downtown *Passagen* (arcades), the distinctly turn-of-the-century architecture of consumption where Therese works as a shopgirl. While uniformed officers swagger through the shopping mall and look at the goods available in the display windows, prostitutes troll for business outside the shops. In an Imperial order where the military man commands the top ranks of society, woman is an easily acquired and discarded commodity. The film argues against any conservative bourgeois morality that might serve to challenge this system, and it even uses the rhetoric of gender equity in arguing for a liberalization of sexual relations. Grethe Weiser, the immensely popular wisecracking Berliner, gets the supporting role in *Die Geliebte* and her familiar task of taking on bourgeois prudery. Playing Therese's colleague at work, she reassures Therese that she should not accept the double standard when it comes to sexuality. "*Moral*, that's a foreign word!" she insists, "And that's good for men . . . and it means that what men are allowed to do, we aren't allowed to do by far." The true German should not accept this foreign concept of morality, the film suggests. Instead, she should have the liberty to offer herself freely to soldiers and not be bound by, in Hitler's words, the "hypocritical morality" of an "outdated, past world."[42]

In the end Therese decides to make the ultimate sacrifice for her lover and drowns herself so that she will no longer stand in the way of a class-appropriate marriage to his wealthy fiancée. After a flashback sequence with a montage of happy images of the affair, the final shot of the film is that of a hand placing flowers on Therese's beautiful corpse. Rather than demonstrating a punishment for extramarital sexuality, this sadistic narrative was intended to idealize the woman who delivers herself completely to the erotic needs of the soldier. Its final shot is thus the reverential image of a melodramatic martyr. Through *Die Geliebte*'s martyrdom the spectator was again supposed to draw a distinction between the restrictions of the Wilhelmine era and a more "enlightened" Third Reich. Under the Nazis, the spectator should infer, women could subjugate themselves without necessarily having to commit suicide directly, since the "foreign" word "morality" was being banished from the German fascist vocabulary. Among other goals, the Nazis were working on obviating the need for monogamous marriage.

Indeed, *Die Geliebte* seems to offer a genuinely Hitlerian vision of romance. As Hitler once told his table companions, the worst part about bourgeois marriage is that it gave women too much bargaining power: "So it's better not to get married. The worst part of marriage is that it creates a sense of entitlement! The right thing to do is to have a mistress. The burden falls away and everything remains a gift."[43] Many men among Hitler's entourage supported this view, and *Die Geliebte* seems to have been produced with the personal interests of some members of the Nazi leadership in mind. Indeed, Goebbels's own mistress Lida Baarova was originally cast in the role of Therese, but she was ultimately replaced when the casting threatened to cause a public scandal. The narrative of *Die Geliebte* also bears a striking resemblance to the real romantic history of Reinhard Heydrich, the director of the Security Service branch of the SS.[44]

The leadership's private antipathy toward the rights of wives, as limited as they were in the Third Reich, explains in part Nazi cinema's obvious interest in adulterers. Even when the films ultimately reinstate the legitimate marriages at the end, it is significant that so many Nazi love triangles are narrated from the position of the rival rather than the legal spouse or legitimate fiancée. As we have seen in *Die barmherzige Lüge,* wives are sometimes also disposed of in favor of rivals, especially if the rivals are single mothers and thus have already proven their reproductive capacities. But even when the rival does not get the man at the end of the film, she usually gets most of the camera's attention. In the romance melodrama *Das Mädchen von Fanö (The Girl from*

Fanö, 1941), for example, a married nurse has an affair with a married sailor, and both consider leaving their spouses. The film clearly prefers the childless adulteress of its title, as indicated by the amount of screen time and space that she occupies. The deceived wife of the heroine's lover, on the other hand, barely shows up on the screen and is not treated to any engaging character development, although she is the mother of a couple of blonde children.

A limited exception to Nazi cinema's preference for the unmarried was Veit Harlan's extramarital romance *Die Reise nach Tilsit* (*The Journey to Tilsit*, 1939), starring Harlan's own mistress at the time, Kristina Söderbaum.[45] Unlike in *Die Geliebte,* the camera stays mainly with the legitimate partner of the philandering man, although she is also threatened with death by drowning at the end of the film. The romantic triangle in *Die Reise nach Tilsit* is drawn between a German man, his German housewife, and his Polish girlfriend, so the erotic rivalry also takes on nationalistic significance. Here, the foreign rival is characterized as a dangerous cosmopolitan femme fatale in a similarly clichéd form as in German director F. W. Murnau's American-made film *Sunrise* (1927), of which Harlan's film is a remake. Both the camera and the narrative outcome of Harlan's film favor the legitimate (and racially/sexually "pure") wife, while the Polish mistress undergoes a brutal chastisement by the German community when she refuses to give up her lover. Since the rival Polish woman is identified as being from Warsaw and the film premiered only weeks after the Germans bombed and invaded that city, Harlan's melodrama directly supported Germany's vicious military campaign by manufacturing a Polish threat to domestic peace.

That this threat was equated with sexual desire, however, meant that the film's position in regard to marital fidelity and domesticity still remained somewhat muddy. Since no film by the "*Erotomane*" (erotomaniac) Harlan could unequivocally condemn sexuality (especially of the extramarital kind),[46] the conflict between duty and desire is particularly tortured here. Domesticity, although threatened, does not appear entirely idyllic in this film either, but is once again pictured as confining. The husband is portrayed convincingly as a man suffering from domestic asphyxiation, and the shots of the couple in their house are excruciatingly tight. The photography of the grim, swampy winter landscape around the couple's home also adds to the suffocating atmosphere of the marriage. Compared to Murnau's idyllic rural American village, this East Prussian landscape is much less idealized.

Correspondingly, the city is also more exciting than threatening in Harlan's film, and the contrast between rural and urban environments is not clearly defined as one of purity and decadence. In fact, to some degree it is the experience of tourism that motivates the positive outcome to the narrative. The husband chooses not to drown his wife, Elske, in favor of her Polish rival and falls in love with her again at the end of the film, but only after the couple has taken a trip to the city of Tilsit and the wife becomes urbanized by means of new clothes and bottles of champagne. She thus adopts some of the outward traits of the foreign mistress in order to regain the erotic interest of her husband.

Goebbels, however, was not at all satisfied with this resolution and attempted to ban the film before release. Apparently he identified too strongly with the dilemma of a married man unable to separate himself from a foreign mistress and saw both his own situation with his Czech lover Lida Baarova and Harlan's affair with the Swedish Söderbaum laid bare on the screen. Magda Goebbels, who was then losing the competition for her husband to a Slavic woman, likewise believed that the melodrama was a commentary on their own domestic situation, and she protested.[47] Nevertheless, the film was eventually released, and the SD claimed that female audiences reacted positively to the film: "Women in particular reportedly feel that the clear delineation of the concept of honor and the deeply humane behavior of Elske as mother are valuable."[48] For once, the romantic triangle was resolved in favor of an unsophisticated housewife, and it was the relative rarity of *Die Reise nach Tilsit*'s apparent support for traditional family (as well as nationalist) values to which spectators responded. Observers were later presented with the same popular ending to Goebbels's own real-life extramarital romance when Baarova was forced to return to Czechoslovakia.

Elsewhere proponents of marriage and monogamy felt that their interests were under attack. Heinrich Himmler's articles in the SS journal *Das Schwarze Korps* revealed the leadership's lack of genuine commitment to traditional family structures, and his Lebensborn (Spring of Life) maternity homes for the pregnant girlfriends of SS men appeared to many to be scandalously immoral breeding farms.[49] Even if Himmler often paid lip service to a notion of "respectability" in public, he voiced his opposition to it in private. As Himmler reportedly told his associates:

> Marriage in its existing form is the Catholic Church's satanic achievement; marriage laws are in themselves immoral. The case histories of monogamy so often show up the woman as thinking: "Why should I take as much trouble with my appearance as before I was married?" . . . But with bigamy, each wife would act as a stimulus to the other so that both would try to be their husband's dream-woman . . . The fact that a man has to spend his entire existence with one wife drives him . . . to deceive her . . . The result is indifference between the partners. They avoid each other's embraces and the final consequence is that

they don't produce children . . . On the other hand, the husband never dares to
have children by the woman with whom he is carrying on an affair . . . simply
because middle-class morality forbids it.[50]

If Himmler held antipathies against monogamous marriage because he saw it
as inherently unerotic and thus as an impediment to reproduction, he clearly
had some support from Third Reich filmmakers.

Veit Harlan, the Third Reich's highest-ranking melodramatist, worked on
the leadership's antibourgeois morality project in most of his films. *Opfergang*,
probably the most stylistically excessive melodrama of the Third Reich, made
a particularly colorful contribution to this end. *Opfergang* replays the familiar
competition narrative in which a married woman is rivaled by her husband's
mistress. Here, the film's focus once again returned to the rival, and this time
Kristina Söderbaum was recast as the "other woman." Although *Opfergang*
offered a conventional solution to the triangle by having the rival die at the
end of the film, it is the adulteress who is the heroine of the film here, not
the deceived wife. The names of the two female protagonists announce this
preference. While the wife carries the imposing Latin name Octavia (the
eighth), Söderbaum's character is named Aelskling, Swedish for "dearest" or
"loved one." The camera clearly also prefers the rival. We rarely see shots of
Octavia when she is not accompanied by another character, but Aels commands sequences on her own. Thus, the spectator is given privileged access
to the interiority of the adulteress by means of sequences that are primarily
interested in the development of her emotions, while the speech and the gaze
of Aels often motivate camera movements and cuts, so that the spectator is
situated in her position. Hallucinatory sequences that indicate Aels's subjective
visions further engage the spectator in an identification with her character.

The two characters are also aligned along the most common axis of Nazi cinema's sympathies; the wife represents a suffocating domesticity and a stifling
bourgeois morality while the rival represents a liberating natural eroticism.
As Söderbaum explained in regard to Harlan's concept for *Opfergang*: "Stiff,
rigid lifestyles were supposed to be confronted with freshness and naturalness."[51] The wife is the representative of the old order while the mistress is
the fresh young type preferred by German fascism. Octavia, a model of *haut
bourgeois* domesticity and sexual prudery, first makes her appearance in the
film by descending the staircase of her airless Hamburg villa dressed as a vestal
virgin in a long white gown. Her room, to which she brings the film's central
male protagonist, Albrecht, before their offscreen wedding, is also entirely
decorated in frozen white and has tightly shuttered windows. Although Albrecht admires the luxury of the décor, he appears somewhat overwhelmed

Colonial mistress: Kristina Söderbaum as Aels in *Opfergang* (1944). Source: Deutsche Kinemathek

by Octavia's excessively feminine domesticity as he wades through her shin-high white shag carpet. Octavia's bourgeois world is also represented as being choked by sedentary decay in the following sequence, in which her father reads Nietzsche aloud and contemplates death in the dark downstairs sitting room, in the company of Octavia's morose mother and aunt. The nuclear family with its middle-age female members is thereby associated with morbidity and sterility. The reference to Nietzsche in this scene serves as a shorthand critique of a "decadent" bourgeoisie and suggests the need to reinvigorate German society through Dionysian, amoral physicality.

Accordingly, Albrecht quickly becomes agitated with this deadening familial confinement and throws open the windows to escape to the sunny outside world of virile action. It is there that the sympathetic adulterer makes her entrance in the film, once again by means of a boating scene, as in *Die Geliebte*. Appearing as a nude swimmer in her first scene and most often pictured outdoors in subsequent scenes, Aels is connoted as more "natural" than the prim Octavia and is correspondingly unconcerned with marital morality. When Aels appears on screen fully clothed, it is most often in equestrian fashions. Since female sexuality in Nazi cinema is so often associated with the iconography of horse riding, this costuming also indicates that Aels is the more stimulating partner. She races horses "for victory" only, as she tells Albrecht, and is willing to "go to battle for happiness," as she tells Albrecht's meddling puritanical friend, Mathias. *Opfergang*'s script gives Aels privileged use of the preferred fascist vocabulary when she employs the words "*Sieg*" (victory) and "*Kampf*" (battle), thus associating her unbound sexuality with a militarist lifestyle. Importantly, both Aels and Albrecht are also associated with Germany's colonialist ambitions, which are set against Octavia's primarily domestic concerns. Aels is described in the film's dialogue as a "migratory bird" who spends winters in Africa, while Albrecht is introduced at the beginning of the film as an explorer and an illustrious member of a German colonial association. As Susanne Zantop has argued, *Opfergang* is principally "a film about recasting past German colonialism as a moment of national 're-masculinization' and proposing colonialism as an attractive 'idea' to strive for."[52] As Zantop adds, Aels is to be understood as the agent of re-masculinization: "The contact with the tropical woman/ colony provides the man with what he needs to become a German man: a turn to sunshine, movement and space . . . the film reactivates both long-held beliefs about the benefits of physical exertion . . . and colonial fantasies concerning the rejuvenating effect of the colonial adventure on individuals and the national body."[53]

Aels's openness to engaging in colonialist fantasies and her more adventurous way of living provide the prototypical fascist man's way to happiness, Harlan's script further insinuates. When Mathias insists to Albrecht that the principle of monogamous marriage must be upheld and that Octavia must be respected as an ideal spouse, Albrecht answers: "That doesn't do anything for me, not at all. I can tell myself that a hundred times, but when I'm with Aels, I'm just happier. It's as if there's always an arm's distance between me and Octavia." Albrecht thus indicates that Octavia's chaste lack of desire hinders the consummation of the marital relationship. The result of Octavia's sexual purity is ultimately a sterile marriage, and the couple remains childless. The rival Aels, on the other hand, is presented as a single mother, which is intended as proof of her erotic and reproductive superiority. This fact is underlined in the key sequence in which Octavia stalks Aels in order to discover the secret of her rival's attractiveness. When Octavia witnesses how men turn around in the street to gaze at Aels with desire, she moans, "She is simply superior to me!" Mathias, the unsympathetic representative of upper-middle-class propriety, immediately arrives on the scene to hold Octavia back from pursuing Aels and tells Octavia that she should be happy that men do not look at her the way they do Aels, since she is "pure" (*rein*). Octavia, however, counters, "No, but she is too!" Octavia thereby converts Mathias's bourgeois sense of the word "pure" as indicating chastity to the Nazi sense of "*rein*" as indicating racial purity. This shift in terms effects a shift away from the middle-class morality criticized by Himmler, Hitler, and Goebbels. The pursuit scene is set up to have a causal logic: Octavia attempts to discover the secret behind Aels's attractions, and the repeated cutting between Octavia and Aels builds suspense. The resolution and the end of the sequence comes as Aels's child emerges from her nanny's house, and Octavia realizes the reason for Aels's superiority: her sexualized and fertile body.

However, the rivalry between the two women appears to produce some desirable results; Octavia slowly learns to become more like her husband's mistress and aspires to become less homebound. Octavia's transformation is effected by her participation in an orgiastic, stylistically excessive masquerade ball sequence. After leaving domestic confinement to go to the carnival celebration, she gives up her usual piano playing and decides to take riding lessons. At that point the camera also begins treating Octavia more voyeuristically and spies on her as she undresses in her bedroom, which signifies her willingness to finally become sexualized. In this way *Opfergang* seems to covertly argue for bigamy, because the wife competes here with the mistress to dress and undress like the romantic hero's dream woman—or, perhaps, dream man. In the pursuit sequence—the only one in the film in which the camera stays with Octavia and cuts are matched on her gaze—there is a strong homoerotic undertone to the stalking. While Octavia's scenes with Albrecht show her somewhat frigid and struggling to feign desire, when she pursues Aels she is shown as virtually possessed by attraction, panting and fixing Aels with an intense gaze. The scene is prefigured in the carnival sequence, when two women dressed in riding gear flirt with Albrecht and lock arms with each other, a phantasmagoric doubling of Aels and Octavia

as bisexuals ready to engage in triangular desire. As Slavoj Žižek has commented, *Opfergang* depicts "the supreme 'male chauvinist' fantasy: that of
the mistress and wife, each sacrificing herself for each other . . . the wife wins
her husband back precisely by accepting his illegitimate passion for another
woman, and even by taking upon herself his desire."[54] By the end of the film
Octavia has absorbed so much of her husband's desire that she is styled in the
last sequence as a copy of Aels, costumed in an equestrian blazer and bowler
while riding next to the ocean. The result of the competition in *Opfergang* is
that the German wife undergoes a process of eroticization and masculinization and takes on attributes of her "tropical" counterpart. The seaside setting
of the final sequence and Octavia's aristocratic riding attire (much like the
costuming in *Man spricht über Jacqueline*) connote her readiness to leave the
confined domestic spaces of Germany and to support her husband's potential
future as colonial master.

At the end of the film the bigamous triangle is narratively dissolved when
Aels dies of a mysterious illness. This conclusion has been read by some
scholars as evidence of a Nazi condemnation of premarital sexuality and
adultery.[55] However, this reading overlooks many cues to the contrary. According to the logic of *Opfergang*'s narrative sequencing, sexuality is actually

The bourgeois wife transformed: Octavia in *Opfergang* (1944). Source: Deutsche
Kinemathek

the source of health. After the carnival sequence Octavia and Albrecht return to Hamburg, and Octavia proves her transformation once more by sending Aels a suggestively shaped pink orchid as a greeting. The next sequence opens with a close-up of the flower in Aels's hand, followed by a tracking shot back to reveal her desiring look. Shortly thereafter Aels recovers enough from her bout of illness to energetically march out of her house with a howling pack of man-sized dogs and to whack trees with her riding crop. Later, when Aels falls ill again, Octavia dresses like a man and passes by Aels's villa on horseback to greet her with another riding crop, which gives Aels enough strength to get up and press herself ecstatically against the window. This event is ostensibly explained as a "ride of sacrifice" that proves Octavia's willingness to surrender her own interests and in effect to tolerate her husband's bigamy, but the mise-en-scène also manages to invest this act with homoerotic desire (one that mirrors the health-giving lesbian desire in the similarly excessive 1933 melodrama *Anna und Elisabeth,* discussed in the last chapter).

Sacrifice in *Opfergang* in effect becomes power as the phallic riding crop is transferred from one female character to another. In Hermann Kappelhoff's assessment, what is characteristic about Harlan's "politics of emotion" is the manner in which the fascist director departs from melodramatic conventions established by the eighteenth-century bourgeois theater: instead of offering the spectator the sentimental pleasures of a suffering heroine, Harlan apotheosizes sacrifice into heroism.[56] However, it is not only political power that is alluded to here but also the supreme pleasures of erotic intensity. Aels's death is simultaneously pictured as an act of sacrifice and an orgasmic moment of union in which the image of her lover is superimposed over the image of her own impassioned face, a shot that effectively sutures shot and countershot into one image and thereby undermines certainty about whose fantasy is expressed in the final hallucinatory dialogue.[57] As will be further elaborated in the epilogue of this book, desire and narrative position remain curiously free-floating throughout *Opfergang,* enabled and intensified by the plot device of feverish illness.

Aels's tuberculosis-like illness is a recycling of the conventional motif long employed by melodrama and opera that allows a female protagonist to express strong sexual needs. As Susan Sontag has asserted, tuberculosis "was conceived as a variant of the disease of love" and "was also a way of describing sexual feelings—while lifting the responsibility for libertinism."[58] In the classical Hollywood melodrama, Mary Ann Doane asserts, death is often the only solution for a desiring and desired woman, the only solution to the "impossible signs" she creates: "The woman associated with excessive sexuality . . . is unrepresentable and must die."[59] The resolution to *Opfergang,* therefore, was entirely conventional within the classical system. However, it was not the only solution to excess desire that was considered possible by the Nazis, and the narrative outcome of *Opfergang* should not be read as a Nazi condemnation of adultery or a categorical equation of eroticism with illness. Rather, it is her impending death that allows the heroine of *Opfergang* to live beyond the bounds of bourgeois morality. As Veit Harlan explained in an oblique reference to the Nietzschean critique of middle-class restraint, he intended the character of Aels to represent the experience of a "Dionysian and self-incinerating frenzy of joy."[60] *Opfergang* certainly eroticizes death, but death is not proposed as a substitute for repressed sexuality here. Instead the film argues that the risk of death facilitates a more intense and more militaristic form of life that in turn intensifies erotic experience.

This was a potentially useful piece of propaganda for wartime audiences, and as we will see in the next chapter, similar messages could be found elsewhere in Nazi cinema and media. In 1938 senior Nazi Party official Martin Bormann proposed a related solution to the love triangle that would supposedly better serve the interests of an imperialist war economy than either monogamy or chastity. As Bormann commented:

> We have to wish that the women who do not have or cannot get a husband after this war will have the possibility of entering into a marriage-like relationship with a man, out of which as many children as possible will grow. We must, for the sake of our people, carry on a veritable mother cult . . . By special request, a man should have the right to enter into a long-term marital relationship with not just one wife, but also with an additional one . . . since the more numerous the births are among a people, the more secure its future and its life."[61]

Hitler was in agreement with Bormann and had made informal plans to legalize polygamy after the war as a reward for decorated soldiers and party officials. To encourage the scheme, the Nazis planned to offer tax credits and state jobs to any man practicing polygamy; in compensation to women, first wives would have the right to the title "Domina."[62] Excess women were therefore to be reintegrated into a new marital and martial order. The fact that such a plan was never directly narrativized in *Opfergang* or in other extramarital melodramas of Nazi cinema, but only covertly suggested, was due to both generic convention and audience resistance.

Nuclear Destructions: Family and Maternal Melodramas

The Nazis had plans to allow the postwar construction of new family structures, including that of a patriarch in charge of multiple wives, but they also gave indications of being suspicious of all forms of family unity. According to Herbert Marcuse's analysis, the Nazis consciously exploited anti-domesticity and anti-patriarchy rhetoric in their attempts to build military dominance. They promised to liberate Germany from the sexual repression of the nuclear family, a message for which there was already a receptive audience:

> The destruction of the family, the attack on patriarchal and monogamic standards and all the similar widely heralded undertakings play upon the latent "discontent" in civilization, the protest against its restraint and frustration. They appeal to the right of "nature," to the healthy and defamed drives of man ... They invoke the "soul" against soulless mechanization, folkish solidarity against paternal authority, the open air against the smugness of the "bourgeois home," the strong body against the pale intellect. This inevitably implied the granting of easier opportunities for satisfaction, but the new liberties are just as many duties to the population policy of the Reich; they are rewarded contributions to the campaign for a larger supply of labor and war power.[63]

In this way Nazism co-opted arguments that had been launched against restrictive traditional values by the communists and women's movements in the Weimar period, and then directed mass desires for freedom to their own ends. Patriarchy was attacked in order to make room for a more dynamic and militarily efficient order, a corporatist model of social organization.

For this reason the family melodrama was not a popular genre in the Third Reich, in contrast to the (premarital or postmarital) romance melodrama. When families were shown in Nazi melodramas, they were most often depicted as the central source of problems for the hero or heroine to overcome rather than being a fundamentally stable unit that experiences a temporary disturbance or intrusion from without. In this respect Nazi melodramas deviated from international norms. According to Noël Carroll's analysis, classical Hollywood family melodramas ultimately reinforce the ideology of family even if they narrate familial disruptions: "the existence of these stories reinforces prevailing beliefs in the idea by symbolically rehearsing a faith in the family through fictions that train, or, at least, further inculcate audiences in this particular way of ordering everyday human events."[64] Family melodrama in the Third Reich often had exactly the opposite intent: rather than strengthening the ideology of family, many melodramas of the Third Reich argued for the destruction of this way of ordering the everyday.

In particular the family was shown as interfering with the building of the fascist order itself. A well-known example is the early propaganda film *Hitlerjunge Quex* (*Hitler Youth Quex*, 1933), which represents the nuclear family as dominated by communist tendencies. The young hero of the film,

Heini, is initially trapped in the dreary environment of his family's small Berlin apartment, where both he and his downtrodden mother are subjected to abuse by his father, a committed member of the Communist Party. After befriending several teenage members of a Hitler Youth gang, who seem to be remarkably free of parental control since their mothers and fathers never make an appearance on screen, Heini experiences the outdoor group activities of the young Nazis as liberating. The film in effect argues that children belong first and foremost to the various organizations of the Nazi state rather than to their parents. As Eric Rentschler has suggested, it is a family film that manages to subvert its own generic conventions by undermining faith in the family: "*Hitler Youth Quex* begins only as a family drama; by its end both parents have disappeared, the dead mother briefly mourned, the father having surrendered his son to the brigade leader . . . Hitler's order redefines family and social configurations to become the dominant source of allegiance."[65] Rentschler's reading here corresponds to Max Horkheimer's assertion that the Nazis were hostile to the nuclear family: "totalitarianism in its German version tried to dispense with the family as an almost superfluous intermediary between the total state and its social atoms."[66]

Similarly, another of the most important family melodramas of the Third Reich was actually an advertisement for the destruction of the nuclear family. *Der Herrscher* (*The Ruler*), another Veit Harlan film and the winner of the 1937 highest regime honor for a film, the *Nationaler Filmpreis,* was ostensibly a genius/leader biography, but like *Das unsterbliche Herz,* it was primarily interested in the leader's domestic problems. *Der Herrscher* has been discussed by film scholars mainly as an example of the *Führerprinzip,* as an inculcation of the masses in the principle of submission to hierarchy in both politics and industry.[67] But the film also attempts to propagandize against what it presents as the primary impediment to this submission: the conventional bourgeois family. The main protagonist of the film is the CEO of an industrial firm, Matthias Clausen, who is modeled after Gustav Krupp. In Hollywood the family melodrama often centers on dynastic disputes and is primarily concerned with male oedipal conflicts.[68] Correspondingly, *Der Herrscher* is a sort of "male weepie" about a misunderstood man suffering from insubordinate family members. Unlike most Hollywood dynastic family melodramas, though, *Der Herrscher* invites the audience to identify with the sufferings of the tyrannical patriarch rather than those of his children. At the beginning of the film, Clausen (played by Emil Jannings) is shown at the funeral of his wife. While his children sob bitterly at their mother's grave and one of his daughters attempts to throw herself onto the coffin, close-ups of Clausen's stony face make it apparent that he does not mourn the death of the housewife and wishes the death of his children as well.

At home after the funeral, the family gossips disapprovingly about how little emotion Clausen shows for his deceased wife. The mise-en-scène of this domestic space is designed to convey an image of the bourgeois family as confining, antiquated, and unhealthily female-dominated. Clausen inhabits a classically melodramatic mansion with an imposing central staircase, yet the interior is filmed to give an impression of restriction rather than large spaces. In most of the interior scenes, family members crowd or lurk in the darkly lit limited space around the staircase, which leads up to a second floor with a small library and a collection of antiques. The camera does not travel into adjoining rooms, so there does not appear to be any private space in the house. Instead the camera remains mostly in the central downstairs area, which is dominated by a large portrait of the dead *Hausfrau* hung over the family hearth. Clausen clearly resents the fact that the mother still exerts postmortem authority in this domestic space, as her painted eyes continue to enforce the family's sexual repression.

Generically *Der Herrscher* stands in direct relation to the Hollywood family or domestic melodrama as epitomized by the Eisenhower-era films of Douglas Sirk. But there are some telling differences between Harlan's use of melodramatic convention and Sirk's later American developments of the genre. According to Noël Carroll, Sirk's films conform to the Hollywood faith in the nuclear family by "catechizing receptive audiences in courtesy, stoicism, humility, and charity."[69] This faith is reinforced by the mise-en-scène of Sirkian melodramas such as *All That Heaven Allows* (1955), which naturalizes the nuclear family through the inclusion of flowers in the domestic space and shots of the garden outside the family house; the nuclear family thereby becomes, as Carroll states, "part of the cosmic order" with "naturally revivifying powers."[70] In contrast, in *Der Herrscher* the family is denaturalized by means of a domestic mise-en-scène dominated by antique sculptures that serve to indicate that the nuclear family is an outmoded institution in which its members age too quickly and become like lifeless museum artifacts. In *All That Heaven Allows* it is the dead husband who continues to exert control over the sexuality of the widow, via objects on the mantelpiece that serve as reminders of patriarchal authority in absentia. *Der Herrscher*'s scenario is a curious reversal of this Hollywood version, as it recasts the nuclear family as an intrinsically matriarchal structure.

Consequently, the upper-middle-class family, as in *Opfergang,* is also portrayed here as overly intellectualized and lacking in virility. One of Clausen's sons is an effeminate professor dominated by his scheming wife. Bettina, one of Clausen's daughters (played by Harlan's second ex-wife, Hilde Körber, in a characteristically sadistic bit of casting), is a hysterical spinster with one paralyzed arm and a pathological attachment to her dead mother. Bettina is also aligned with Christian morality and its repression of sexuality, since she is costumed in ecclesiastic black dresses with white collars and a cross around her neck; Christian-bourgeois sexual morality is thereby equated with paralysis. Clausen does possess a large family of four children, ostensibly the Nazi ideal, but these children only serve to maintain the deceased mother's authority. In one scene Bettina screams at her father to think of "mother's jewels" and to not violate her memory by taking a new lover, thereby dispossessing the dead mother of her previous material and sexual status. In another scene Clausen's son admonishes him to think of his responsibility toward his grandchildren, four of which—two boys costumed in sailor suits and two girls in white dresses—file into the room to greet their grandfather. In response Clausen only grimaces, and when the children are marched out of the room again, he sighs in relief, "So, that's finally over!" Here, *Der Herrscher* reveals succinctly how little affection lies at the bottom of the fascist obsession with children, who are seen as little more than future warship personnel or reproductive instruments. The fascist man, the film argues, should not be forced by convention to take lifelong responsibility for children. As Veit Harlan explained, *Der Herrscher*'s hero is to be understood as an "exemplary man who throws all 'bourgeois garbage' overboard."[71]

If the nuclear family and its domestic space have revivifying powers in Hollywood melodrama, it is, in contrast, the workplace that has this power in Nazi melodrama. The space of the family is antiquated and deadening in *Der Herrscher,* but the corporation is bursting with virile energy. In a sequence in which Clausen musters his factory workers, muscular men are shown pumping rods into flaming furnaces to a sound track of throbbing and humming machines. Clausen then remarks, "Children, wives? No, one should have machines as companions! Machines are decent creatures!" A willing machine-like woman soon appears in his office, a new secretary named Inken (played robotically by Marianne Hoppe). Although young enough to be Clausen's granddaughter, Inken decides to serve the captain of industry unconditionally, working tirelessly at her typewriter and offering to sleep with him without demanding marriage. The audience is again invited to identify with the mistress, since she is portrayed as admirably selfless, an employee who asks nothing in return for the privilege of working around the clock, in contrast to Clausen's demanding and avaricious family. Indeed the main focus of *Der Herrscher* is its hero's quest to divorce his family for a younger woman, a fact emphasized by the program booklet that was distributed along with the film. The text of the program concealed *Der Herrscher*'s fascist content with the emotional language of romance and personal fulfillment:

> Matthias Clausen is a man who seems to possess everything necessary for happiness, and yet he has become increasingly isolated on the inside, until, on the downward side of existence, he finds a person who gives him the wondrous gift of a new youth . . . For the first time, Matthias Clausen has the experience that a person demands nothing of him, but only wants to give him a gift: herself. Hesitantly, but deeply delighted, he takes this most beautiful human present.— But Clausen did not reckon with his family. With their peculiar egotism they immediately raise an alarm at the first appearance of Inken, and the family is already determined to ward off this danger. The fight breaks out passionately.[72]

Similarly, *Der deutsche Film* called *Der Herrscher* "a political film" that nevertheless thematized a primarily domestic war: the film, the reviewer stated, was about the "battle with the family" and the "battle for the girl."[73]

The Hollywood domestic melodrama, especially in what Thomas Schatz calls the "family aristocratic variation" of 1950s melodrama in the manner of Sirk's *Written on the Wind,* also thematizes the struggle for power within the nuclear family and the problem of individual desire. Conventionally in this version, a motherless family threatens to break apart due to "inadequate male heirs and sexually frustrated daughters."[74] An intruder with "redemptive powers" then appears and eventually stabilizes the family, providing for dynastic continuity. By the end of the film, the tyrannical patriarch has been eliminated or reeducated to become more humane, and the nuclear family as an ideally functioning system is reaffirmed. *Der Herrscher,* however, is informed by a very different ideology, and in no uncertain terms it argues for the destruction of traditionalist family values. The "battle for the girl" reaches its most climactic moment as Clausen unleashes a fit of male hysteria and rages up the staircase of his house to smash the antique vases and slash the portrait of his dead wife. He then screams programmatically, "I was never married! I never had a wife, I never had children!" Such dialogue echoes statements reportedly made by Hitler himself, who insisted that the demands of work and man's essential nature were incompatible with marriage.[75] *Der Herrscher* is in no way concerned with reeducating the patriarch. Instead the bourgeois family, *Der Herrscher* suggested, must be eliminated because it endows its members with a sense of inherited rights.

Furthermore, *Der Herrscher* suggested that the housewife should be eliminated as well. While the housewife/mother is a privileged figure in the classical Hollywood melodrama and the home is viewed as a refuge from

Battle against the family: Clausen assaults the housewife's portrait in *Der Herrscher* (1937). Source: Deutsche Kinemathek

the alienating experience of modern urbanity and industrial capitalism,[76] the German fascist melodrama argued in favor of the destruction of the domestic space, in which women held too much influence. In the corporate workplace, on the other hand, authority structures were more rigidly defined than in the home. As an employee, the woman was defined by contract and low wages to an inferior position of subordination and could be fired at will. The fascist man, *Der Herrscher* argued, did not need a space of refuge from industry, because this is where he was most alive. Instead he needed refuge from the family. As Laura Mulvey has further pointed out, bourgeois ideology of the nineteenth and early twentieth centuries viewed the housewife as the guardian of private space: "It is the mother who guarantees the privacy of the home by maintaining its respectability, as essentially a defence against outside incursion or curiosity as the encompassing walls of the home itself."[77] Since Nazism intended to dissolve the walls between the private and the public spheres and attacked previous notions of respectability, the bourgeois housewife and mother lost her original value.

For the fascist man, passionate commitment was best sought outside the walls of the home. At the end of *Der Herrscher* the hero becomes engaged to his secretary, but since she goes back to her stenography immediately after the proposal, there is no indication that she will produce a new nuclear family for the industrial leader. Instead the secretary herself performs all familial and corporate roles, becoming an entirely subservient worker as well as a combined child/lover figure. For this reason most of the contemporary reviews of *Der Herrscher* emphasized Inken's youth to an exaggerated extent. *Filmwelt* described her character as "a young, childlike creature that demands nothing for itself, but only wants to live for him, the beloved man, and gives him the gift of youth and love."[78] Thus, through the girl's battle-won gift of youth, the hero regains his own virile energy, which in turn benefits the nation. At the film's conclusion, Clausen disinherits all of his sons and daughters and dictates to Inken his final will, mandating that a new leader for the corporation should be found in the *Volksgemeinschaft* rather than in the family.

The problem of negotiating production with reproduction was revisited six years later in another Emil Jannings production, *Altes Herz wird wieder jung (Old Heart Becomes Young Again,* 1943), which replays many of *Der Herrscher*'s themes and makes its perversions even more explicit. Here, Jannings once again plays an industrial CEO, in this case a never-married seventy-year-old who seemingly begins an intergenerational romance with a twenty-year-old girl who takes a job in the corporate main office. Later it is revealed that the young woman believed to be his fiancée is actually his granddaughter, the progeny of an interclass premarital pregnancy from many decades past. The girl's grandmother, the working-class woman whom the hero made pregnant long ago, relinquished all claims on child support in order not to interfere with the hero's career and is described by the script as "a pearl," a forward-looking woman who knew how to raise a child with no male help. This film, like *Der Herrscher,* thereby plays on a male Nazi fantasy of dynasty without family while reinforcing the privileges of male capital. In a scene at the end of the film in which a group of BDM girls dance around a fountain with a few gray-haired friends of the hero, *Altes Herz wird wieder jung* furthermore suggested that the German "race" could survive and renew itself regardless of total war. Genetic lineages could continue in the absence of marriage, and in the absence of the young men killed at the front, because some old German men would always be available as fountains of insemination.

Thus, the incestuous fantasies of Nazi cinema actually worked in concert with its hostility to the bourgeois nuclear family, since such scenarios allowed for the separation of motherhood from the male world of industrial and military action. It is remarkable how often Nazi narratives include suggestions of incest or actual consummations of it. They appeared on stage as well as in the cinema: a 1942–1943 touring Kraft durch Freude (the state-sponsored leisure institute Strength through Joy) operetta, for example, was titled *Das Glück im Kreuzgangwinkel* (*Happiness in the Cloister Corner*) and featured a romance between a seventeen-year-old girl and her fifty-five-year-old adoptive father.[79] Incest, it seems, was a peculiar fascist fascination. It was certainly one of Veit Harlan's obsessions, as *Der Herrscher* and his other melodramas testify. The married couple in *Opfergang,* Albrecht and Octavia, are also first cousins. In Harlan's *Jugend* (*Youth,* 1938) Kristina Söderbaum's character is impregnated premaritally by her cousin and is driven to suicide by the repressive morals of a rural, clergy-dominated society. In the *Heimatfilm*/romance melodrama *Die goldene Stadt,* the same occurs (though here it supports a racial argument instead of an attack on Christian hypocrisy, since the lecherous cousin is Czech). As in *Der Postmeister,* there is also a clearly incestuous relationship in *Die goldene Stadt* between the young female main protagonist and her father. The heroine's mother is yet another of Nazi cinema's drowning victims, long dead before the start of the film plot. Indeed, *Die goldene Stadt* visualizes perhaps the most characteristic fascist form of incestuous desire, in opposition to Hollywood's more commonly eroticized mother-and-son relationship.[80] While Hollywood was dominated by the classic oedipal scenario, Nazism's family romance fantasized an even more sinister reversal in which the patriarch kills the mother in order to possess the daughter.

According to Stephen Lowry's analysis, *Die goldene Stadt* served to indulge a specifically fascist fantasy of reproduction without women in its elimination of the woman as "mediator between generations of men."[81] Indeed Nazism's perverse imaginary seems to center on the elimination of wives and mothers from any claims to male dynastic continuity. Instead Nazi films covertly imagine the possibility of reproduction of the fascist order with unmarried girls—usually with employees, but sometimes with cousins, daughters, or granddaughters. This imaginary is perhaps only natural. Incest fantasies can be seen as an extension or radicalization of the ideology of racism, which seeks an elimination of foreign elements and a purification of blood, and no blood was considered by the Nazi male to be more pure than his own. *Die goldene Stadt* crystallizes its racist argument in a father-daughter kiss on the lips in close-up, followed by a dissolve that suggests a continuation of incestuous relations off screen. The girl's attempts to escape this Nazi fantasy once again end in drowning.

But death in Nazi cinema was not only enforced as a punishment for racial "impurity" or illicit desire; in fact, there is a symptomatically high mortality rate for all mothers and wives in Nazi cinema. Female characters are eliminated from the diegesis even when they do exactly as Nazism asks and give birth to four or more children, as in *Der Herrscher.* Indeed traditional motherhood plays a curiously underrepresented role in Nazi cinema, a surprising omission that has been repeatedly noted in recent scholarship.[82] Likewise, even contemporaries have sometimes acknowledged that there was a gaping discrepancy between Nazi plans to develop a "mother cult" and the images of motherhood actually presented in the cinema. In 1943 an anonymous reviewer for *Film-Kurier* commented that nuclear families with mothers were barely seen in German films, since they preferred to focus on the romantic fates of younger individuals: "Usually one has the impression that the heroes and heroines of our films have traveled the world solo before they fall into each other's arms happily as lovers or with serious intentions in front of city hall. The family is generally suppressed . . . Still, we are pleasantly surprised that people are gradually acquiring a taste for it and have discovered the 'Woman around Forty,' not the exceptionally interesting woman with her individual destiny of love, but rather the wife and mother."[83] It is telling that films featuring married mothers in main roles were still considered a new discovery two years before the end of the Reich. But as the *Film-Kurier* article indicated, for Nazi cinema motherhood was a slowly acquired taste.

In most Third Reich melodramas with middle-age mothers as heroines, the woman is not married, and the woman's relationship to her children and to her new male partner are placed into opposition with each other. Such films corresponded to what Thomas Schatz has called the "widow-lover varia-tion" of the classical Hollywood family melodrama, which thematizes the conflict between mothering and sexual desire, but the Third Reich variant of this melodramatic subgenre intensifies this conflict further.[84] In *Moskau-Schanghai* (*Moscow-Shanghai*, 1936), *Zwei Frauen* (*Two Women*, 1938), *Frau Sixta* (*Mrs. Sixta*, 1938), and *Mit den Augen einer Frau* (*With the Eyes of a Woman*, 1942), the conflict between mothering and sexuality becomes so exaggerated that the child directly becomes the mother's sexual rival, pro-ducing another peculiar version of Nazi cinema's incestuous attractions.[85] *Frau Sixta*'s main protagonist is a recently widowed rural postmaster who begins a new relationship with a military officer. When her teenage daughter demands to be liberated from the strictures of her convent school and moves back home, her mother's lover begins giving the daughter horse-riding les-sons and rhapsodizing about the superior attractions of youth. The mother then bravely prepares herself to sacrifice both. In the final sequence of the film, the camera remains with the melancholy Frau Sixta as she watches her daughter and her former lover cross the Alpine border into emigration together, leaving her with nothing but her work. Thus, in this melodrama, as in most Nazi widow-lover films, the mother's sexuality is sacrificed in order to make room for more fertile youth, but these films also take leave from the maternal role itself.

As a consequence, there are few "pure" maternal melodramas in Nazi cinema. Most Nazi films that feature mothers as protagonists are primarily concerned with the problem of sexuality and social status rather than with mother-child relationships. Maternal duty is rarely the source of passion but functions rather evasively as its justification. Films that use sacrifice for the sake of a child as their ostensible crux are generally much less interested in the child itself than in the mother's romances and efforts to gain professional recognition. Heroines in Nazi cinema, like the Zarah Leander character in the 1943 melodrama *Damals,* are allowed to travel the world and carry on passionate extramarital romances in the name of maternal sacrifice, while the child for whom the supposed sacrifice is being carried out remains safely distant and receives only a few minutes of screen time. Children in Nazi cinema are instrumentalized and become a source of melodramatic suffering and conflict rather than objects of desire. In contrast, the interest in children in classical Hollywood appears much more genuine, since they more often remain at the center of the camera's attentions and are given speaking roles. Most Nazi children come in either of two forms: as three-year-old doll-like creatures who cannot yet talk and who are usually referred to as "*das Kind*" (the child), and are thus genderless and without individuality. Or they are portrayed as clearly sexed young adults who are on the brink of coupling themselves. Children presented as children are rare in Nazi cinema, and this fact did not go unnoticed at the time. A 1942 editorial in *Der deutsche Film* made exactly this point and asked why, if Germany was supposed to be the "land of children," the cinema did not represent it as such:

> Where have families ever been shown in a German film that have more than one or two children? . . . Usually it is only the single child that is privileged, and even here it stands "between the parents" or is born out of wedlock. Thus it only becomes a source of conflict around which everything revolves, and as such, it only has the task of bringing more confusion into the plot through its very existence. In what film, though, have children appeared only as children, that is, as a natural part of a family? When has the family life of more than one to three children ever been shown, and created the subtle impression in spectators that these many children were the pride of the family? . . . even in *Unser Fräulein Doktor*, which was in many respects a very charming film, the child actors often appeared like wound-up dolls, like props.[86]

Characteristically also, the undifferentiated male children in the comedy *Unser Fräulein Doktor* were not part of a family but rather the students of the heroine, objects of fascist education rather than familial affection. Since children were viewed as future war instruments by the Nazis, it was logical that they should not be treated as uniquely valuable individuals.

As Goebbels wrote in 1940, it was the primary task of German women to manufacture this materiél: "Women too wage war, by bearing children."[87] However, he was as squeamish about representing this part of war as all other aspects of its production. Visibly pregnant women were generally banned from Third Reich screens, and film producers were instructed to avoid any representation of childbirth. Goebbels ordered part of a scene cut out of *Kolberg* that attempted to visualize his call for female warfare by showing a woman giving birth in the middle of Napoleonic bombing.[88] Similarly, in 1944 a film that Terra Studios intended to produce featuring a midwife as a main character was terminated in the early censorship stage. The Reichsfilmdramaturg Kurt Frowein stated that a film featuring a Red Cross nurse would be preferable so that the focus would not be on mothers giving birth but rather on nurses and soldiers (thus allowing for more erotic attractions).[89]

All classical cinemas had a similar prohibition on the representation of pregnancy and childbirth. While Hollywood justified this prohibition with the need to maintain standards of "decency" and divinely ordained morality,

Nazi cinema's evasions were more obviously motivated by a plain distaste for mothering. In Hollywood, as Mary Ann Doane has stated, the universal, psychoanalytically determined horror of the maternal is repressed in fetishistic form: "The threat of the maternal space is that of the collapse of any distinction whatsoever between subject and object . . . The horror of nondifferentiation is suppressed through a process of attaching a surplus of positive attributes to the maternal."[90] Hollywood was required by the Hays Code to allow the bourgeois family to profit from the surplus value of mothering. Nazi cinema, on the other hand, subverted Hollywood's standards of decency and attempted instead to isolate the space of the maternal and to contain it away from fascist masculinity. It was certainly this motivation that lay at the heart of Nazism's championing of single motherhood.

Overtly, however, the Nazis took up the issue of extramarital pregnancy as a war strategy. While the thematization of illegitimate children became increasingly impossible in Hollywood after the institution of the Production Code, Nazi filmmakers took on the theme as a favorite cause célèbre.[91] Nazi cinema, following the Nazi leadership, defended single motherhood against the condemnations of Christian tradition and the bourgeois morality of the masses.[92] As Rudolf Oertel claimed in his 1941 book on German-Austrian cinema, the Nazis had successfully done away with the old formula of the "fallen woman": "Nowadays, when a girl has a child out of wedlock, we do not view her with hypocritical lust and see the titillating fate of a fallen woman, but rather we see the mother-to-be."[93] Oertel was speaking in his book for the leadership, however, not for all the spectators in the cinemas. The more traditionally oriented masses often objected to the Nazi leadership's support for extramarital mothering; in one case parents in Brandenburg brought their complaints to court after a party official had assured their daughters at a BDM meeting that each one of them could have babies without ever having husbands.[94] Nevertheless, the leadership continued to cautiously push forward its departure from the nuclear family, since it viewed extramarital procreation as a nationalist necessity. As Hitler told his tablemates, Germany's pre-bourgeois history validated this approach: "Let's remember that after the Thirty Years' War polygamy was tolerated, so it was thanks to the illegitimate child that the nation recovered its strength."[95]

If children were to grow up within monogamous marriages, he insinuated further, these marriages should be contracted only after a girl had proven herself worthy through a term of premarital sexuality. A reinstitution of the supposedly rural Germanic tradition of the *Probier* (trial relationship), according to which fiancées came to their weddings already pregnant, Hitler argued, would ensure that no marriages remained childless.[96] Douglas

Sirk's 1935 melodrama *Das Mädchen vom Moorhof* (*The Girl of the Moors*) apparently supported this plan. In this north German *Heimatfilm,* the main protagonist of the title is a single mother who falls in love with a farmer and competes for him against his virgin fiancée, eventually winning the competition. Sirk's defense of the illegitimate mother arguably may have been motivated by hidden leftist sympathies, but they coincided with Nazi leadership's own interests (as did most of Sirk's other Third Reich films).[97]

Many Third Reich melodramas suggested that mothering was best done in solitude, without male participation past the act of insemination. It is telling that in the regime's most widely publicized film about motherhood and one of the few pure maternal melodramas of the period, the parenting is done by the woman alone. *Mutterliebe* (*Mother Love,* 1939) attempted to provide a more encouraging vision of motherhood than the previous year's *Frau Sixta* (both films were directed by Gustav Ucicky), but the film did not imagine motherhood occurring in the same space as marriage. An absurd deus ex machina puts a quick end to the nuclear family within the first ten minutes of the film, as the father gets struck by lightning during a family picnic. The young widow is then left to care for her three young children on her own, slaving away at building a laundry business and resisting an offer to remarry. Shortly thereafter the film flashes forward about fifteen years to a moment when all of the children are adults with their own budding love lives and the mother has become a successful businesswoman with a luxurious downtown Vienna apartment. Soon one of her sons almost goes blind with an eye disease, and in a tear-jerking story line she gives up one of her own to save his sight. At the end of the film, all of her children and her longtime suitor are assembled around the table to honor her birthday, and operating in her usual self-effacing mode, she forgets to set a place for herself at the table.

The film was released on Mother's Day in 1939, and there were official orders to make the most of it.[98] Predictably the press advertised the film as a testament to the noble sacrifices of all German mothers. *Filmwelt* enthusiastically praised the film's heroine for doing all the parenting work alone and without complaint: "What a mother! . . . She washes and irons until the dead of night, she works until she falls over, she gives up the temptations of life, she only thinks about her children, she sacrifices her youth and her desire for love. She suffocates her private wishes and passions, in order to give the world an example of a mother. Without complaining, she carries the enormous burden of raising children."[99] Nazi film commentators attempted to sell this example of maternal sacrifice as a new role rather than a return to tradition. The reviewer for *Der deutsche Film,* suspecting that serious maternal melodrama might not sell in the Reich, assured audiences some-what apologetically that despite the kitschy title of the film, it was not as bad as Weimar-era maternal melodramas (such as the 1929 Henny Porten melodrama of the same name): "The title is perhaps appropriate for spread-ing the smell of cinematic sentimentality. Memories from earlier times are to blame for that . . . It awakens all the horror images of palpable ideology and gaudy effects; it hides plenty of tear-jerking traps. But [the subject] was mastered by Ucicky and his colleagues with tact and superior skill, with the right dosage of seriousness and humor."[100] The film reviewer, required by higher authorities to assure audiences of the film's quality, could not entirely hide his distaste for such manipulative maternal melodrama, and certainly not all viewers were convinced by its intent either.

Despite its title, *Mutterliebe* did not offer an attractively sentimental im-age of the joys of mothering, but instead attempted to sell the principle of sacrifice for sacrifice's sake. In this respect, *Mutterliebe*, perhaps even more than most Third Reich melodramas, appealed to the "surplus-enjoyment" of renunciation that Žižek has defined as the very basis of fascist ideology.[101] However, it was not presented entirely without instrumental value. Sacrifice in *Mutterliebe*, as in *Opfergang*, is also power: its fantasy compensations for single motherhood are authority, respect, and wealth. The mother runs a business while maintaining a loyal male companion, and not remarrying effectively allows her to maintain autonomy over her finances. When she melodramatically gives up her eye to her son, this act also forces him to see things her way, further consolidating her authority over him. When her other son impregnates one of her laundry employees, she demands that he show some respect to the mother-to-be. By these somewhat duplicitous means, *Mutterliebe* was supposed to represent the newly raised status of motherhood under Nazism and was the cinematic equivalent of press propaganda that as-sured women that the Third Reich respected the mother more than any other member of society. The principle of maternal sacrifice came with falsified guarantees of female power over fascist men. *Der deutsche Film* commented that the ending of the film indicated a new spirit of the times that "gave back to the German woman and mother her proper place of honor."[102] However, the gap between this official propaganda and the reality of conditions in the Third Reich must have been apparent to masses of female viewers. According to SD reports, many BDM girls who had attended compulsory screenings found the film grim rather than encouraging.[103]

Mutterliebe's propaganda could not disguise the fact that single mothers and mothers of many children did not have the advantage of wealth and status in the Third Reich. The Nazis handed out medals to mothers of four or more children but not much else. Little space was allocated to large families, both on cinema screens and in reality, and large families continued to be at a material disadvantage.[104] The upper and middle classes realized, despite all the press propaganda, that having many children would indeed result in unappealing forms of sacrifice. Consequently, the number of children born to each married couple actually dropped during the Third Reich so that the average couple had only one or two children, far from the ideal minimum of four.[105] And despite Nazism's constant pro-natalist rhetoric, the birthrate during the Third Reich never reached the level of the Weimar Republic's baby boom, and by some accounts the abortion rate actually increased to more than five hundred thousand each year.[106] The Nazi militarist elite showed even less interest in getting married and having children than the general populace: by 1939 only 39 percent of SS men were married, and of those who were, each fathered an average of only 1.1 children.[107] Nazi cinema's failure or refusal to make the large, nuclear family appear desirable may have played some role in these statistics.

Furthermore, there was a very noticeable gap in the supposedly improved status of mothers in the Third Reich and their actual social position. The regime's lack of genuine commitment to the welfare of mothers became increasingly apparent to many women during the war, particularly to those from the lower classes. While lower-class women with four or more children were often forced by the regime to work a minimum of ten hours a day in munitions factories, childless upper-class women could avoid work entirely. The grumbling of proletarian mothers became increasingly louder. They objected to the blatant discrepancy between the official ideology of the classless *Volksgemeinschaft* and the reality of Nazism's stratified society; as the SD reported in July 1940: "The women comment to this end, that the so-called 'better circles' still have one or more servants, sit around in restaurants and cafés, populate the beaches, tennis courts and sports fields and are already sitting in the garden in lounge chairs by the early morning. According to a report from [the city of] Stettin, conscripted women of the munitions factory Löcknitz literally remarked that 'it's always the little man who gets swindled.'"[108] Nazism's antibourgeois rhetoric, it was clear, aimed at a male-oriented liberalization of sexual morality, but not an extension of economic privilege. The lower classes continued to carry the simultaneous burden of both production and reproduction for the Reich.

The Domestic Protest: Audience Responses

According to Herbert Marcuse's analysis, the Nazis exploited German culture's longstanding "'anti-bourgeois' mentality" and its opposition to "Christian civilization," converting both forms of protest into "powerful instruments for training in technological rationality."[109] The Nazi leadership, however, was often disappointed by the fact that petit bourgeois mentalities and Christian loyalties remained rooted in vast sectors of the population, particularly in provincial towns and rural areas. As a result, Nazism's cinematic technologies of desire did not always function according to plan.

Audiences who were still under the influence of Christian tradition were most likely to reject Nazi cinema's erotic attractions. The Catholic Church repeatedly objected to what it saw as a decay in moral standards, at least in terms of sexuality. While the Church remained largely silent about the mass murder of European Jews, it did dare to battle the Nazi state on the sexual front. In March 1942 the archdiocese of Leitmeritz held a protest sermon, the text of which reportedly included the following: "Nowadays, lust has found an extensive breeding-ground in unbelief . . . One is succumbing to a cult of the body, which sees the highest values or even divinity itself in the strengths and drives of the body . . . Marriage is being made into a ridiculous old-fashioned institution, [and] infidelity and divorce are being glorified."[110] In 1943 the bishops of Cologne and Paderborn joined forces to denounce once again the "free love" of the Nazis: "This godless spirit of the times is making the widespread weakness of character into a right, and making sexual offenses into a virtue . . . the sanctification of infidelity and divorce . . . is undermining the premarital chastity of the youth through its demands for the release of 'free love' and the equality of legitimate and illegitimate motherhood. It is undermining marital purity through its endorsement of infidelity and its justification of and support for divorce."[111]

Similar protests had been registered for years, even if they had not been so publicly voiced. Goebbels and his RMVP were at pains not to provoke audiences whose sexual morality was more conservative than that of the leadership. By 1940 there was clear evidence that the policy of liberalizing sexuality was not universally successful. Security Service reports on public opinion repeatedly documented audience objections to nudity in films and variety shows. There was particularly a split in the reactions of urban and rural viewers. For example, an SD report in September 1940 summarized: "We are particularly hearing increasingly negative comments among the farming population about 'half-naked women,' variety shows and 'dirty jokes' that are mainly designed for urban conditions."[112] Goebbels identified entirely with the tastes of urban audiences and was frustrated by the way in which rural values sometimes opposed his own preferred version of modern Nazi culture: "The farmers are betraying us. They are too preoccupied with blood and soil," he wrote in private.[113]

However, in the interest of successful propaganda, Goebbels had to respond to the objections. In early 1940 he had received other reports of strong complaints regarding Nazi-Party-sponsored Kraft durch Freude (Strength through Joy) shows that had featured barely dressed dancers and sexual jokes as their main attractions. Goebbels then readjusted his earlier policy regarding the substitution of sexual for political humor and said that the jokes should cease. On April 1, 1940, Goebbels gave the following instructions in his daily meeting at the Reich Ministry of Propaganda: "Herr Gutterer should make sure that Strength through Joy announcers resort to dirty jokes less than before. The principle should be that they can be liberal in exposing the female body, but should be more restrained with the alleged 'joking around.'"[114] The naked female body was henceforth to be exploited in all seriousness, and erotic imagery was to remain uncommented. Goebbels followed with further directives on December 5, 1940, that no more nude dancers were to appear in shows in small provincial towns or the countryside, as a concession to the more traditional sensibilities of rural audiences.[115] Similarly, melodramas about single mothers also generated negative spectator responses among more conservative segments of the population, and in April 1941 Goebbels ordered that the "problem of illegitimate children" should not be treated in upcoming film projects.[116]

The risks involved in the Nazi eroticization of the public sphere included the loss of support from more traditionally oriented Nazi Party members as well as nonparty Christians. Nazi women were a particularly unreliable factor; many of them who had supported the party in the belief that it would defend traditional values and return the wife and mother to her proper place of esteem were deeply disappointed by the regime. Nazi women who had been disgusted by the pornography marketed during the Weimar Republic were similarly disillusioned when they realized that the Nazis had no intention of completely halting the production of arousing film imagery. Two letters that survived the bombing of the RMVP building at the end of World War II and are now preserved at the German Federal Archives document one female spectator's protest against the objectification of women in Nazi cinema. The woman, a resident of Vienna and a member of the Nazi Party, wrote the first letter of complaint to the *Frauenschaftsleiterin* (women's group director) of the Vienna District on March 14, 1940, the partial text of which follows:

> For a long time, I have been harboring the desire to raise an issue in an appropriate forum, one which must deeply concern all women and girls, but it is often the case that we are not informed about the ways such things must be done . . . What has been preoccupying me is the programming of so-called "entertainment centers" in our city and others, programs that continue to be humiliating to women. I first want to emphasize that I am not at all prudish and that nudity itself is a beautiful, natural thing . . . [But] the fact that naked women are praised in advertisements for the nightclub Achmed Bey on Peter's Square as "crowd-pleasers," that in the revue shows of the Reich (above all in

Munich, according to the illustrated papers, but also in Vienna), female flesh is sold by the kilo by greedy directors in unchanged vulgar-Jewish fashion—these are things that should be abolished . . . On the one hand, they make such an enormous fuss on Mother's Day, they make the most wonderful appeals to the male youth and military recruits to value and respect the woman as a mother and a sister, and on the other hand they give free rein to the dirty speculation of white Jews on the raw, lower instincts of men . . . We as women must defend ourselves against everything that assaults our dignity.[117]

The *Frauenschaftleiterin* responded by informing the letter writer that she had little chance of bringing her complaint to responsible authorities, since she was a woman, and the opinions of women were generally not heeded in these matters.

But the woman persisted and wrote another letter addressed directly to Goebbels. She told him that she had recently seen a film in which, as she wrote, the set was "decorated by half-naked women functioning as candelabra figures." The worst aspect of this, she said, was the fact that young people in the audience were being corrupted by this objectification:

Among these people are also young people, unspoiled youth. Though also young people who, until recently, received the best education about honoring women. Then they come to this revue show and see what "life," even more, what the "amusing" life is like, and many of their previous opinions will certainly change for the worse. So much randiness and lecherousness is being aroused that might never have been brought into the open if it weren't for this shameless provocation. If they think that they are going to elevate the birthrate through this display of women, then I believe that I can say with absolute certainty that such provocations will only help raise the rate of venereal disease.[118]

This female viewer clearly recognized that the use of eroticism in Nazi cinema was a conscious policy and that it was manufactured to support the state's reproduction goals. Revue films and stage shows were the main focus of her anger, but this letter reveals how some spectators could indeed see the discrepancy between the officially proclaimed Nazi "mother cult" and cinematic representation of all genres. Underlying her anti-Semitic slurs was the recognition that the Nazi claim to having rid German culture of Weimar-era decadence and indecency was nothing but fascist ideology's marketing scam. In the Holocaust-era absence of Jewish film producers, the contradictions of Nazi culture were laid bare, and even fanatical Nazi spectators could sense that what had long been displaced onto an instrumentalized concept of "Jewish smut" was actually German masculinity's own desire. Apparently one of the bureaucrats working under Goebbels sent this spectator only another dismissive reply.

However, such protests clearly led to uncertainty within the ministry about censorship standards, particularly in regard to productions that addressed controversial domestic issues. There was a sense in Goebbels's office that the masses were not yet entirely ready for a full-scale attack on bourgeois morality. A script that Tobis Studios submitted for preproduction censorship to the RMVP in 1944 provides an example of this cautiousness. The planned film, titled *Das Erbe* (*The Inheritance*), was a melodrama about a childless married couple with an aristocratic estate who are in need of an heir and discover that their failed attempts to conceive stem from the husband's infertility. After much melodramatic wringing with jealousy and against the wishes of his traditionalist parents, the husband finally decides to encourage his wife to have an affair with another man in the hope that her lover will successfully inseminate her. The wife then departs with her new lover, and the affair is represented idyllically by the script: "The two young people spend magical weeks together and become completely one with each other."[119] After the wife does indeed become pregnant by her lover, her husband decides to sacrifice himself by committing suicide in order to make room for the child, and the lover disappears somewhere abroad. She then raises her boy alone as a single mother. When the boy grows up, he becomes a soldier, and in the course of a deployment in Iraq, he finally meets his biological father, now a general under whose command he fights.

The minister who reviewed the script, Kurt Frowein, wrote to Goebbels in a tone that indicated he generally approved of the ideological intent of the script, but he also expressed concern that audiences might react unpredictably to such a film: "It should indirectly propagate the idea that war-related human losses may be remedied through eugenic measures which go beyond previous family morality. This thesis has a double edge. There is no clarity among the authorities about its value. Considering the immediate risk of the dissolution of moral bonds, it seems premature at this moment to explore upcoming population policy issues in the medium of film."[120] It was too early to attempt a full-scale overthrow of bourgeois family values, he suggested, since carrying out such an unfamiliar project would be risky during wartime. The Nazis' attempted liberalization of sexual morality through the media threatened to provoke uncontrollable protest on one side and uncontrollable excesses on the other. Therefore the Nazis intended to wait until after the war to continue their eugenic solutions to family structures with fuller force. By 1944 they had realized that despite their desire to knock down the walls of bourgeois domesticity, upholding the status quo of marriage was still a strategic necessity.

Conclusion

This chapter has examined the domestic melodrama and has argued that it was used by the Nazis in a genre-contradictory manner to effect a departure from the nuclear family, in accordance with the antibourgeois antipathies of the regime's leadership. In melodramas featuring an adulterous love triangle in which one of the partners is married, camera work and narrative structures align spectator identification with the adulterers more often than with the legal spouse, and the use of mise-en-scène suggests that the extramarital relationship is actually the more legitimate one. In many Third Reich melodramas, the design of domestic spaces suggests that the marital home is an inherently confining environment and the nuclear family is a suffocating institution, unlike the workplace. This stands in strong contrast to classical Hollywood melodramas of the same era, in which the middle-class home is invested with regenerative powers and marriage is viewed as the very foundation of social cohesion. Evidence from advertising materials proves that Third Reich melodramas intentionally appealed to desires for liberation from middle-class domesticity, and that the antibourgeois message was stressed in paratextual discussions more heavily than any capitulation to convention at the ends of the films. Therefore Third Reich melodramas ultimately undermined the status quo of monogamous marriage. Some extramarital romance melodramas also supported the 1938 liberalization of divorce laws or indirectly suggested support for the Nazis' planned legalization of polygamy.

Family and maternal melodramas in the Third Reich likewise argued for the dissolution of family bonds in favor of more corporatist forms of social organization. Revealing an underlying aversion to mothering, Third Reich maternal melodramas suggested that reproduction was best done outside of marriage and without the assistance of men. Children were scarce on the screens of the Third Reich, because reproduction and familial demands stood in conflict with industrial production and colonialist ambitions in the fascist male imagination. Other Nazi melodramas do violence to mothers and housewives, encouraging fantasies of reproduction without wives, and even hinting at incestuous relations. Evidence of spectator response demonstrates that not all viewers shared this erotic imaginary. Catholic, rural, and conservative female spectators in particular felt that the sexual and family morality of Nazi cinema and Third Reich society was deteriorating at an intolerable pace. Ultimately spectator resistance interfered with official plans to promote polygamy to an even greater degree. The next chapter compares how home front melodramas in Nazi Germany differed from their Hollywood counterparts in their address to spectators, particularly with regard to their visions of sexuality, domesticity, and nuclear family relations in wartime.

4. Germany's Great Love
vs. the American Fortress:
Home Front Melodrama

When the United States entered the Second World War in 1941, the American film melodrama went to battle against the Nazis, and Nazi cinema continued to fight for supremacy over Hollywood. After he saw Hollywood's first major home front melodrama of World War II, *Mrs. Miniver* (1942), Goebbels ordered German filmmakers and screenwriters to study the film and adapt its exemplary propaganda devices to Nazi use.[1] *Mrs. Miniver* remained a standard against which the Nazis measured the success of their own films; in 1944 they triumphantly reported that their extramarital romance melodrama *Opfergang* had brought in more box office receipts in neutral Switzerland than *Mrs. Miniver* had.[2] However, Nazi filmmakers never managed to counter *Mrs. Miniver* with an equally popular and nationalistically invested Frau Müller.[3]

Home front melodramas featuring female main protagonists, contemporary settings, and a thematization of the war were produced in Hollywood and in Babelsberg, but the form and extent of this treatment was not identical in the two cinemas. There were some distinctions in genre preferences: Hollywood spoke to home front viewers primarily through the family melodrama, while the wartime Nazi cinema specialized in the love story. German and American war melodramas also had varying methods of recruiting the energies and ordering the emotions of their viewers. While Hollywood addressed viewers in the languages of advertising and direct propaganda, Nazi films attempted to disguise propagandistic intent in visions of romance. And while Hollywood tried to press the public sphere into the domestic melodrama, Nazi melodramas often attempted to repress it through narratives of private life.

These respective approaches to visualizing the war were determined in part by filmic genre and in part by historical experience. Since the battlefields remained far from the American continent, Hollywood cinema had to work more intensely to bring the war closer to the viewer's consciousness than did the Nazis, who wanted instead to contain the damage to spectator morale caused by the ever intensifying bombing of German cities. Thus, Nazi films underplayed the collapsing of home into front while Hollywood films worked in the other direction. For most Americans the war existed only on screen; in comparison with all other combatant nations, the United States suffered relatively few casualties.[4] Hollywood therefore sought to unify soldiers and civilians through film, for fear that the American public could too easily retreat into the isolationism of their own homes, armed only with a false sense of security. Thus the war moved with more rhetorical force into the domestic interiors of American home front films than in their German counterparts.

In radio speeches and newspapers the Nazis addressed the wartime masses in hyperbolic language and demanded that they sacrifice themselves for the survival of the German race and nation. Feature films, however, usually avoided the explicitly patriotic tones of much of the print media, and they visualized sacrifice in attractive and even self-serving forms. Nazi home front films were visually and narratively less puritanical in their sexual morality than their Hollywood counterparts, in keeping with their calculated strategy to control spectator desire to the benefit of the fascist militarist order. The Hollywood home front film, in contrast, argued that the sublimation of desire was required if all civilian and military energies were to be successfully focused on winning the war. As noted in previous chapters, the Nazi strategy scored some victories at box offices in the Reich and in occupied territories, but it also led to internal battles over film content and the management of spectator response. The Nazi leadership's antipathy toward bourgeois morality gave rise to propaganda difficulties during the war as viewers responded in either an excessive or contradictory manner from what was intended.

To varying extents Hollywood and Nazi film producers expressed particular concerns about female spectatorship, since the cinema was viewed as vital to securing universal support for the war. In cooperation with the advertising industry, Hollywood developed wartime appeals directed primarily to middle-class housewives. American home front films insisted that the war was being fought above all to preserve suburban domesticity as well as family values and Christianity. Hollywood's somewhat contradictory goal was to recruit these housewives and mothers as active participants in the war effort while simultaneously reinforcing traditional nuclear family structures in an effort to tie the stability of the home to the security of the nation. Nazi cinema, on the other hand, following the regime's much more ambivalent attitude toward the bourgeois family, did not posit stable familial relations as the precondition for national strength. Instead Nazi cinema imagined a national community unrestricted by the walls of domesticity as it attempted to unify the home and the front in a common romance of war.

The conventions of melodrama lent some support to both American and German purposes but created a few complications as well. Since melodramas usually focus on the conflict between an individual's desires and the standards of society, spectators of such films are generically preconditioned to accept the sacrifice of a desired object in the name of some transcendental or ideological purpose. Whether in love or war, melodramas instruct spectators to bear their suffering bravely, and sometimes they even succeed in reattaching desire to the act of suffering itself. However, neither the Nazis nor the Americans were entirely convinced that the pleasures of masochism that melodramas offer spectators were enough to recruit direct participation in the war, so they sought to add other compensations. The melodramatic genre also posed difficulties on both sides, which had to be negotiated through rhetorical and visual means. Because Hollywood's task was to elicit active and voluntary forms of sacrifice, American home front films had to work against generic conventions that support female passivity. On the other side, the Nazis employed the home front melodrama, a genre of domesticity, to endorse the regime's colonialist fantasies. In order to further compare how the Hollywood and Nazi cinemas enlisted the film melodrama in their war strategies, we will consider the approaches to cinematic propaganda advocated by the leadership of both sides, look at the paradigmatic Hollywood home front films *Mrs. Miniver* and *Since You Went Away* (1944) in detail, and then examine Nazi home front melodramas in relation to conventions established by these Hollywood films.

For God, Consumption, and Domesticity: Hollywood Home Front Films

The United States government never possessed the level of control over film production that the Nazi RMVP exercised, and yet much of American film production very effectively served war goals. Long before the war, of course, Hollywood producers had been making entertainment films with ideological effects in mind. Many Hollywood executives recognized that even light entertainment features had potential effects on the worldview of their spectators and that all films can be ideologically formative. When the Production Code was drawn up in 1930, a nationalist and even eugenic reasoning buttressed its proscriptions: "Wrong entertainment lowers the living conditions and moral ideals of a race," the code stated, and it forbade miscegenation at the same time as it made film producers responsible for "much correct thinking" in the United States.[5]

Thus, the transition to making entertainment features as a form of mass influence at the start of the war was not an entirely abrupt one for American studios. In fact, Hollywood jumped the gun on World War II propaganda, producing antifascist films and violating the official governmental position of neutrality in the years before the United States' declaration of war in December 1941.[6] By the end of the war, the politically independent American film industry had produced at least ten times more World War II features than the Nazi-controlled studios.[7] Starting in June 1942 a U.S. government agency also held some degree of influence over film production. The Bureau of Motion Pictures (BMP) in the Office of War Information (OWI) had advisory functions, though it lacked censoring powers. Producers voluntarily submitted scripts to the bureau for review, and many of the BMP's suggestions were translated directly into film dialogue. The bureau also worked out propaganda tactics. Elmer Davis, the director of the Office of War Information, seemed to emulate Goebbels's strategies when he claimed in 1943, "The easiest way to inject a propaganda idea into most people's minds is to let it go through the medium of an entertainment picture when they do not realize that they are being propagandized."[8]

Both the OWI and Hollywood producers were aware that quite a lot of entertaining propaganda would be necessary to convince Americans to fully support the war. Before the attack on Pearl Harbor, up to 40 percent of the population held strongly isolationist views and believed that keeping the country out of the war was more important than controlling the spread of fascism. Only a small minority felt that the United States should enter the war for the purpose of coming to the aid of Britain.[9] Hollywood immediately began redesigning genre film to recruit the American public's support, churning out familiar narratives with current events projected into their backgrounds. While the new historical situation could be relatively easily written into most other prewar genres, there was some risk involved in producing war-related features that were specifically targeted to female audiences, since war was not a conventional element of domestic melodrama.

Hollywood producers, unlike their Nazi counterparts, had a clearly gendered concept of film genres and spectatorship and believed they could not afford to neglect female audiences when planning high-budget productions. Some industry sources estimated, though erroneously, that up to 70 percent of film audiences were female, and they reported that women dominated men's moviegoing decisions.[10] In contrast to the Nazis, American film producers conducted systematic public opinion polls and planned film titles, stories, and casts according to spectator questionnaires after controlled previews rather than relying on the random recordings of Security Service spies. Not surprisingly, the American polls reported that female spectators generally reacted negatively to war films. As one Chicago woman who was interviewed in a poll during the war reportedly said, "A big tank or bomber gets my boy friend all excited, but it leaves me completely cold."[11]

Leo Handel, the director of the Motion Picture Research Bureau, explained female spectators' reactions to war films in the following way:

> First of all, women feel that war pictures, as a rule, confine themselves mainly to fighting, that they lack thorough characterizations of the men and therefore human interest drama . . . War films also create in some women a feeling of insecurity . . . [A] woman's fear of loss of her man may increase her emotional dependence upon him. The greater the feeling of dependence, the greater the fear of loss which in turn may result in pathological effects. A woman, unable to identify herself with her husband (boy friend, etc.), can easily regard the Army as her enemy."[12]

Such an analysis of the female spectator would have created difficulties for a pro-war producer or screenwriter. If all war films threatened to trigger "hysterical" effects in female viewers, how could female support of the war be effectively elicited? Even if a writer added some melo- or "human interest" drama to a war film script, this would not be sufficient to make a woman actively support the war, since, according to Handel, "it is logical that you can imitate only a person of your own sex."[13] Thus, following this model, real female identification with male soldiers was excluded even in the best of circumstances, and by extension, this precluded any identification of a woman with a male character's fight against fascism. Worse, the energies that a war film mobilized in the female spectator threatened to turn against her own country's military and thus potentially undermine her man's morale. Furthermore, Handel said, women categorically reject war films due to their generic conventions, because such films "stress too much the mechanics of battle and strategy of fighting which [women] neither understand nor care for."[14] What women did care for, according to his research, were "Love Stories" and "Serious Drama"—which were also the two categories lowest on male spectators' list of preferences.[15] Handel's research indicated that Hollywood producers needed to address female and male spectators separately, in the divided spaces of genre cinema.

The governmental Office of War Information offered further suggestions to Hollywood producers regarding wartime appeals to male and female spectators. Among the suggestions that the OWI gave to the Walt Disney Studios was to appeal to all audiences by concentrating on the following "basic propaganda themes": characterizations of the enemy and the Allies; the necessity of work, fighting, and sacrifice; and images of Americans and their values. When characterizing the Nazi enemy, the OWI suggested, Hollywood producers should make use of Nazism's known opposition to Christian tradition and bourgeois family values; war-related films should show that the Nazi "hates religion" and that he "smashes home life."[16]

A large contingent of the OWI's advisors came from the advertising industry, and they were particularly confident of their ability to package the war for female consumption. James Webb Young, a member of the OWI staff and partner in a New York advertising firm, claimed that advertisers had no difficulty in reaching their target audiences: "We have within our hands the greatest aggregate means of mass education and persuasion the world has ever seen," he said.[17] The selling of ideology could thus be approached in the same manner as the selling of consumer goods. In fact, the advertising industry did perform a great deal of propaganda work; at the same time as it sold products, it attempted to explain the goals of the war to American housewives, creating both national and brand loyalty at the same time. According to Dana Polan's analysis, wartime advertising worked in concert with Hollywood and pitched its appeals to American female audiences by stressing in particular the themes of what "'we' are fighting for: the home, the building of healthy families, the consumption of products."[18] The war was thus effectively marketed as a struggle of the American middle-class family against an enemy who threatened its purchasing power and the integrity of its private, domestic space. The heightened sense of insecurity and dependence that supposedly defined wartime female audiences was thus countered with the concept of the family as the temporarily endangered, but still essentially unshakeable, foundation of the American nation.

By some accounts the American strategy was ultimately more effective than the Nazi appeals to German audiences. According to Leila J. Rupp's comparative analysis of American and German propaganda during World War II, this was particularly true of media directed to female viewers: "An examination of appeals to women shows that the legendary Nazi propaganda machine was in fact less effective, in this area, than the Office of War Information in the United States. American propaganda was far more intensive and persuasive," she concludes.[19] Specifically, American propaganda was more effective in recruiting women to participate actively in the war effort. By connecting the war with family values and patriotism with consumerism, Hollywood and its advertising allies contributed to the much higher level of volunteering for work in war-related industries in the United States than in Nazi Germany. Although the United States, historically, had a lower proportion of women in the workplace than Germany, the wartime increase in American women working outside the home was substantial.[20] American propaganda primarily addressed middle-class housewives and reassured them that work outside the home would actually reinforce rather than disrupt their familiar domestic order, since it would speed the end of the war and the return to normalcy. As Michael Renov has asserted, American propaganda managed to combine exhortations to work outside the home with the maintenance of the status quo of domesticity through its "portrayal of factory work as the industrial equivalent of domestic labor."[21] U.S. government-sponsored campaigns were often designed to reassure working women that their temporary jobs would not undermine the institution of marriage.[22] In the imagination of American war propaganda and advertising, Rosie the Riveter was a temp worker who was fighting to become a safer and wealthier "Rosie the Housewife" after the war was won.[23]

American propaganda and advertising defined the war as an essential struggle for an ordered domesticity, and the defense of the patriarchal family was also a key concept for addressing male viewers. A 1942 advertisement from a Chicago ad agency made its war-related appeal in a characteristic manner: it pictured a couple with three children assembled around a dining table, the mother gazing at her husband reverently as he takes a sip from a cup, along with the message: "This is America . . . where the family is a sacred institution. Where children love, honor and respect their parents . . . where a man's home is his castle. This is your America . . . Keep it Free!"[24] The image of the suburban home as a male castle was apparently a power-ful one for American military men. According to John Morton Blum, most American soldiers, when asked about their main motivation for fighting the war, responded with some variation of the concept of "home": "soldiers usually talked about creature comforts, secure routines, even affluence."[25] Thus, many Americans felt they were principally fighting for the attainment or maintenance of bourgeois domesticity rather than more abstract ideals such as the fight for democracy.[26] And it was this motivation that both the American government and private industry worked together to manufac-ture. In 1942 the governmental Office of Facts and Figures produced a series of radio broadcasts called "This Is War" in cooperation with a New York advertising agency. One broadcast in the series was a drama titled "To the Young," in which part of the script offered a pro-domesticity rationale for the war: "Then the voice of a boy: '. . . That's one of the things this war's about.' Girl: 'About us?' Boy: 'About all young people like us. About love and gettin' hitched, and havin' a home and some kids, and breathin' fresh air out in the suburbs . . . about livin' an' workin' *decent,* like free people.'"[27] If "decency" was considered a goal of the war for masses of Americans, this necessarily implied the domestication or repression of the erotic drive in favor of nuclear family relations.

Indeed, Hollywood worked continually to discipline desire, as sexuality was linked to the war economy. Dana Polan has argued that Hollywood home front films functioned to sublimate eroticism in the following ways: "In a first discursive strategy, sexuality will be represented as something that most appropriately belongs to the other side, to the enemy . . . In a second move, desire will be represented as the province of romantic young women who haven't yet learned the importance of denial . . . In a third move, desire is admitted but as something to be held in abeyance."[28] Polan has further suggested that romance and the war narrative were essentially incompatible within the Hollywood film; citing the battle film *Prisoner of Japan* (1942), which ends with a military man and a woman dying together in an explosion, he notes that death is offered as a substitute for sexuality in Hollywood World War II films.[29] For the home front, repression for the duration was the norm, and thus the melodrama of domesticity triumphed over the love story in wartime Hollywood cinema.

Mrs. Miniver, the most popular Hollywood home front film, was a family melodrama featuring a British housewife and mother of three children as the heroine of its title. Released in May 1942, the film was enlisted to characterize the nature of the enemy and the Allies and to confront challenges to the Anglo-American domestic order. *Mrs. Miniver*'s preamble announces its intentions: "This story of an average middle-class family begins with the summer of 1939, when the sun shone down on a happy, careless people, who worked and played, reared their children and tended their gardens in that happy, easy-going England that was so soon to be fighting desperately for her way of life and for life itself." This introductory text indicates the familial-national logic with which *Mrs. Miniver* aims to mobilize identificatory impulses in its viewers. Through the description of England as female ("her way of life"), the viewer is invited to associate the nation with a threatened woman, in this case a housewife whose prewar bliss is represented by a shopping trip in the first sequences of the film and whose easygoing consumption is soon to be interrupted by German bombs. When Mrs. Miniver (Greer Garson) finds a wounded German aviator hidden in the bushes of her well-tended garden halfway through the film, Nazism's threat to the British (and, by extension, American) way of life and to the life of its citizens is made concrete as a threat against the protagonist's body, as a stand-in for the national body.

Nazism as an attack on the nuclear family: *Mrs. Miniver* (1942). Courtesy the Kobal Collection at Art Resource, New York

The female spectator's identification with the protagonist Kay Miniver is then set up to slide smoothly into an identification with the British nation, the desperate existential struggle of England becoming the struggle of the American spectator as well. The introductory text also makes an appeal to the viewer's maternal feelings by describing the English in infantilizing terms, as a "happy, careless people, who worked and played" outside in the sun. Of course, to describe the British as naturally "easygoing" required a reversal of more usual images of a dominating country from which the Americans had to violently separate themselves less than two hundred years before. The family order is overturned: America becomes the parent who must protect the threatened British child. The female spectator's supposedly primary desire for "healthy families" is thereby mobilized and rerouted to a conception of a family of nations.

The family in *Mrs. Miniver* may be threatened from the outside, but not by any apparent internal divisions. Marriage and the family are shown in this film as the unshakeable foundations of the nation, in keeping with Production Code values that commanded Hollywood filmmakers to defend the "sanctity of marriage and the home."[30] The domestic peace is not disturbed by any battle of the sexes in *Mrs. Miniver*; neither men nor women must be forcefully reconciled to their roles in this film. The main male protagonist, Clem Miniver (Walter Pidgeon), presents an ideal model of a devoted husband and father. As an architect he is as concerned with the construction of well-functioning domestic environments as Kay Miniver the housewife. This harmonious image of married life serves to legitimize the nation's struggles as well as to assert the unity of the Allies in their battle against fascism. If the Nazi enemy's goal is to "smash home life"—by which is meant the destruction of both architectural space and marriage—it is in large part the solidity of the institution of marriage that gives the Allies their will and their superior right to win the war, the film suggests. When Lady Beldon, the aristocratic villain of this melodrama, mutters, "war can't be any reason to rush into marriage," the spectator is asked to think otherwise. The Minivers' son, Vin, subsequently proposes a rush wedding to Lady Beldon's teenage granddaughter, Carol, a marriage that survives for only two weeks before Carol is killed by the Nazis. But as Carol asserts in a dialogue, even a brief period of marital bliss is enough to compensate for the loss of life, and it is principally marriage that allows the Anglo-Americans to find the strength to face death.

Accordingly, *Mrs. Miniver* works to construct an appealing mise-en-scène of domesticity. As Laura Mulvey has pointed out, the "home" in Hollywood melodrama is heavily furnished with ideological significance, since it stands not just for a private space but also for an "ordered national consensus."[31] While the introductory shopping sequence shows the city as chaotic and slightly threatening with its aggressive traffic, the Minivers' semirural village home is the very image of a peaceful and ordered domesticity. Many scenes are filmed with the characters assembled around a table to convey the sense of complete familial unity. It is around the dining table that Vin proposes to Carol while they are surrounded by the rest of the Minivers, thus effecting her simple—and desexualized—transfer into Vin's nuclear family. In the background of the table sequences, there is usually a servant visibly laboring to produce this image of consensus, but the film works to define servitude as the natural order. The décor of the Minivers' home is dominated by floral motifs: floral curtains, fresh flowers in vases, paintings of flowers, and flowers attached to the clothing of the female family members. These interiors not only naturalize the bourgeois nuclear family (as did the Sirkian family melodrama of the 1950s[32]), but they also nationalize it. The rose is, of course, a symbol of Britain, and Mrs. Miniver also becomes a stand-in for her embattled nation by lending her name to a competition-winning rose. The village community comes together and all social classes are unified by means of this flower contest at the end of the film, so the floral motifs in the Miniver household are signs of this perfected ordering of the national community into a harmonious unit.

In many other instances as well, *Mrs. Miniver* attempts to organically link images of the family and the home to images of war so as to domesticate the nation's struggles. Since most of the film takes place within the Minivers' home, the entire war unfolds in its vicinity; Kay Miniver and her husband watch from their bedroom window as their son, Vin, goes to battle in the skies over their garden. Similarly, when Mr. Miniver joins a civilian boat brigade to rescue British soldiers stranded in Dunkirk, the film carefully links the space of battle to the space of the home. Since Mr. Miniver is shown docking his boat next to the garden lawn, the water of the English Channel appears to flow directly to the Miniver house. While Mr. Miniver is gone, Nazism invades the Minivers' kitchen in the concrete, physical form of the German pilot. Later in the film the family becomes the target of enemy aggression again when the Luftwaffe bombs the Miniver house. Thus, in a directly physical and spatial manner, the film imports the battle front into the private home.

The English Channel sequence also moves in the other direction, flowing from the private to the public in an effort to militarize the civilian. The Miniver family's motorboat is first joined by other boats from their village, and then, in a high-angle shot of monumental proportions, more are added from all over the country. The individual boat thus quickly becomes part of an abstract mass, a national community. Emotional effect is produced by repetition and accumulation as ever more volunteers are added to form an abstract pattern, and the shots of the masses from overhead alternate with close-ups of individual men's faces as they listen to the voice of their leader. In its visualization of the nation as ordered mass, this sequence shows formal similarities to Susan Sontag's definition of fascist aesthetics, even if its aim was a contrary one.[33] Here, the invisible leader's orders issue from an imposing battleship, thus suggesting that the disembodied voice emanates from a god who commands the national community to go to battle against a godless fascism.

The OWI, as we have seen earlier, recommended that film producers appeal to American audiences by arguing that the Nazis intended to destroy Christianity. Correspondingly, religion is presented as a further foundation of the nation, site of collectivity, and source of identification in *Mrs. Miniver*. It is in the church space that the film offers another image of the national community as an extended family. In the two crucial church sequences at the beginning and end of the film, the pews are occupied by the Minivers and their servants along with the Beldons, to whom they are eventually joined by marriage. It is here that the start of the war is announced in an emotional scene as the vicar interrupts his previously scheduled sermon and begins to preach patriotism. In offering his parishioners a "prayer for our beloved country," he also offers an ideological frame for the nation: "Our forefathers have fought for a thousand years for the freedom that we now enjoy, and that we must now defend again. With God's help . . . we shall not fail," he says. Britain is thus christened the Land of the Free, bringing it closer to America's own self-image, and the war is granted divine legitimation. With its frequent references to religion, the film appeals to spectators who were presumed to be—like the Minivers—white, middle-class, Anglo-Saxon Protestants. Such appeals were, of course, a common element in Hollywood World War II films, even those that described the United States in terms of democratic plurality. The language of religion was clearly deemed to have a strong emotional pull for American audiences. *Mrs. Miniver*'s scriptwriters were perhaps somewhat self-ironic about their own methods in this regard; as they have Mr. Ballard say, "You can't beat the Bible—can you—for deep feelings?" However, there is little irony in the final sequence of the film, also set in the church. As the . community joins together to sing the hymn "Onward Christian Soldiers," the camera tilts to offer the last shot through the bombed-out roof of the church, a view of warplanes crossing the sky, flying eastward. The war is thus finally coded as Crusade.

If *Mrs. Miniver* addressed itself primarily to white, female, middle-class American Protestants and attempted to assure them that the Allies belonged to a family of nations with common values, there was some troubled territory to cover. The description of the Minivers as an "average middle-class family" in the introductory text was, of course, a bit deceptive. Fearing that the average American might not identify with protagonists who were genuinely average, middle-class (and thus urban) Brits, the filmmakers moved the Minivers out to the country and gave them a house and a lawn with which an American suburbanite might feel at home. The purchasing power of the Minivers was certainly above average, so the film clearly attempted to appeal to audience reverie and desire for luxury at the same time as it asked for a self-sacrificial attitude from its spectators.

A major fault line of the film's argument runs along class barriers, and they threatened to shake up the film's pro-war rhetoric. When the vicar describes the war as a defense of Britain's thousand-year-old freedom, this was likely to set off some alarms in spectators who did not easily equate liberty with a long history of feudalism and monarchy. Instead of simply ignoring the contradiction, the film attempts a difficult maneuver, first bringing class conflict to the surface and then sinking it again in a mixture of negation, emotional distraction, and compensatory offers. Any potential objections by viewers are articulated openly by Vin, who arrives home from Oxford at the beginning of the film with vaguely Marxist objections to his own family's wealth. Vin questions the concept of freedom and suggests that the Minivers' maid, Gladys, is as indentured as any serf of centuries past. His demand that something be done about the class system is immediately neutralized by discrediting his character: he is called a useless "talker" who is simply "suffering from an acute case of immaturity." The film's script even manages to reverse the logic and recuperate Vin's and the viewer's objections for its own purposes, suggesting that class conflict is actually one more reason to fight the war rather than an impediment to patriotism. When Vin's soon-to-be fiancée, Carol, concedes that his critiques may be valid but that talking is useless and "a little bit of action is required now and then," two types of activity are proposed: charity and battle. The former is performed by Carol and thus marked out as an appropriately female response to social inequities, while the latter is the male alternative. Later in the film, after Vin has apparently overcome his immaturity by enlisting in the air force, Carol asks if he will be "going into action," which links his dissatisfaction with class privilege to his aerial defense of his village's private properties.

The debate between the aristocrat Carol and the bourgeois Vin soon dissolves into conventionally melodramatic means of resolving ideological and narrative conflict: the formation of the couple. The two characters are married, and thus the problematic public sphere is domesticated by means of an emotionally satisfying private union; the upward mobility of one of the film's characters thus compensates for the immobility of the class system as a whole. The resolution of ideological contradiction is also achieved by means of distraction during the flower show. When Lady Beldon decides to surrender her feudal privilege and allow Ballard's commoner rose to win the show, this is staged as a highly emotional event, a touching solution to a personal conflict as a substitute for social revolution. Despite Lady Beldon's concessions regarding the flower prize and the marriage between Vin and Carol, however, the social order is more reaffirmed than altered by the war. Vin joins the aristocratic Royal Air Force, while the Minivers' maid's proletarian husband fights lower down, with the ground troops. By the end of the film, the original balance has also been fully reestablished through the war, since two figures of social integration have been killed off: the noble Carol, who dared to marry down, and the lower-class Mr. Ballard, who dared to challenge feudal traditions. These deaths are instrumental, since both figures are invested with utopian energies, and spectators may convert this sense of lost utopia into anger toward the Germans responsible for the deaths. The originally implied promise of the film—that class conflict may be resolved through the war—is fulfilled only through a thinning out of the conflicting classes by violent means.

Another solution and another form of compensation are ultimately offered by the film: material goods as a postwar promise to spectators. After the preamble text at the beginning of the film announces that Britain is fighting for its "way of life," the shopping sequence immediately follows. All appear to participate: while Mrs. Miniver acquires her new hat and her husband his car, the village vicar gets his pricey cigars. It becomes clear, then, that the way of life to which the introductory text refers is one principally comprised of consumer pleasures. Commodities are also clearly the prime objects of libidinal energies in the film, in accordance with the dominant Hollywood assumption that female audiences experienced the most visual pleasure through images of luxury goods.[34] While Mr. Miniver lies alone in his single, Production Code–approved bed, Mrs. Miniver turns off the light and crawls into bed with her hat, gazing at it lovingly. The camera first shows the hat in close-up, and then there is a decent dissolve, as if on a kiss.

The representation of Mrs. Miniver's consumer desires ostensibly functions to mark a later transformation in her character as she adapts to war circumstances, but there is no indication that her basic values have been altered by the war in any way. Rather, she stops shopping only for the duration (and as the wife of an architect, she will certainly profit from postwar reconstruction efforts). Indeed the film suggests—like much of American wartime advertising—that the war was being fought expressly to defend consumption. If money is "the power to buy ourselves a little something that will make us a little happier," as Mr. Miniver says, victory guarantees a return of national happiness in the form of increased purchasing power. Consumption is even marked as a leveler of class difference at the beginning of the film when Lady Beldon complains: "Shopping is impossible these days . . . I spent the whole afternoon being pushed around by middle-class females buying things they can't possibly afford . . . I don't know what this country's coming to: everyone trying to be better than their betters . . . No wonder Germany's arming!" The purchasing power of the middle class is thus presented as a challenge to both aristocratic privilege and to fascism, and consumerism becomes an expression of the "freedom we now enjoy." *Mrs. Miniver* suggested to its middle-class female audiences that a personal investment in the war effort would be repaid later in expanded shopping possibilities. This, of course, was not a false promise, as the postwar economic strength of the United States would prove.

Since *Mrs. Miniver* invests most of its signs of desire in commodities, it simultaneously achieves a sublimation of eroticism. The film perfectly fulfills Hays Code ideals by sanctifying marriage and avoiding suggestions of indecency. The romantic relationships in the film are tender and balanced, but de-eroticized; the closest approximation of fetishistic physical displays that the film allows is the bedroom scene in which Garson is costumed in a floor-length nightgown cut at the top to reveal her exposed collarbone and arms. The spectator's attention, however, is redirected to the fetishized commodity as Garson's desirous look motivates a pan to the close-up of the hat.

However, the sequence with the German aviator does show signs of the strain of sublimation. While her husband is at the front and Mrs. Miniver is left without masculine supervision, the German slips into her garden and passes out in her bushes before invading her kitchen and demanding milk. Mrs. Miniver proceeds more or less voluntarily to feed him, wrap him in her husband's coat, and wipe his feverish head. Her actions are apparently to be interpreted as an instinctive maternal nurturing, revealing the superior humanity of the Allies in the face of brutal Nazi fanaticism. However, the way the scene is staged creates a suspicious level of erotic tension between the two. Mrs. Miniver and the German are placed in extended two shots that intensify the suspense of their physical proximity, and as he breathes heavily, they seem to gaze at each other with some palpable passion that is not exclusively fear. When he passes out again on her kitchen floor, a tender close-up shot of his face with closed eyes (framed from Mrs. Miniver's position above him) shows the momentarily peaceful German to be a surprisingly good-looking young man. Then he regains consciousness, and Mrs. Miniver, who has relatively little physical contact with Mr. Miniver throughout the film, takes hold of the German from behind, in a gesture that appears almost like an embrace, and moves him to the table—the film's preferred site of familial unity. When the Nazi remains defiant, Mrs. Miniver slaps him across the face and finally refuses his intense eye contact, like a jilted lover. It is perhaps this subtle suggestion of misplaced, sublimated desire that contributed to a British reviewer's assessment of the film as "unconsciously pro-fascist propaganda."[35] If Hollywood's strategy was to show that sexuality belonged to the enemy, it certainly ran the risk of accidentally attaching desire to the other side.

In *Since You Went Away*, often called the "American Miniver," there is a tighter control over the management of desire, and the film ultimately stresses sublimation and sacrifice more than compensation. The writer and producer of this family melodrama, David O. Selznick, took much direction from the government as well as from the responses of audiences in prerelease screenings when deciding how to package its messages most effectively.[36] *Since You*

Went Away is remarkable for the sheer amount of ideological work that it performs openly. As Clayton Koppes commented, the film was a "virtual compendium of OWI-approved vignettes of American unity."[37] *Since You Went Away,* like *Mrs. Miniver,* is framed by an introductory text that announces some of its intentions. As in the earlier film, the nuclear family is presented as the essential foundation of this national unity. An authoritative voice-over informs the spectator that the film is "a story of the Unconquerable Fortress: The American Home, 1943." Immediately the favorite catchword of Hollywood's propaganda campaign is called up, and the family home is linked to the nation. Here again it is the task of the disciplined housewife to ensure that un-American ways of life never successfully colonize the suburbs.

Seemingly echoing the ever repeated logic of the OWI and advertising men, *Since You Went Away* addressed the question of why America was fighting the war. Rather than naming fascism's atrocities, the script offered a more familiar rationale: placing a soldier next to a living-room fireplace, it explained that the American man enlists in the military not to defend "the four freedoms," but to preserve domesticity: "it all added up to a simple corny phrase that I couldn't laugh off: 'Home Sweet Home,'" the uniformed character Tony says. As in *Mrs. Miniver,* this privileged locus of national identity serves as the primary motivator and justification for America's war against the Axis powers. Also as in the earlier film, "home" is exclusively defined here as the living space of an upper-middle-class married couple, along with their children and servants. At the beginning of the film, the camera examines the house and registers the combined evidence of marital and military life, traveling across a plaque commemorating the wedding of the film's heroine, Anne (Claudette Colbert), before resting on a close-up of her husband's mobilization orders. The letter is addressed to the Hilton family house on "Suburban Drive," thus emphatically locating the American home in the new spaces of WASP homogeneity. As in *Mrs. Miniver,* the camera stays in the house and garden for most of the film, observing the interactions of the protagonist and her children. The favored site of collectivity in *Since You Went Away* is the familial fireplace, the symbolic nature of which is underlined by its inclusion in the title sequence of the film. This burning hearth indicates the importance of feminine nurturance to the American war effort. A voice-over revealing Anne's thoughts at the beginning of the film assures the audience that she intends to keep her marital affection burning "like a warm room" awaiting the return of her deployed husband. The American housewife's task is thus to maintain a comfortable domesticity as the primary generator of military morale.

The sexually sublimated housewife as the heart of the American nation: *Since You Went Away* (1944). Courtesy the Kobal Collection at Art Resource, New York

Since the American nation is constructed out of nuclear familial units and depends on the solidity of each one, as the film suggests, being unmarried is treasonous. The film relies on a basic pedagogical structure, presenting a desired model for behavior pitted against a negative one. Anne Hilton's positive example is juxtaposed with that of her friend Emily Hawkins, a promiscuous and apparently childless divorcée who is suspicious of wartime "flag waving" and interjects French phrases into her speech. The film's script directly reproaches the unmarried woman for failing to make sacrifices and for showing insufficient patriotism. Her divorced status and interest in multiple men is connected to her refusal of fidelity to her country's flag, effectively equating sexual promiscuity with sabotage. The patriot Anne, on the other hand, pledges absolute loyalty to her husband, bravely battling the advances of Tony, the attractive naval officer continually stationed in her presence. The film thus serves as a training manual for the sexual conduct of home front women. In a home remodeled as a fortress, the bedroom must be as orderly as a barrack, and the friendly fire of single soldiers on leave threatens to undermine the morale of married men on the front lines.

If it makes the repression of sexuality in the married woman into a strategic necessity, the film's strategy is also to discipline the drives of unmarried Americans of both sexes. The Hilton women are all costumed modestly and are positively contrasted with the tartish styling of background characters. Anne's eldest daughter, Jane, provides a model for younger spectators as she learns to subjugate her own desires to the war effort—as Tony tells Jane, men fight the war "largely for their dreams of girls like you." However, male fantasies in this film are not composed of unlimited sexual access. Rather, what *Since You Went Away* suggests men genuinely want is marriage, and the film correspondingly presents marital devotion as a goal of the war. Tim Hilton writes to his wife that he went to fight the Japanese with the assurance that he would have her love as the prize for American victory. The function of the character Tony, in addition to exercising the married woman's powers of restraint, is to direct male desire away from sexually assertive and foreign women and toward the chaste American housewife and mother; in one of his scripted admirations of Anne, Tony insists that no Italian woman's physical charms can distract him from his unrequited love for her, a desire that feeds entirely on the fact of its own repression.

Since You Went Away also attempts to ensure the falling in line of female desire through the fetishization of men's uniforms and the militarization of private spaces. Most characters in the film show a great interest in reading the signs of rank and division written on men's chests, and officers hold a special appeal for the film's heroines. Only the bad example Emily disregards uniforms, preferring to evaluate men's individual characters rather than their military rank. Such undisciplined desire is described as a lurking home front threat, since it negates the system of exchange by which men's military accomplishments are to be rewarded by female fidelity. Jane, whose desires are successfully contained by the end of the film, pledges to marry and have a baby immediately after her first kiss with the uniformed soldier Bill. Indeed, *Since You Went Away* aims for a full sublimation of eroticism to the benefit of patriarchal family values. As Mary Ann Doane has asserted, the indexical traces of the deployed husband that the camera registers at the beginning of the film "do not connote the erotic," but rather "act as memory traces of authority-in-absence."[38] By invoking and maintaining the presence of a physically absent patriarchal authority, the film reinforces the presence of the nation's war in the everyday of its model female citizen. The full militarization of the domestic realm takes also directly physical form when a retired army colonel moves into the Hilton house and replaces the authority of the missing husband. Outside of the house as well, the standard iconography of patriotism follows the Hilton women wherever they go, with national symbols repeatedly inserted into the set design and the national anthem and march music cut into the sound track.

Even if the American suburbs were much farther from the battlefield than the British village in *Mrs. Miniver, Since You Went Away* still attempts to bring it closer to the spectator's consciousness. No Nazis show up in this film, so the war does not threaten the American family in the same manner as in *Mrs. Miniver,* but its direct physical presence is still felt. The war is made tangible in the opening shot of the veteran's hospital where Jane works as a nurse: a medium close-up of an amputee with a prosthetic arm. Equally discomforting is the dialogue's invocation of the "mangled bodies" Jane must touch while at work. Even though *Since You Went Away* does not dare to kill off the main protagonist's husband, it also does not entirely conceal violence and death from its female audiences, much in contrast to Third Reich home front films.

The film's willingness to reveal some unsettling aspects of the war is not matched by any challenging treatment of social conflicts on the home front, however. Like *Mrs. Miniver, Since You Went Away* also attempts to neutralize the threat that the lower classes presented to the wartime domestic order, although in a less rhetorically direct manner. Since class is determined here largely by race and ethnicity, the film's ideological maneuvers are even more dubious. When the Hiltons' maid, Fidelia, volunteers to serve the family for free and explains that she simply wouldn't be content if she left them for a paid job, the film suggests that a reinstatement of slavery-like conditions would be a patriotic policy. As Clayton Koppes has commented, the fact that (the fittingly named) Fidelia is played by Hattie McDaniel, who also appeared in the Selznick production *Gone with the Wind,* adds an important element of intertextuality: "Miss Scarlett's devoted slave-turned-servant in one war, she is still Mrs. Hilton's live-in maid in another conflict."[39] While *Mrs. Miniver* managed to recuperate the opposition presented by class conflict, *Since You Went Away* could only deny racial tensions.[40]

Some compensation was offered to the middle classes, however. While it proposed that men be offered stable marriages in return for war participation, *Since You Went Away* suggested less substantial rewards to its female participants. The protagonist Anne, believing that a woman's true duty is to remain a housewife and mother, at first resists Jane's plan to train as a Red Cross nurse. Eventually, Anne becomes convinced that war work can also be a form of feminine service and enlists herself as a welder in a munitions plant. The film is careful to insist that both of the Hilton women who take on war jobs do not do so for the monetary compensation. In a mass ceremony for newly inducted nurses (conducted in the shadow of a monumental mural depicting Christian apocalypse and resurrection motifs), Jane explicitly pledges to work for free. Working outside of the home is redefined here as a sanctified form of female sacrifice, albeit a clearly temporary one. Since it argues that the war was being fought to preserve domesticity, the film has to perform a rhetorical about-face to encourage the housewife to take a war job. It is careful, though, to assure spectators that Anne's part-time transformation into a "lady welder" has the approval of male authority. Her decision to go to work is validated by the two men in uniform who keep her under their watch while Mr. Hilton is gone, and when the camera enters the factory, a tracking shot follows a male supervisor as he inspects and approves the women's work.

Unlike the housemaid Fidelia, Jane and Anne experience a certain social integration through this war work, an inclusion into the image of the nation. During Anne's time in the factory, a high-angle shot of a large number of non-individuated workers indicates her unity with the mobilized masses. Outside of the home, Mrs. Hilton comes into contact with immigrants and lower-class women who are, as she writes to her husband, "nothing we ever heard of at the country club." There is a suggestion here of the risk of class contamination, of a dissolving of the borders of her comfortably isolation-ist identity. However, the film compensates for this risk when an Eastern European coworker reverently tells Anne, "You are what I thought America was," and associates her with the Statue of Liberty. *Since You Went Away* offers this image of the housewife as national icon and proposes it as the American woman's ultimate satisfaction. Patriotism becomes its own reward as the home is renovated to become the homeland.

The Romance of War:
German Fascist Home Front Films

Hollywood home front films, as we have seen thus far, usefully connect mother-ing to the political sphere. As Mary Ann Doane has stated in relation to *Since You Went Away*: "The identification of America with the ideal wife and mother allows a political discourse to expropriate an entire constellation of connota-tions associated with the maternal—comfort, nurturance, home, containment/ stasis, community, closeness, affect—in the service of a nationalistic cause."[41] Nazi cinema, reflecting a fundamental distrust of femininity, domesticity, and the maternal, avoided such expropriations. The Nazis apparently did not believe that German soldiers would be willing to fight to defend bourgeois domestic-ity or to identify Hitler's Reich so intimately with the figure of the housewife.

Mary-Elizabeth O'Brien has commented on the suspicious discrepancy between official ideological pronouncements regarding the German family and its representation in the Nazi home front film *Wunschkonzert*: "The German nuclear family, conceived in Nazi ideology as the bastion of Aryan virtues, is almost nonexistent in *Wunschkonzert*. Because of the military struggle, not one household remains intact. War dictates a new definition of kinship. Rather than extolling the individual family, Nazi war propaganda stressed the need for disparate groups to bind together."[42] As demonstrated in the last chapter, the shift to a corporatist organization of social relations actually occurred in Nazi cinema years before the outbreak of military struggle. Films such as *Hitlerjunge Quex* and *Der Herrscher* attempted to break open the self-contained nuclear family and assaulted the authority of the maternal image.

Despite the general scarcity of World War II–related films in Nazi cinema, Third Reich filmmakers did attempt to project the war into the background of films with female protagonists on a few occasions. In the 1941 home front melodrama *Annelie*, the main protagonist is a mother, but she is no Mrs. Miniver. The film's narrative resembles *Mutterliebe*, since it is a tale of a mother's sacrifices to give birth and raise children through hard times, although it ends with the mother's death just as the Second World War is beginning. Thus, instead of showing a nuclear family functioning as the very foundation of a nation at war in the Hollywood manner, the resolution of this Nazi melodrama suggested that maternal nurturance is no longer necessary in wartime. According to the German fascist perspective, the Nazi cause was best served by the disappearance of the no-longer-reproductive woman in favor of the *Männerbund* (male society) of self-sufficient soldiers. The war thus largely obviated the need for family melodrama.

According to Karsten Witte's analysis, the revue film was instead the most characteristic feature film genre of German fascism. The abstracted arrangements of dancers' bodies in musicals and their revealing uniforms were the equivalent of Leni Riefenstahl's ornamental masses of soldiers on parade at the 1934 Nazi Party rally in her propaganda film *Triumph des Willens* (*Triumph of the Will*, 1935). The stage shows of revue films, Witte claims, were essentially war dances of the "female reserve army."[43] I argue, though, that revue films were not just a metaphor for the readiness to go to total war. Rather, the militaristic formations of Nazi dancing girls were more literal: their legs were themselves the weapons of German fascism. The revue show dancers were never meant to trade in their toy rifles for real ones; instead, they would use their displayed bodies, and the shooting would be done with cameras. In Witte's analysis the Nazi revue film functioned, like the Hollywood melodrama, to de-eroticize sexual relations and to redirect the repressed libidinal energies into war. However, he underestimated the extent to which libidinal energies were produced by Nazi films and how such energies supported the Nazi occupation of the minds of both domestic and foreign audiences (as we have seen in the case of the Belgian reactions to Nazi films). Rather than aiming for a complete repression of sexuality during wartime, Nazism exploited its audiences' erotic drives. Militarism in the Nazi cinema was not offered as the substitute for sexuality, as it often was in Hollywood; rather, the male-centered consumption of sexuality was offered as an incentive to fascist militarism.

A brief sequence in the propaganda film *Ohm Krüger* (1941) reveals the Nazi strategy. A historical drama/genius film about a leader of the Boer rebellion against the British in South Africa, the film's fin-de-siècle war served as a double and precursor to Nazism's war forty years later. The film incorporated the Dutch Boers into a common Germanic *Volk* and posited their opposition to the British as an ongoing German battle against British imperialism. Germanic peoples know how to win war dances, the film suggests in a sequence in which a troupe of Boer women are performing on the stage of a large theater. Shots of the audience appreciating the show alternate with voyeuristic shots from under the dancers' skirts. One man in the audience, a British officer, then remarks to another: "I don't know what we have against the Boers. I think they're charming. Particularly the one on the left—she has delightful legs!" The camera then gives the film spectator a reverse shot from the perspective of the converted (diegetic) enemies.

Goebbels himself had experienced a similar moment a year earlier and had realized once again the propagandistic value of visual pleasure. In 1940 he had written rapturously of a stage show he saw in Paris that featured "lots of beautiful women and disarming nudity."[44] The fact that Goebbels called this enticing display of female bodies "disarming" is not an accident, since he was interested in the strategic possibilities of eroticism. The display of beautiful bodies might ultimately induce the enemy to desert his loyalties to his own national culture while simultaneously recruiting the energies of domestic audiences. The Nazis, it seems, intended to facilitate an intensified eroticism not only on the screen but also in reality. Hitler, more concerned with action than representation, said that he would not allow bourgeois morality to interfere with the German soldier's love life: "Battle and love belong together. The uptight bourgeois [*Spießer*] who grumbles about that should just be happy if he manages to get the left-overs."[45] The warrior, Hitler felt, had a superior right to sexuality and should also have the freedom to consume and consummate it without the restrictions of traditional family morality.

Evidently the secure marital relationship between Mrs. and Mr. Miniver was not the Nazis' idea of love in war, so Hollywood's image of the happy bourgeois couple was not translated for use by Nazism's wartime propaganda. As we have seen throughout this book, domesticity itself was suspect, and marriage was usually problematized rather than naturalized in Nazi cinema. Early in the war Goebbels attempted to do away with this topic altogether and instructed Fritz Hippler in an April 1940 meeting at the Propaganda Ministry to make sure that "marital problems and marital conflicts" would no longer be a major theme of film production. As Goebbels claimed, marriage—happy or unhappy—was not interesting to the fascist masses, since "people in our time are only interested in masculine conflicts."[46] These last words, however, were crossed out of the minutes of Goebbels's meeting. Clearly something had changed his mind. The problem of marriage simply would not go away, and neither would feminine conflicts.

The Nazis would have preferred to ignore the issue of female spectatorship. Unlike the OWI, the staff of the RMVP did not develop specific strategies for addressing female spectators, and Goebbels wanted to imagine that the German public was a unified audience. However, evidence to the contrary continually poured in. If the letter to Goebbels from the female spectator in Vienna that we considered in the last chapter is any indication, the exploitation of eroticism and objectification of women in Nazi visual culture undermined even fanatical Nazi women's support for the regime. Most dangerously, the letter writer connected this Nazi culture with the war effort. Infuriated by a filmed revue show, she added:

> Soldiers also come to this theater. They now see *this German culture* (and for how many naive souls is theater culture!), which, according to propaganda, they are defending against Bolshevism. Mr. Reichsminister, just from this perspective, there simply cannot be any more rubbish in the entertainment programs of the German people. "Good moods at all costs," the clever people say once again. No, we don't need that. It's not all over for us. That may give our enemies ideas. Our morale may still be raised by the glorious heroic courage of our troops, but it certainly goes to hell in the face of the kind of filth that is poured out on the "inner front," since it just resembles too much the evil products of the Jewish World War mongers of the past . . .
>
> Just look at the get-ups of all those endless dancing girls, who should rather be working in the armaments industry, with their repulsive dancing "gigolos" in white tuxedoes! How it embitters and enrages to think that our best young blood is being spilled out there right now and lives are being lost (in order, among other things, to make this display of "culture" possible)!

> Even if Berlin eats up this trash, why must it also be filmed and shown in
> excerpts in all cinemas of the Reich, so that everyone everywhere can see how
> Berlin amuses itself?[47]

The writer ended her letter by telling Goebbels that, despite her objections to Nazism's modern home front entertainment, he should not simply dismiss her as a reactionary: "I hope you don't lump me together with all those prudish idiots they used to ridicule."[48] Even if Goebbels did indeed dismiss this woman's letter, it was hard to completely ignore other reports that indicated dissent among female spectators in regard to both the war and its representations.

According to the reports of Security Service spies, German women's support for the war was less than certain, and many expressed impatience with the war's duration.[49] As a result of this anxiety about women's willingness to tolerate the war and the possibility that they might spread defeatism to soldiers, the SD recorded the responses of female spectators in the cinemas separately. And to the SD it appeared that German women were generally less infected with war fever than men. SD agents reported intense enthusiasm for war-related *Wochenschau* newsreel footage during the first two years of the war, but they also observed important gender differences in audience response. It is interesting to note that the alleged reactions of both men and women gave the SD cause for concern: men for their excessive responses, and women for their failure or refusal to respond as expected. Men in particular, the SD wrote, seemed to be seized with an intense scopophilia, or *Schaulust,* in 1940.[50] For them, the newsreels showing German soldiers marching through France and Belgium were a source of entertainment akin to cinematic action thrillers. On June 17, 1940, it was noted: "Occasionally, it already appears that the bourgeois man [*Spießer*] in the safe movie theater is forgetting that the war newsreels are not entertainment or horror films, but rather an experience of a special kind that should make him feel reverential and committed."[51] While this report reiterates the usual Nazi contempt for the bourgeois "philistine," it also expresses disgust for voyeuristic men who enjoyed participating in the war vicariously rather than directly.

Some women, on the other hand, reportedly refused to participate entirely and turned their eyes from the screen. The SD noted on May 27, 1940, the following response to newsreels covering the Nazi occupation of Holland and Belgium: "It has been reported on various occasions that these newsreels have had such an upsetting and alarming effect on women who are thinking about their family members at the front that they are sometimes refusing to go to see the newsreels altogether."[52] Reactions were particularly mixed when it came to images of death. Pictures of dead German soldiers were carefully excised from the newsreels so that they would not unsettle spectators and undermine support for the war. But even images of dead soldiers on the enemy side reportedly elicited feelings of pity among women. On May 14, 1940, the SD reported: "What is being revealed by all war films has often been apparent with the film *Feuertaufe* [*Baptism of Fire*, 1940] also, namely that a uniform reaction cannot be achieved with all spectators, no matter how a film is structured. While part of the audience wants more battle action and actual war scenes, above all it is women who have expressed sympathy with the Polish, and the images of destroyed Warsaw have not created heroic pride, but rather a depressed, anxious mood in regard to the 'horrors of war.'"[53] There thus arose a similar dilemma for the Nazis as for Hollywood producers as to how they could sell the war to all spectators and simultaneously control the response to its representations. Some female viewers apparently could not identify with the pride of conquering soldiers, but rather, as in America, were filled with anxiety in the face of war imagery. If they were to successfully manage spectator response, the Nazis had to represent the war without creating sympathy for the enemy and without excessive recourse to heroic feeling.

Of all spectators in the Reich, it was probably the lower-class women working in war industries who posed the greatest threat of dissent. The Security Service repeatedly documented the ever growing frustration among the lower classes as proletarian women with large families were forced into hard labor following the decree of June 20, 1941, which mandated compulsory war work for all women who had previously held jobs. Middle- and upper-class women with no children, on the other hand, were not forced to work, leading to bitter complaints among those who were. The SD reported in February 1942 that this policy was creating a dangerous level of class conflict and that the poor health of overused workers was also becoming publicly visible: "The cases in which women have simply collapsed at their machines or behind store counters have been increasing recently."[54] The regime showed little concern for the individuals involved, but as the rate of miscarriage, contraception, and suspected abortion escalated, the Security Service raised an alarm about a possible wartime birth strike.[55]

Hitler and Goebbels's response to this problem, however, was to repress it. While Hollywood wartime melodramas attempted to negotiate class troubles, the Nazis simply evaded this topic. Rather than using the melodrama to encourage middle-class housewives to take jobs in factories as American films did, the Nazis continued to increase the burden on lower-class women.

Eventually, after the Allies advanced ever closer to Berlin, the middle classes were also brought into the war effort. Although he called for mass sacrifice in total war, Goebbels resisted the idea of extending his total war to German cinema. He saw the film industry and the performing arts as a "reservation" for female beauty (and as a private petting zoo), but the air raids were threatening these reserve units of German culture. As Goebbels reportedly remarked toward the end of the war: "It's such a sad situation that actresses, dancers and singers have to be released from work duty through special order of the Führer, in order to at least create a sort of reservation in Germany in the field of the fine arts, where female beauty and grace, unthreatened by the work-related brutalization and masculinization of our women, can carry on a modest but secure existence."[56] The task of the German actress was not to model work in war industries, but to maintain the desires of the masses, and Goebbels did not want too much realism to interfere with the cinema's erotic attractions.

Consequently, the production of the war remained hidden from Third Reich cinema screens. Nazi cinema continued to promote the middle-to-upper-class career woman, but it did little to advertise women's work in war industries. Nazi melodramas certainly romanticized the militarily useful medical profession, but they did not represent the masses of female war workers who manufactured the weapons of war. Hollywood cinema was much more effective in this regard, as *Since You Went Away* and other American home front films featured women working in munitions factories or costumed in Women's Army Corps uniforms. The only German film that presented women doing specifically war-related work was the short *Wochenschau* newsreel/propaganda documentary *Wir helfen siegen* (*We're Helping for Victory*, 1941). Nazi feature films, on the other hand, were largely reserved for the production of visual pleasures. In the few Nazi films that represented the domestic situation to wartime audiences and attempted to recruit home front support, the war and its industrial production were disguised and rewritten with romance.

In a characteristic manner, Helmut Käutner's 1941 home front melodrama *Auf Wiedersehen, Franziska* narrated the prehistory of World War II as a love story. Unlike the Hollywood home front films *Mrs. Miniver* and *Since You Went Away*, in *Auf Wiedersehen, Franziska* there is no text at the beginning to frame its interpretation or to announce it as a film about the war. The propagandistic intent was disguised and the war theme carefully dosed in *Auf Wiedersehen, Franziska*. The film pretends to be private in nature and reveals the public act of war only at the end of the film. For most of its length it is a tale of romance between a young woman from a Bavarian village and a cosmopolitan photojournalist who repeatedly flees their relationship, much to the frustration of the female protagonist. This prewar romance is clearly a rehearsal for the war situation, and the film does attempt to address some wartime female conflicts. Like Hollywood home front films, *Auf Wiedersehen, Franziska* served as a training manual for self-sacrifice and the surrender of female desire. However, in contrast to those family melodramas, this Nazi version did not insist on a surrender of sexuality, but instead negotiated a suspension of marital relations. Also unlike American home front films, *Auf Wiedersehen, Franziska* did not attempt to settle the class conflict that threatened to rupture the unity of the wartime Reich. Here, as in most German home front films, it is the domestic sphere itself that appears to be the main site of trouble.

It is significant that the film does not feature an already formed and stable nuclear family as the Hollywood home front films do; instead it plots the stormy path to the formation of the couple. The film's couple provides a model for Nazism's version of modern love, drawn in militarily useful forms. The taglines used in the film's advertising described the romance as a sort of battle, but they repressed the war itself: "Marianne Hoppe, charming in the role of a courageous young woman who succeeds in holding down the adventurous man who wants to live life to the full. Modern people speak to us, the air of our world flows through this film, and through seriousness and cheerfulness, a great love shines. A bold dare-devil conquers a girl, but then she conquers him."[57] "Great love" is a product of battle, it seems from this advertising. Significantly, the taglines do not indicate that this couple is engaged in a struggle for the preservation of traditional or national values. Instead, the language appeals to a sense of modernity defined by aggressive sexual relations and a spirit of imperialist conquest transferred into the private realm.

Although it attempted to be contemporary, *Auf Wiedersehen, Franziska* did not risk sending its protagonist to the munitions factory at the end of the film. The heroine, Franziska, instead manufactures wooden models of trains that her love interest, Michael, calls "small fetishes for big people," thus naturalizing the industrial vehicle that transports him to various battlefronts. Michael, the romantic hero played once again by Hans Söhnker, is a more technologically advanced fetish maker, manufacturing sensational images of war, catastrophes, and sports. As a world traveler and colonialist of imagery, Michael is also an ideal peacetime prototype for the soldier. He specializes in making images of military conflict, but he also hunts women with his aggressive lens, photographing Franziska against her will at the beginning of the film and pursuing her through the streets of her village. Marianne Hoppe, who plays Franziska, gives this character a seemingly liberated and somewhat defiant energy that derives from her masculine appeal. She "conquers" her mate by anticipating his strategy, showing a rare capacity to understand the psychology of the male hunter. Franziska is thus a model for the war bride, since she shows herself willing to tolerate and match male adventurism.

Just like Hoppe's role four years earlier in *Der Herrscher,* this romantic heroine again represents the Nazi youth in rebellion against an older generation of bourgeois respectability. Her modern nature is encoded in her costuming, which consists of structured suits and pants instead of Bavarian dresses. (On her first meeting with Michael, she wears almost the same khaki raincoat and stiff hat as he is wearing.) She also expresses opinions that the film presents as almost revolutionary tendencies in the matter of sexual morality. After knowing Michael for only a few days but aware of his history of casual affairs, she goes to his house and takes the initiative. As he sits in an armchair, she leans over him and asks if she can spend the night. The suggested sex that follows occurs in the ellipses between matched close-up shots of one of her "small fetishes"—an ironic play on the function of the Freudian fetish as an object of disavowal. Crosscutting during this seduction scene to Franziska's father's house, where her professor father sits with Christoph, Michael's rival for Franziska, indicates that this premarital sexuality is to be understood as an exemplary act of defiance against patriarchal authority. Both the father and Christoph, an antiques dealer, are styled as sedentary academics of a similar brand as in *Opfergang* and *Der Herrscher,* and they are shocked by Franziska's independent behavior. The next morning, Michael's elderly housekeeper is similarly scandalized that there is a woman in his bed, but Franziska shows no shame about the one-night stand and instead fakes a lack of interest in continuing the relationship as a show of autonomy.

Of course, this sexual "modernism" was not genuinely intended as an argument against all authority or as a promotion of female pleasure, but rather as a departure from bourgeois morality for the benefit of the Reich's imperialist strategies. It conformed to the attitude of party leaders who insisted that traditional standards of propriety no longer applied under the Nazi martial order, since reproduction had to be maintained under all circumstances. As Rudolf Hess wrote in 1939, unmarried mothers should be honored "who, perhaps outside the bounds of bourgeois morality and custom, contribute to compensation for the blood sacrificed in the war . . . for . . . the life of the nation comes before all principles thought up by men, all conventions which carry the mark of recognized custom . . . The highest service a woman can render to the community is the gift of racially healthy children for the survival of the nation."[58] Thus, the rhetoric of American cinema that equated wartime sexual promiscuity with sabotage was entirely missing in this Nazi film.

Unlike in comparable Hollywood films, the home is not a solid fortress braced for attack in *Auf Wiedersehen, Franziska.* The home is not really even a stable location, since the heroine moves three times in the course of the film, from her father's house to a Berlin apartment, before finally settling alone into Michael's house. After the first seduction night, Franziska confronts her father and demands to be released from paternal authority (the mother is once again missing from this household but is easily replaced by another hired housekeeper). Speaking about the stifling provincial domesticity in which her father and Christoph live, Franziska says: "I want to get out of here! I can't live with you two anymore. I feel like I'm imprisoned. Outside, the world is passing us by and we don't hear anything and we don't see anything of it. I don't want to get old with you two before I had the chance to be young." Franziska then escapes to Berlin to experience an independent youth—at least until Michael returns her to her original incarceration.

According to Sabine Hake's analysis, the modernist design of the Berlin apartment in *Auf Wiedersehen, Franziska,* like that of related Nazi films, conveys a sense of new fascist gender roles: "the man's initial opposition to domesticity is portrayed as a sign of healthy masculinity . . . By contrast, the women use interior design to express their principled opposition to traditional female role definitions."[59] These domestic spaces are unlike the house of *Since You Went Away,* in which all objects testify to marital fidelity and an unproblematic fusing of identities into the familial and national unit. Instead, Michael's house contains two separate spaces: hers and his, a clash of feminine design and photographic technology. The space of the house in *Auf Wiedersehen, Franziska* is not visibly militarized, however, and there are no implied eyes of state authority watching over it. Instead the home is rather curiously cut off from the rest of the world, separated by editing from the front and other sites of the public sphere. But the film's image of domesticity is in its own way oppressive. When Franziska moves into Michael's house, she appears no less imprisoned than before she fled paternal authority. While she clearly had a social circle in Berlin, in her seemingly depopulated provincial hometown she is left entirely alone, once again without the accompaniment of any sights or sounds of urban modernity. A flashing marquee sign illuminates her Berlin studio, indicating the presence of the modern forms of entertainment that still gave an illusory sense of connection between the Reich and abroad, but provincial Germany in this film appears lacking in any extrafamilial community. There are no rural festivals pictured here, and no more than a handful of (mostly older) inhabitants of the village make an appearance on the screen.

Unlike Hollywood home front films, therefore, this Nazi film is not at all content to stay at home with the female protagonist. Instead all sequences that describe Franziska's small-town life are impatiently cut short in order to return to the more visually stimulating world outside. The ethos of the film is hypocritical in that it attempts to define German-ness as the intrinsic quality of being rooted in the homeland, yet the mise-en-scène of the film displays a primary interest in the locations of Michael's international career. The stifling stasis of the hometown contrasts with the dynamic movement of worldly action. A rapidly edited montage sequence shows Michael's photographic apparatus turning to capture explosions, burning buildings, and airplanes. These visions of destruction, set to energetic music and superimposed over an image of Michael's rapturous face, merge with Michael's body and rhythmically stimulate the spectator as well.

Correspondingly, erotic adventure appears to be a particular advantage of the cameraman's profession. Even after Michael has Franziska securely installed in his house, he continues to pursue other women, including his American colleague Helen (a woman who competes with her camera but also offers her own attractive sights). When Michael receives a letter from Franziska telling him of the (premarital) birth of a son, he is in a nightclub in a North African port, surrounded by scantily clad women. A dark-skinned woman in a bikini dances through the nightclub space, and instead of a scene coded as thoroughly sinister and threatening by means of dark, fragmented lighting, the film offers a fully lit spectacle so that the viewer can fully relish the dancer's body. As Michael stumbles drunkenly past the dancer, he also ogles her and passes her some money. Since he gains access to such sights by means of his war-related camera work and his wealth, the film maps them for German spectators as the enticing territories of war and the potential locations of future German colonialism. Such scenes, not uncommon in Nazi cinema, were what gave rise to the objections of blood-and-soil Nazis like Peter von Werder to the eroticization of non-"Aryan" women on Third Reich screens.[60]

Clearly the nuclear family is anything but solid here and is not represented as a bulwark against the enemy as in the Hollywood home front films; instead it exists in a rather precarious arrangement. The news of the birth of a son briefly inspires a sense of duty in Michael, since it motivates him to push off the prostitutes on his lap and return home to Germany to marry the mother of his child. Characteristically for Third Reich melodramas, though, the wedding is not shown on screen, and the subsequent year of marital domesticity, referenced only by the dialogue, is likewise relegated to ellipses. The plot skips ahead to the moment when Michael is once again dissatisfied with his bourgeois life. Standing in the upstairs bedroom, a confining room with small windows and a low ceiling, Michael tells his wife that he has tried to stay home and carry on the marriage, growling: "But I can't do it! I can't and I don't want to! . . . I've just been sitting around here doing nothing the whole year, looking at the small windows and gritting my teeth!" These windows are also covered with heavy drapes; *Auf Wiedersehen, Franziska*'s set design once again conveys the idea that marriage and provincial domesticity are spaces of limited vision. Craving the sights of international conflict, Michael then returns to the pleasures of his career, leaving Franziska essentially a single mother. Finally she refuses to tolerate her husband's disappearances any longer and files for divorce. Since the camera follows the characters to the office of the divorce lawyer but not to the wedding ceremony, the film is clearly more interested in the techniques of marital separation. The divorce lawyer questions Franziska to find a legal basis for divorce, asking if her husband provides enough financial support and if the couple still has sexual relations, but warns that the court will see Michael's frequent absences as justified because they are necessary for work. This Nazi home front film thereby defines marriage as a financial and reproductive arrangement, not as the bourgeois/classical Hollywood conception of the wife and mother as a nurturer responsible for maintaining her family's continuing capacity to engage in the public sphere, including that of war. Instead, the wife in the Nazi melodrama retards the male energy that would otherwise be applied to creative production or conquest. And here it is clear that it is not sexual relations themselves that act as the retardant on production, but rather other familial duties and dependencies.

By the end of the film, both characters have gone through a conversion process and the divorce proceedings have (at least temporarily) ceased. After Michael's colleague Buck gets hit by a grenade splinter on a battlefield in China, Michael returns to Germany in the following sequence with a renewed interest in settling down. His apparent conversion to domestic-ity, however, threatens to interfere with his engagement in the Nazi public sphere. In a dialogue sequence that was edited out of the copies of the film now in circulation, Michael at first resists joining the war because of his renewed sense of responsibility to his wife and children, but Franziska convinces him that it is his duty to leave her behind once again.[61] Franziska's conversion consists of a release of her desire to "hold" her adventurous man for her own private, familial use. When she takes Michael to the train sta-tion after he receives his mobilization order, she reverses his often-repeated phrase "auf Wiedersehen, Franziska!" ("good-bye, Franziska!") and this time says, "auf Wiedersehen, Michael!" indicating that she is now the one who finally embraces their separation. As Friedemann Beyer has com-mented, the romance in *Auf Wiedersehen, Franziska* is "a marriage on call that is endangered by his fulfillment of duty in the shadow of the war, but which also becomes the woman's chance for emancipation."[62] The film thus ends with the ambivalent suggestion that family and gender relations may be rearranged through war. The promise to female spectators that wartime experiences may make men less egotistical is balanced by the suggestion to male spectators that battle may provide a more or less welcome respite from banal domesticity. In any case the war situation requires a certain degree of female autonomy and allows the heroine to continue to fulfill this potential. Contemporary viewers therefore could have mistaken the film as an endorsement of appealingly modern gender roles, even if the woman's role here is actually that of complete subservience.

Since the film ends at the train station, *Auf Wiedersehen, Franziska* does not show its hero in combat for Nazism and instead represses the actual conflict. But the images of Michael's glamorous life as a war reporter are designed to transfer to the imagination of war itself so that war becomes simply another form of male adventure, one that facilitates erotic adventure. By narrating the prehistory of World War II as the embattled but stimulating "great love" of a German couple, *Auf Wiedersehen, Franziska* covers war with romantic appeal, reducing it to an event that is ultimately beneficial for the private lives of the characters. It is war that provides narrative closure and puts a halt to the divorce, at least temporarily. But *Auf Wiedersehen, Franziska* also indicates that the ultimate resolution of the problematic issue of marriage would have to wait until after the war. Until then, female spectators were advised to continue to work and produce "Aryan" babies on their own.

Another home front film of the following year, *Zwei in einer großen Stadt* (*Two in a Big City*, 1942), made a similar argument about female subservience disguised in seemingly liberatory images. A film about two soldiers on furlough in Berlin, it provided a falsified account of the benefits of wartime life. After entering a city seemingly untouched by bombing, the soldiers immediately find willing girlfriends and take them along to a sunny lake in the forest just outside the city. The two couples enjoy a day of summer pleasures in what is possibly a Nazi remake of the late Weimar weekend romance *Menschen am Sonntag* (*People on Sunday*, 1930). The Nazi film intensifies the effect of the situation by providing the audience with voyeuristic shots of the two women as they undress and put on swimsuits. In one scene the camera is placed very close to the action occurring in the small space of a changing cabin, giving the spectator the impression of a privileged access to the striptease. The tease is later consummated when the soldiers convince their dates to provide them with further pleasures. Heide Schlüpmann has compared the use of female sexuality in this film to the effects of food; sex is presented a means of regeneration for the

The Nazi eroticization of war: *Zwei in einer großen Stadt* (1942). Source: Deutsche Kinemathek

male soldier in this film, and it suggests that a woman's patriotic duty is to maintain a passive position of "constant readiness" to serve these needs.[63] The access to and consumption of sexuality were posited by this film as soldiers' privileges. Unlike in Hollywood home front films, however, this access was not connected to the precondition of marriage.

The reception context of both of these Third Reich home front films was the beginning of the offensive against the Soviet Union, so their lessons in waiting and constant readiness clearly came at an opportune time. Although both Hitler and Goebbels expected to conquer the Soviet Union in the same *Blitzkrieg* style as was used in Western Europe, it soon became clear that this could not be carried out within a few months as originally planned.[64] In late 1941 the press continued to lie to the German masses about the war against the Soviets—who were generally described as uncivilized and barely armed Bolsheviks—claiming that the conflict had already been decided in favor of Germany and that there remained only a bit of cleaning up to do. At the same time, letters from soldiers arrived in home front mailboxes and told another story, the illicit truth of retreat. By December trainloads of wounded men with frostbite were arriving back in the Reich. The clear evidence that the Eastern campaign was badly organized cracked the image of an invincible German army, and this shock rippled through the home front populace. SD reports registered an increasing distrust of the media in late 1941 and early 1942 along with an increasing mood of panic.[65]

The limited dose of war offered in *Auf Wiedersehen, Franziska* and *Zwei in einer großen Stadt* was only slightly increased later in *Die große Liebe* (*The Great Love,* 1942). This home front film seems to have been produced with the SD reports in mind and largely follows a strategy of denial. *Die große Liebe* is a romance melodrama and is more about the war of the sexes than any public struggle. In opposition to *Mrs. Miniver,* which was showing in Allied cinemas at the same time, the protagonist of this Nazi hit was not an "average" house-wife representing a nationalized domesticity, but rather a famous international entertainer. The film narrates the love affair between the Danish singing star Hanna Holberg (Zarah Leander) and the Luftwaffe officer Paul Wendlandt (Viktor Staal). Conflict erupts when the heroine's lover continually disappears in order to fulfill his war duties and breaks off the couple's engagement before Germany's attack on the Soviet Union. Eventually the heroine learns to delay her marital demands. Although the film's main ideological task is the usual one for home front melodrama, that of educating female spectators to subvert their own desires in deference to the war, there is simultaneously an attempt to mobilize desire as a war strategy.

Die große Liebe admitted more of the contemporary wartime situation into the script than most of Nazi cinema's World War II evasions. The film makes reference to air raids and food rationing, though the actual dangers of the war and the material shortages are deemphasized. The home front in *Die große Liebe* apparently does not have to sacrifice much except a choice of desserts at restaurants, and there is a deceptive level of material abundance in Leander's costuming and the mise-en-scène of wartime Berlin, much in contrast to the increasingly dismal situation outside the cinemas.[66] The war itself is also never pictured with unsettling imagery. The romantic hero is not depicted here as a foot soldier on the Eastern front (which might have better served the interests of realism), but rather as a pilot and member of the more elite branch of the military—and thus less prone to frostbite. The film starts with scenes from the North African front as Wendlandt heroically saves his plane from an impending crash. But the way this scene is filmed makes it appear absurdly unlike battle. The hero's comrades watch his maneuvers from their beach chairs, sunning themselves on a war front that looks more like a vacation colony. Wendlandt and his fellow soldiers return from Rommel's field trip with attractive tans and no wounds. The catastrophically cold Eastern front is likewise represented only by a reassuringly short shot of a plane landing in a summery forest landscape. This refusal to imagine the true nature of combat can be seen as the general Nazi approach to war representation, with its tendency toward romanticization and trivialization. The enemy remains hidden in most Nazi war-related films, leaving the spectator with the impression of battle as merely an expression of dynamic energy, like an exercise without human adversaries and few consequences. [67]

As a result, there are no onscreen deaths in *Die große Liebe*. Although the hero does suffer a minor injury at the end of the film, being shot down by Soviet pilots only lands him in an Alpine hospital that looks more like a ski chalet, a set design reminiscent of Staal's earlier romantic adventure in *Umwege zum Glück*. It is significant that in neither *Auf Wiedersehen, Franziska* nor *Die große Liebe* is any character killed off in whom the narrative has invested much emotional energy. The death of Wendlandt's friend Von Etzdorf is not shown and is barely mourned, unlike the heavily melodramatic moment when Carol is killed on screen in *Mrs. Miniver*. The deaths in the Hollywood films are moral outrages that call for revenge, but in the Nazi films, casualties are simply part of the sport of battle. In fact, the only war casualties we actually see in *Die große Liebe* other than Wendlandt in his picturesque hospital are the bandaged extras swaying cheerfully in a grand Parisian ballroom to Zarah Leander's hit song "It's Not the End of the World." In comparison, the shots of the war wounded in *Since You Went Away* are considerably more anxiety-inducing; while Hollywood films attempted to prepare women for their postwar roles as self-sacrificial healers of returning veterans, *Die große Liebe* does not dare to touch such issues. Rather, it simply attempts to reduce the home front populace's anxieties about family members' participation in the war, and it does so by deceptive means. Part of the film's work is to replace front soldiers' unsettling firsthand narratives with more innocuous filmic ones—images more resembling summer camp than the soon-to-come Stalingrad.

Indeed the depiction of death and its true affective consequences are generally avoided in German war films. In a 1941 article addressing the question of whether death should be excluded entirely from filmic representation, Fritz Hippler, director of the RMVP film department, answered in the negative. But Hippler emphasized that the camera should keep its distance from any actor performing death: "The elemental phenomenon of dying and the majesty of death elude direct representational re-creation to such an extent, that one should . . . as a matter of principle abstain from all shots of the face, and especially from the unjustifiably popular close-ups of 'dying' actors, and should instead only make use of indirect means of representation, of which film of course has no lack."[68] Although Hippler asserted that death was so sacred an experience for the fascist that it was essentially unrepresentable, the reason for the avoidance of shots of the dying was primarily the RMVP's nervousness about viewer reactions. As discussed earlier in this chapter, images of death threatened to elicit unreliable spectator responses. Any images of war threatened to backfire, particularly with female audiences, who were on the whole eager for the war to end. SD reports repeatedly underlined that women tended to react more often with anxiety or pity to images of dead soldiers than did men, or at least they were perceived as doing so. Another war-related film of the same year, *Der große König* (*The Great King*), for example, was apparently well received by male audiences, but was rejected by many female spectators. The SD gave an account of the film's reception on May 28, 1942, and noted: "As was repeatedly reported, women rejected the film with the explanation that there was 'too much war' in it and that the film was too intense a strain on the nerves."[69] Female spectators threatened to undermine the propagandistic effect of this expensive production. As the reports added, in some places women had "started a 'real underground propaganda [campaign]'" that turned others against the film.[70] For the most part, such a risk was avoided with *Die große Liebe,* and it was rewarded with high attendance numbers and a large profit margin.[71] Perhaps following Hippler's instructions and the SD reports on spectatorship, *Die große Liebe* avoided any direct representation of death or violence. It did admit some indirect thematization of melancholy and mourning, however; the scene in which Hanna walks through ancient Roman gravesites in Italy effectively relocates the possibility of death far away from the Berlin *Heimat.*

While the horrors of war were kept out of sight in *Die große Liebe,* so were their justifications. Unlike in *Mrs. Miniver,* in *Die große Liebe* the enemy remains completely invisible. No Soviets or Allied soldiers ever physically appear during this film, perhaps to avoid the spectator effects of visualizing the enemy as a man with a body, a vision that might give rise to unmanageable feelings. The heroine, Hanna, does not even name the source of the air raids, so the film does not attempt to generate anger against the British for bombings. Since the British planes are never pictured, the air raids appear almost as a sort of inclement weather, an impersonal, virtually natural force, much unlike the dread generated by the shots of low-flying Nazi warplanes invading *Mrs. Miniver*'s home. There is also little explicit discussion of the political goals or origins of the war in *Die große Liebe* and no framing of the war as a communal struggle comparable to the shots of the unified masses in *Mrs. Miniver*'s boat sequence. Although the attack on the Soviet Union is announced in *Die große Liebe* in a similarly disembodied fashion as a voice from loudspeakers, the receivers of the message are not framed in close-up and are visible only for a brief moment as passers-by on a Berlin street; the film thus avoids any emotionalizing or identification with these anonymous German citizens. A rather disorienting cut follows and brings the spectator back to the heroine of the film, and as she sits at the desk in her Roman hotel room, she only sighs tiredly, "war with the Soviets!" but does not articulate any reasons why they must be fought.

Thus, the rhetorical and emotional effects of the rousing church congregation speeches in *Mrs. Miniver* and *Since You Went Away* are generally missing here, and instead of a call to public action, *Die große Liebe* simply attempts to generate an inwardly focused attitude of war tolerance. The most significant reference in this film to Nazi political ideology is the mention of the national/racial community while Hanna's maid, Käthe, is scuffling with a man in the air raid shelter over her package of coffee. "The national community [*Volksgemeinschaft*] doesn't go that far!" she says, snatching the package from the greedy man's hands. The Nazi concept of community here is the basis of a joke that appears irreverent enough to pass for honesty, although not enough to inspire real critique. But it does foreground the issue of private investment in the war effort. As Stephen Lowry has concluded, *Die große Liebe* makes its main appeal not to a sense of patriotism but to more private desires: "It is no longer only the abstract ideals of nation or ethnic group that are the main focus, rather the fulfillment of duty is connected to the promise of private happiness."[72]

This promise was differently packaged in Nazi home front films than in their American counterparts. In contrast to Hollywood, happiness is not exclusively located in the nuclear family in Nazi melodramas, and the marital home does not serve as a similarly privileged site of national collectivity. Like *Auf Wiedersehen, Franziska* and many other Nazi melodramas, *Die große*

Liebe reflects a deeply ambivalent attitude toward marriage and domesticity. Here again the "home" is not even a stable location, and the heroine actually spends more film time in her hotel room in Rome than in her Berlin apartment. When Hanna moves into a big house in the wealthy Berlin district of Schlachtensee and throws an engagement party there, the house is shown as still being in a literal state of remodeling. The conversations of the party guests are interrupted by the sound of construction workers hammering on the roof, and even before the guests begin smashing glasses in celebration, the wedding is called off once more because of war maneuvers. The home then looks particularly transitory and tenuous, since the scene suggests that both the planned marriage and the house are continually threatened with collapse. Such a space is barely suited to representing "an ordered national consensus."[73] National consensus is not located in the home in this Nazi home front film, and here again domesticity interferes with rather than supports male action. During the wedding party, Wendlandt's comrade Von Etzdorf asks him if he might not want to reconsider getting married, and a subsequent scene shows the groom-to-be helping Hanna in the kitchen, which certainly generated for some male viewers a sense of unbearable feminization through domestication. Shortly thereafter Wendlandt is seated in a large chair next to his fiancée in front of a somewhat foreboding closed and inactive fireplace, and at that moment the telephone rings with orders to return to the front. Masculine energy for military duty does not generate from the housewife-warmed home and hearth in *Die große Liebe,* unlike in *Since You Went Away.* Rather, duty provides an escape from a domesticity that threatens to entrap the military man in the banal maintenance rituals of daily life.

However, in an earlier sequence the mise-en-scène of the domestic space in *Die große Liebe* did suggest a unified home and front of a more spectacular kind. As Hanna is singing for Wehrmacht soldiers in the ballroom of a massive Parisian palace decorated with Baroque gilding and crystal chandeliers, her lover, Wendlandt, arrives at her Berlin apartment, the décor of which is contiguous with the interiors of occupied France. Hanna's domestic space is designed as *grand luxe,* with ornate gilded mirrors, Baroque antiques, candelabra lights, and a crystal chandelier over the grand piano. When Wendlandt enters her living room, he switches on a lamp in the shape of a female nude and sits on Hanna's silk brocade couch, positioned in front of a wall mural in early eighteenth-century style. This is the design of aristocratic aspiration, not the bourgeois domesticity of floral prints and tartans that mark the mise-en-scène of the homes of *Mrs. Miniver* and *Since You Went Away.* Rather than reinforcing traditional gender roles, therefore, the interior design of *Die große Liebe* suggested the German appropriation of French styles of cultural dominance.

Imperialist pleasures: Wendlandt and Von Etzdorf on the Western front in *Die große Liebe* (1942). Source: Deutsche Kinemathek

In comparison to those of Hollywood, Nazi home front films did not fetishize commodities as explicitly or make reference to future middle-class shopping opportunities. Instead the war primarily appears as the means to two kinds of consumption: cultural and erotic. As the Vienna woman's letter to Goebbels correctly surmised, the war was conceived as a way of spreading German culture to new territories and increasing spectatorship possibilities.[74] Specifically, the war made expansion possible as the German film industry gained hegemony over Hollywood in Nazi-occupied territories, annexing new studio space and colonizing the minds of new populations. Goebbels wanted German cinematic imagery to become more attractive than Hollywood's, and *Die große Liebe* contributes to this effort by making wartime life appear desirable for both soldiers and civilians. The war seems to exist primarily to provide a stimulating backdrop to romantic relations.[75]

Although marriage and domesticity are delayed or even made impossible by the war in *Die große Liebe*, sexuality is actually promoted by it. The unequal lovers come together as a result of wartime fuel shortages that force even a celebrity to ride the subway and expose herself to advances she would not have experienced in a private car. An unexpected air raid then leads straight to a one-night stand. As he is standing in front of Hanna's open window during the air raid, Wendlandt describes the war in seductive terms, suggesting to her that both love and war are "beautiful, precisely because there are risks." War is again trivialized as romantic adventure in *Die große Liebe,* but at the same time it is presented as a form of heightened experience capable of generating intense emotion and erotic opportunity. As the director of the film, Rolf Hansen, suggested in an interview publicized when the film was released, the message of *Die große Liebe* was that war can increase erotic pleasures: "The realization that three weeks might have to suffice for great happiness nowadays, but that these three weeks can make happiness even stronger and more intense through their temporal limitation: that is the insight into the demands of the time, which Hanna Holberg gradually gains in our film and which all of us must someday gain as well."[76] The condensation of love affairs into short periods of military furlough rather than lifelong marriage removed the drag of banality from the lover's experience, Hansen proposed. Most of the film makes war appear like an ideal opportunity to see the world's most romantic getaways. The heroine meets her lover in Berlin and then travels across Europe to join him for wartime duties. Hanna is chauffeured around Paris in a Wehrmacht convertible while a back projection with monuments of the conquered city recasts Nazi aggression as luxury tourism. Besides sunning himself in North Africa, Wendlandt spends the rest of the war taking a puppy to the theater in Berlin, drinking champagne with occupying officers on the Western front, and going with his comrades for a dip in the waters off the coast of France.

Such scenes also serve to explore the body of the military man while softening the image of the soldier. Throughout the film, Wendlandt is repeatedly shown lying on couches or baring his chest, his reclining positions and exposed skin inviting erotic contemplation. If *Mrs. Miniver* worked to militarize essentially unsoldierly civilians, *Die große Liebe* attempts the opposite by disavowing the hero's participation in brutality. And while *Mrs. Miniver* eroticizes consumer commodities, the Nazi home front film commodifies erotic relations. The beach sequence opens with a close-up of a line of empty combat boots, and the missing bodies of the boots' owners may create a momentary shock for the spectator who reads this image as evidence of offscreen violence. But a camera pan to a shot of the undressed men playing in the waves promptly defuses the dread as it reinstates the bodies of the soldiers and demilitarizes them. A following framing has Wendlandt and Von Etzdorf lying on the sand in their swimsuits with the camera positioned for a view of the pelvic region of the two men, emphasizing the virility of these stripped soldiers, but also suggesting an eroticism of a more civilian than sublimated nature. The discussion of the soldiers on the beach revolves entirely around romance rather than war as Wendlandt and his comrade argue about the desirability of marriage. Von Etzdorf says that he prefers to seek part-time amusements and makes a case against monogamy. Comparing women to ties, he adds that once he buys one, all the others in the shop windows suddenly look much better than his. An officer's status clearly makes such consumption possible; in an earlier French palace scene in which Wendlandt occupies a sofa, Von Etzdorf empties a wine bottle and discusses plans for the night's operations: "let's just amuse ourselves with someone, anyone," he says.

Nazi films apparently endeavored to enlist spectator desire to the benefit of the fascist militarist state by collapsing war into romance or sexual adventure. Here a somewhat different process was at work than the eroticization of death that has been diagnosed by Susan Sontag and others as being central to fascist aesthetics.[77] Instead of a sublimation of sexual energies and their release through death or self-subjugation to Führer figures, these images suggested that war allows for the release or living out of (male) sexual energies because it is an extraordinary circumstance that dissolves the bonds of the peacetime bourgeois moral order. Such images support Foucault's argument that modern Western culture, far from repressing sexuality, actually produced it in the interest of power relations: "The Faustian pact, whose temptation has been instilled in us by the deployment of sexuality, is now as follows: to exchange life in its entirety for sex itself, for the truth and the sovereignty of sex. Sex is worth dying for. It is in this (strictly historical) sense that sex is indeed imbued with the death instinct."[78] When Hanna sings in *Die große Liebe*, "My life for love . . . Whatever pleases, is permitted!" the proposition is exactly that: an exchange of life for brief pleasures lent extraordinary intensity by the proximity to death.

Die große Liebe did not risk a total dissolution of the bourgeois order, of course, since there was a qualified reinstatement of convention at the end of the film, when the protagonists renew their marriage plans. As Stephen Lowry has also noted, Leander is costumed in white in her final song sequence, and the framing emphasizes her face more than her body, thus reversing the fetishistic quality of Hanna's first vampish stage performance. Lowry concludes from this iconic trajectory that *Die große Liebe* aimed for total de-eroticization, a conclusion that has been echoed by other scholars.[79] However, it is important to consider the narrative placement of this scene: the performance comes just as Hanna's access to sexuality has been removed by the apparent end of her relationship to Wendlandt. The focus on her face intensifies the sense of suffering caused by this removal, setting up the narrative for the happy-end reinstatement of erotic relations at the end of the film. Furthermore, the white gown, adjusted to the narrative setting of Hanna's Italian performance, imitates the clothing of ancient Rome, thus referencing imperialist culture rather than a Christian notion of angelic purity.

Moreover, it is not entirely correct to view the film's intent as a complete purging or domestication of erotic energies. Nazi cinema did attempt to make the femme fatale less fatal, but in the same way that it made the war appear less dangerous. *Die große Liebe* does not attempt to domesticate and de-eroticize the woman so much as invest the erotic energy she produces into the war itself. Notably, the first two love scenes between Hanna and Wendlandt that fade out on expressions of physical passion (as an indication of continued lovemaking off-camera) both use shots of airplanes as symbolic ellipses so that war activity complements sexual activity. Thus, what is at play in *Die große Liebe* is not a complete purging or sublimation of eroticism, but a mutually stimulating exchange. At the beginning of the film Wendlandt sits in the audience of a theater, watching the spectacle of Hanna-as-vamp. At the end of the film he is again sitting in the position of spectator, but his desires are focused on the planes themselves.

Furthermore, as Linda Schulte-Sasse has pointed out, in the sequence in which Hanna herself is shown as a cinema spectator, the conventional position of specularity is reversed: "the usual object of our gaze, Zarah Leander, becomes the subject of a desiring gaze."[80] In this reversal the film followed a generic convention. The female protagonist of the classical Hollywood melodrama, as Laura Mulvey has asserted, often "performs the woman who must perform, and for whom performance is invested in appearance," the result of which is that "performance, appearance, masquerade and their erotics shift from the surface of the screen into the story itself."[81] This shift may thematize but does not entirely invalidate the masquerade as the dominant system. The vamp remains a privileged (even required) mode of femininity as consumable spectacle, and this spectacle is one that is clearly desired by soldier audiences. However, even if *Die große Liebe* reveals the masquerade behind this production of eroticism, it still extracts erotics from narrative once again, by projecting eroticism onto the military man and his machines. As we have seen, it is actually Staal's body, not Leander's, which is *Die große Liebe*'s main object of desire.

The renewed promise of marriage at the film's conclusion, *Die große Liebe*'s submission to generic convention, ultimately appears as distant as peace. The couple is reunited in a studio-set fantasy of a hospital, their reconciliation taking place in front of painted mountains. Hanna's lover tells her that he has three weeks of vacation during which they can finally hold the wedding, to which she replies apprehensively, "Three weeks, and then?" He does not answer, and only looks up at the sky at a group of planes flying over, seemingly entranced by the war machines. Hanna looks up hesitantly and then smiles as if finally accepting an uncertain future. Strangely, though, the positions of the couple's eyes appear to be mismatched, focused on different objects, and marriage appears particularly tenuous in this short moment. No visual evidence that the wedding will indeed take place follows, so the legal consummation of the relationship remains indeterminate. The suppression of Hanna's desires is specifically not a restriction on sexuality but on the legally endowed rights of marriage.

Interestingly, *Die große Liebe*'s final shot of airplanes flying overhead was exactly the same image with which *Mrs. Miniver* ended its cinematic call to action. In the Nazi version, however, this shot was not embedded in a similar mise-en-scène of a divinely ordained national community, but in a scene of romance. Instead of functioning as an ideological crusade, the war remains in the German version, in disavowed form, as a private quest for happiness. Unlike in the Hollywood home front films, unification of the national community is not achieved in *Die große Liebe* inside the single family home or in the church but in the spaces of entertainment. As Linda Schulte-Sasse has observed, the revue theater is the privileged "site of collectivity" in *Die große Liebe,* while the scene showing Hanna in the cinema provides "community feeling" by "allowing the film audience to watch its surrogate."[82] The Nazi home front film imagines the German masses as a unified national community of spectators instead of a mass assemblage of nuclear families fused together through Christianity.

The consensus-through-entertainment model was a wishful fantasy on the part of Nazi culture producers, however. As the dissenting spectator reactions we have encountered thus far evidence, no complete unification was achieved in the theaters. This was especially true in regard to the cinema's attempts to loosen puritanical standards of decency. Spectators, including military leaders and lower-level Nazi Party officials, filed objections to the acts of premarital sexuality written into the scripts of both *Auf Wiedersehen, Franziska* and *Die große Liebe.*[83] For Goebbels, this battle over eroticism and spectatorship became a welcome way of consolidating his influence over more conservative elements of the party. As Goebbels noted in his diary in May 1942, after the Oberkommando der Wehrmacht (OKW, or Supreme Command of the Armed Forces) lodged a complaint against *Die große Liebe*:

> I talked on the phone with Reichsmarschall [Göring], who complained about the OKW because it is protesting against the new Leander film. This film shows

an air force officer who spends the night with a famous singer. The OKW feels morally offended by this and claims that an air force lieutenant does not behave this way. This clashes with Göring's absolutely correct opinion that if an air force lieutenant didn't take advantage of such an opportunity, he wouldn't be an air force lieutenant. Göring makes fun of the prissiness of the OKW, which is very useful to me, since the OKW makes so much trouble for me in my film work.[84]

Goebbels was not willing to remove the seduction scene, because it was central to the propaganda effect of the film. The generals of the OKW knew how to organize soldiers at the front, but Goebbels believed he knew best how to organize the desires of the masses. The military leadership had long interfered with his own cinematic war, and with Göring's support, he was able to continue waging it without too much interference from the leaders of the real war.

Goebbels's adversaries and more conservative spectators were particularly worried about the effects that films had upon the private behavior of individuals. To some it appeared that media messages were indeed causing a loosening of sexual morals. According to Security Service reports and other documents widely circulated among Nazi officials, women and girls in the Third Reich appeared to show an increased sexual appetite during the war and were particularly willing to offer themselves to men in uniform.[85] The SD also reported that a large number of unmarried girls had become pregnant due to the stationing of soldiers in private households.[86] The latter fact was certainly received with some degree of satisfaction by Hitler, Goebbels, and Göring. However, the perceived loosening of the standards of bourgeois morality was reportedly also having entirely unintended consequences. For example, in 1942 the Security Service noted: "A typical case is that of a telephone operator from a middle-class background, 23 years old, who pursued a French prisoner of war because he had 'black hair and a Mediterranean type.'"[87] The fact that this woman was from the educated middle class was alarming to the authorities, because she was a member of the favored target audience of propaganda messages asserting that a woman's greatest gift to her nation was a blonde baby. Despite the antibourgeois ideology of Nazi leaders, middle- and upper-class women were still considered to be the most visually appealing and therefore to possess the most valuable "blood."[88] The case of a German woman with a strong attraction to a black-haired foreigner was described as a typical one and viewed by the regime as evidence of a widespread refusal on the part of German women to conform to the Nazi eugenic policy.

The SD reported repeatedly on the failure of propaganda efforts to universally form female desires for "racially pure" German men. In 1942 the regime estimated with dismay that German women had already given birth to at least twenty thousand children fathered by foreign laborers and prisoners of war.[89] Furthermore, the SD claimed that in most situations it was the woman who was the more aggressive party. Women whose husbands or boyfriends had been at the front for months or years without furlough complained openly of sexual frustration, leading them to initiate relations with foreigners, as the SD reported on July 10, 1943:

> A further argument for the close contact with foreigners is supposedly the lack of men, a lack that has recently become particularly noticeable . . . A farmer's wife justified her intimate relations with a French prisoner of war by saying that her husband had not had furlough for 15 months. At first she resisted the Frenchman, but then she fell victim to her sex drive . . . In addition to the already mentioned motivations, there often appears to be a certain addiction to *the exotic* among the women and girls. They see in the foreigner something interesting and new.[90]

The war that was being waged to "purify" the German "race" was creating the very conditions under which some women could more easily satisfy desires subversive to the regime's racist ideology.

There were also some indications that the sexual morality of Nazi cinema may have negatively affected the morale of some soldiers and civilians. Some audience members objected to the representation of extramarital relations in Nazi films, saying that such narratives only intensified feelings of anxiety among the wartime populace. The Security Service reported that the 1940 romance melodrama *Eine kleine Nachtmusik* (*A Small Serenade*) enjoyed a generally favorable response among audiences, but that its thematization of extramarital love met with some opposition:

> Further reports . . . say, however, that critical opinions are being heard among certain circles of the population. Spectators have pointed out in this regard that it does not make sense during a time of war, in which many families are separated through conscription, to gloss over behavior that is contrary to marriage. To an even stronger degree, reports from [the cities of] Stettin and Allenstein have asserted this viewpoint in regard to the films *Leidenschaft* [*Passion*, 1940], *Eine Nacht im Mai* [*A Night in May*, 1938] and *Ein Mann muß so sein* [*Männer müssen so sein/Men Are That Way*, 1939].[91]

The Security Service, probably realizing that such opinions would be regarded unfavorably by the RMVP, did not represent the objections of provincial spectators to extramarital affairs as moralistic objections, but as potentially ineffective war strategy. Problematic issues relating to marriage simply would not go away, and in fact they did have some strategic implications for the war effort. In the minutes of an RMVP meeting in February 1940, it was noted that soldiers had been receiving anonymous letters reporting that their wives at home were having affairs, and women also received letters saying that their husbands deployed on the Western front were involved with other women.[92] The Propaganda Ministry assumed that these letters were sent by war resisters who used rumors of infidelity as covert oppositional propaganda.

It was this context of sexual anxiety that contributed to the popular success of Veit Harlan's 1943 romance melodrama *Immensee,* which could be viewed as a home front film cleansed of all visible traces of war.[93] Although it may have appealed to soldiers in particular, *Immensee* seemed to endorse more domestic and more peaceful values than usual. It is a choice narrative about a woman (played by Kristina Söderbaum) who is married to the owner of a large country estate and falls in love with another man. The "other man" is a composer, and as usual in Nazi cinema, the musical artist stands for both the supposed superiority of German culture and its soldierly spirit. Accordingly, he travels widely and conquers foreign and domestic women, as well as his artistic rivals. The homebound landowner, on the other hand, keeps bees and is comparatively gentle and passive. Reversing the usual convention of Nazi romance melodramas, the "winner" of this competition narrative, the one who retains the loyalty of the woman even after his death is, surprisingly, the more domestic of the two men. The triumph of the husband in this film conveyed the rather unusual message that marital fidelity would be rewarded, and it also suggested that gentle romantic feeling might actually be regarded as a male strength. Perhaps some soldiers, retreating from Stalingrad, were ready to identify with a character who peacefully maintained a rural idyll rather than becoming an international conqueror of culture. Furthermore, unlike the majority of Third Reich melodramas, *Immensee* made monogamous marriage appear to be a viable institution, and this message was apparently reassuring for male viewers—especially, as Söderbaum suggested, for the pubescent generation who would reach maturity in the postwar Adenauer era.[94] However, this vision of domestic peace was not fully stabilized in Nazi cinema. Harlan's 1944 sequel, *Opfergang,* reversed *Immensee*'s love triangle and was a much more ambivalent treatment of the marital theme.

Late in the war, as the Nazi film press claimed to have finally "discovered" the middle-age wife and mother, there was a partial attempt to shift the focus of melodrama.[95] *Die Degenhardts* (*The Degenhardts,* 1944), possibly an emulation of Hollywood's approach to the home front film, was a late effort to adapt the family melodrama to propaganda purposes. Featuring a Lübeck family bravely facing "total war," the film turned back into the domestic interior at a time when the war was obviously already lost and the front had invaded the home to an extent that many spectators certainly became nostalgic for domesticity. But as Mary-Elizabeth O'Brien has asserted, this was not an optimistic or encouraging view of wartime domestic life. The film, which had a lukewarm reception by audiences, was, as O'Brien stated, a grim "story of an ordinary family that must die to preserve German high culture."[96]

At the same time, many senior Wehrmacht officers were living out the German romance of war. For example, a complaint registered by the SD in 1944 about the behavior of the generalship at the collapsing Eastern front asserted: "As is well known, our Eastern front was very weak . . . The back lines, however, instead of digging in and doing military drills, lived the high life . . . While army reports were already announcing that three formations were charging toward Minsk, they were putting on a [film] premiere with 18 generals in attendance."[97] The military had apparently taken the promises of Nazi cinema to heart, and particularly the upper ranks would not allow total war to interfere with their entertainments. As another Security Service report from 1944 noted, soldiers at the front repeatedly complained about the "pleasure addiction" of their commanding officers.[98] An unnamed soldier quoted in the report added: "'Our officers only think about having a lot of 'amusement.' They very often sit together with Italian women and female artists in their casino and we musicians are very often woken up in the middle of the night to play while they carry on their love games."[99] While their superiors orchestrated orgiastic revelry, foot soldiers were treated to harsh discipline that gave rise to outbreaks of lower-class rage. Many officers were making themselves exactly as comfortable during the war as Wendlandt had in *Die große Liebe*. As another soldier testified: "There is such bitterness among the soldiers, since the officers, with few exceptions, show such arrogance that a national community [*Volksgemeinschaft*] is out of the question. Behind the front lines, they live a gluttonous existence in the officer's casinos, and in the cities you can see the officers wandering around completely drunk. Everyone is hanging around on the back lines, and you can't find anyone at the front anymore. The accommodations of the officers show their luxurious lifestyles, with the finest furniture, porcelain, etc., while the wounded barely even get straw under their backs."[100] As the Nazi officers indulged in their own excessive mise-en-scène of the war, some front soldiers apparently became disenchanted with the Third Reich's illusory promises of liberation through imperialist warfare. On the home front, civilians living in the bombed-out ruins of German cities sat in the cinemas and watched romance melodramas, many still drunk on the visual pleasures of Nazi culture.

Conclusion

This chapter has compared Hollywood and Nazi uses of melodrama during World War II and has demonstrated that the American home front film portrayed the war effort as a defense of middle-class domesticity, while the Nazi home front melodrama suggested that war provided a means to intensified erotic experience. As my analysis of two of the most important American wartime melodramas, *Mrs. Miniver* and *Since You Went Away* highlighted, Hollywood producers (in collusion with the advertising industry) assumed that the normative spectatorial position was that of a middle-class housewife, and therefore U.S. home front melodramas attempted to enlist the emotional identification of viewers by arguing that the war was being fought principally to defend the suburban household, family values, Christianity, and consumerism. The stability of the home and the nuclear family was equated with the security of the nation in Hollywood wartime melodramas, and the threat of fascism was depicted as a threat to the integrity of marriage. Hollywood home front films obliquely acknowledged that internal class and racial tensions posed another threat to the domestic order and worked to defuse these tensions.

In contrast, my analysis of the Nazi home front melodramas *Auf Wiedersehen, Franziska* and *Die große Liebe* demonstrates that the main conflict treated in these films was between the sexes rather than between the ideologies of the warring nations. Unlike their Hollywood counterparts, Nazi home front films did not posit stable familial relations as the precondition for victory. Instead, domesticity is imagined as an impediment to war aims in Nazi films rather than a support for military men. While Hollywood home front melodramas argued that sexual sublimation was necessary for the war effort, Nazi home front films suggested that the acquisition of foreign territories through war enabled a beneficial liberation from repression for the fascist man. Symptomatically, the home is not a stable location in most Nazi home front films. Unlike Hollywood melodramas that pictured the suburban house and church as the core locations of national community, Nazi films presented the communal experiences of theatrical performance and media reception as the prime generators of consensus. Instead of the Hollywood promise of expanded possibilities for the consumption of consumer goods after the war, Nazi home front films promised cultural and erotic domination. Meanwhile, the collapsing of battle into romance in the Nazi home front melodrama served to trivialize warfare and disavow the consequences of violence.

Nazi Security Service reports suggested that spectators may have taken the message of Nazi wartime melodramas even more to heart than the regime anticipated, and that imperious and hedonistic behavior by German soldiers and civilians was viewed as a potential threat to the military hierarchy toward the end of the war. There was a sense among the authorities that Nazi media's production of eroticism was backfiring among German women, who were supposedly engaging in relationships with foreigners to an alarming degree. There is some evidence that the regime began to backtrack on cultural policy late in the war and became more cautious about the depiction of extramarital relations in film projects due to concerns about soldiers' morale, yet the attitude toward marriage and nuclear family domesticity remained ambivalent even in the Reich's final years. The cultural shift from the end of the Third Reich to the restored view of domesticity in postwar West and East German melodrama is the subject of the epilogue that follows.

Epilogue

Reprivatization after Nazi Cinema:
Postwar German Melodrama

In spring 1944, as the Reich was preparing for total war and nervously anticipating the Allied invasion, stories of Wehrmacht officers' lavish lifestyles in occupied territories circulated among the German home front populace, disillusioning many who believed in the mythic power of an ordered and unified *Volksgemeinschaft*. The Nazi "deployment of sexuality" was backfiring on several fronts, and the libidinal, cinematic weapon of war was faulted as a failed technology. In Security Service reports the regime's spies shifted responsibility for military defeat away from the Nazi leadership's imperialist fantasies of mass destruction and toward the supposed destruction caused by excessive sexuality, which the Nazi cinema itself had seemingly produced. Not surprisingly, it was female sexuality that received the brunt of the blame for what was perceived as an abrupt decay in moral standards—defined exclusively in terms of sexual behaviors rather than militarist violence and genocide.

The Security Service raised an urgent alarm in April 1944 about a general outbreak of what it termed the widespread "tendencies toward excessive sexual behavior without responsibility to the community."[1] Wartime conditions had facilitated a complete breakdown in the restraint of German women, the SD agents claimed:

> To a much larger extent than during the First World War, women in the present war have been released from their peacetime life order . . . there are coinciding reports from all areas of the Reich that confirm that it is no longer a matter of isolated phenomena, but rather that a large proportion of women and girls are inclined to live it up sexually to an ever stronger degree. This is primarily noticeably with soldiers' wives. There are reportedly widely known locations in many cities where soldiers' wives go to meet men and to accompany them

home. While their mothers carry on in this way, the children are often left on their own and at the risk of utter neglect.[2]

The message that Nazi militarist culture promoted and facilitated the satisfaction of desires unavailable in peacetime bourgeois society had apparently been received by the female audiences of Nazi films. The SD, overlooking the instrumentality of such messages, directly blamed the Nazi cinema along with other forms of mass culture for what it called the "eroticization of public life" in the Third Reich, an eroticization that had given way to what the Security Service depicted as a widespread and detrimental license that was undermining wartime unity.

As a remedy the SD recommended a complete departure from Nazi cinema's previous gender representations:

> The original values of the German woman should be discussed and emphasized much more in the press, radio and film than they have been up until now. It is not sufficient that books—which are not read by the majority of the population and can no longer be purchased even by those interested—speak of the woman as the "defender of morality," "guardian of life," etc., while films, pop songs, short stories and the illustrated press (joke sections of newspapers, fashion magazines) cultivate the type of the erotic woman who enchants all men.[3]

Apparently this advice was not heeded at the Propaganda Ministry. As we have seen throughout this book, the "erotic woman" was an indispensable element of Nazi cinema's attractions, the basic tool of its ideological and financial goals, and the primary interest of Nazi melodramas. Nazi revue films may have offered the most concentrated provocations of desire with their physical displays and fetishism of the exposed female body, but melodrama transformed these erotic provocations into models for living, moving from iconic image to narrative. And Nazi melodramas, far from offering narratives championing housewives as revered family nurturers and guardians of private life in the manner of classical Hollywood melodrama, continued instead to cultivate the eroticization of the Third Reich public sphere even as it was collapsing.

A few months after the SD circulated its warning, prints of Veit Harlan's domestic melodrama *Opfergang* were delivered to cinemas in the Reich and abroad. The film was enthusiastically received by spectators, and due to its enticing thematization of extramarital relations and its exploration of "natural" eroticism in luxurious settings, it achieved a box office triumph over Hollywood films in some foreign markets.[4] As the Reich general film director noted in a memo to Goebbels on the foreign reception of the film, *Opfergang* was derisively called a "carnival orgy" by a leading film critic in Switzerland, but the melodrama was nonetheless received with enormous popular success in that country.[5] *Opfergang,* perhaps the most paradigmatic Nazi melodrama, narratively dissolved bourgeois domesticity by throwing open the confining windows of tradition, reveling in a sexual masquerade, and ending in hallucinatory eroticized death. The eruptions of stylistic and erotic excess in the film reached a climax in *Opfergang'*s masked ball sequence. Here, as chaotic groups of masquerading women reverse the conventional order of sexual aggression, suggestions of lesbianism are phantasmagorically multiplied. Control over vision and narrative logic threatens to break apart completely under the riot of garish colored lighting, a mise-en-scène dominated by a slide in the shape of a giant clown's tongue, a sound track with dizzying music and the delighted shrieks of female revelry, along with highly disorienting editing. The two blondes in riding gear who wordlessly follow the romantic hero Albrecht at the bar stare at him intensely out of masked blue eyes, move in a synchronized and mechanical manner, and thus seem to be the extreme incarnation of Nazi melodrama's fantasy women. This vision is interrupted by a shot of text dissolving over Albrecht's masked face as his mistress Aels's voice is heard on the sound track: "In the night, the souls are more connected than during the day. Or is it only my desire that is lying to me?" This sequence, ambiguously marked as a possible subjective vision of either the hero or the heroine of the romance, is never securely fixed as the vision of either, and the question of exactly whose fantasy this filmic text may be remains indeterminate. It was a threatening scene, one that another Swiss critic described as being "quoted straight from hell."[6]

The hellishness of the melodrama for the male viewer, we can be sure, arose from the collapse of narrative certainty under the image of female desire. Melodramatic excess was an unintentional by-product of Nazi cinema's attempts to create a uniquely successful German film art and of the inability to completely manage the representation of sexuality and spectator desire within classical cinematic conventions. The occasional failure of this management was evidenced by dissenting viewers and their objections to the sexual morality of Nazi films. Toward the end of the war the Security Service took up this dissent and applied it to an explanation of why the Nazis were losing the war. Much like at the end of the First World War, excessive female sexuality was finally blamed for undermining morale and destroying the unity of the *Volksgemeinschaft.* This time, however, the production of sexuality could no longer be attributed to imaginary enemies of a true German culture. The Nazis had fulfilled their own desires in their cinema and their mass destructions.

The late conviction that the "true nature" of the German woman had not been sufficiently realized in Nazi culture prepared the ground for the renewed postwar cultivation of domesticity and feminine nurturance in West Germany. The return to private life and to puritanical mores in the Adenauer era was partly a response to the attack on "bourgeois" sexual morality that had been carried out by the mass culture of the Third Reich. According to Dagmar Herzog, many historians since the 1960s have inaccurately described the Third Reich as prudish and preoccupied with petty bourgeois family values; thus they have failed to fully grasp the extent to which the sexually repressive climate of the 1950s was not a continuation of Nazi culture but rather an attempt to master the fascist past. As Herzog has commented: "One powerful initial impetus for sexual conservatism in postwar Germany lay in the fact that incitement to sexual activity and pleasure had been a major feature of National Socialism. Turning against nudity and licentiousness in the early 1950s, especially in the name of Christianity, could, quite legitimately and fairly, be represented and understood as a turn against Nazism."[7] Although they may have implicitly understood that the promise of new freedoms and pleasures had provided the Nazis with popular support and an incentive for German men and women to participate in the regime's imperialist and genocidal missions, Adenauer-era conservatives also insisted on a reinstatement of Christian sexual morality as a means of repressing the past. Instead of investing most of their energies in pursuing Nazi war criminals and probing the German conscience about its responsibility for the Holocaust, postwar Christians battled against pornography, homosexuality, and extramarital heterosexuality, thereby displacing efforts to "clean up" German culture from the political to the private sphere.

This "reprivatization" and newly conservative culture left its mark on West German melodramas of the 1950s.[8] The objections of pre-1945 spectators to the Nazi cinema's apparent distaste for domestic and rural settings cleared the way for a postwar retreat into the mountains of the *Heimatfilm*, the most characteristic Adenauer-era melodramatic genre. Here, in Agfacolor daydreams of rural German landscapes untouched by the destruction of carpet-bombing, conventional gender roles and repressive sexual norms were visibly reinstated. As Johannes von Moltke has asserted, the prevalence of the *Heimatfilm* in the 1950s is indicative of "the decade's obsession with domesticity," according to which the image of "home" received new value as a "place of retreat, the realm of privacy, and a key site for the enforcement of outdated gender norms."[9] The popular authority of the church, previously embattled by Nazi secularism, was also reinforced after the war and reappeared on the cinema screen in the 1950s *Heimatfilm* in the form of venerated village priests and copious religious symbols. Accordingly, monogamous marriage once again became the normative ideal and preferred resolution of postwar melodrama's narrative trajectories. As von Moltke has further noted, the "trope of marriage" was central to the 1950s *Heimatfilm* and functioned as the prime figure of "harmony and compromise."[10] West German filmmakers who worked in other postwar melodramatic genres were similarly interested in rebuilding the image of the harmonious German home, though nuclear family unity was to be achieved more through repressive means than through compromise.

Opfergang's director, Veit Harlan, like most Third Reich filmmakers, survived both the war and the halfhearted American de-Nazification measures and continued to make melodramas throughout the 1950s. His postwar films, although produced with the same personnel as his Nazi features, also evidenced some cultural shifts from the Third Reich to the Adenauer-era cinema. After being accused and subsequently acquitted of crimes against humanity for making the notorious anti-Semitic melodrama *Jud Süss,* Harlan redirected his defamatory attacks from Jews to homosexuals in his 1957 film *Anders als du und ich/Das dritte Geschlecht* (*Different from Me and You/ The Third Sex*). Harlan's postwar filmmaking and the public response to it were both paradigmatic for the Adenauer-era tendency to displace guilt for Germany's anti-Semitic genocide onto an obsession with sexual "decency." While the public disapproval of his Nazi past was relatively limited, Harlan did encounter opposition to the sexual content of his early postwar films. Harlan's 1951 melodrama, *Hanna Amon,* was originally scripted as the story of an incestuous love affair between a brother and a sister, thus replaying one of Harlan's favorite Nazi-era themes, but this narrative did not conform to the new climate of conservative sexual morality in the early years of the Federal Republic. As Harlan's wife and lead actress, Kristina Söderbaum, related in her memoir, Harlan's distributor demanded changes to the content of *Hanna Amon*'s script following the hostile reactions to Hildegard Knef's nude scene in *Die Sünderin* (*The Sinner,* 1951) earlier that year: "There were riots in all German cities about this film. The Catholic Church denounced it and the activist group 'Clean Screen' called for a boycott . . . [Our] script had to be rewritten and the material toned down . . . All allusions to a possible brother-sister love were eliminated, and all that remained was the act of Hanna Amon, who killed a woman because she considered her incapable of managing the farm according to the wishes of her parents."[11] Incestuous desire and *Opfergang*-style eroticized death had become unacceptable content for early Adenauer-era melodramas. Murder for the sake of private property and family legacy, on the other hand, was apparently more comprehensible for conservative postwar audiences.

With the return to influence of the Catholic Church came a reinstatement of domesticity, a revaluation of the nuclear family as normative, and a newly puritanical concept of sexual decency. Harlan followed the spirit of the times with his 1958 family melodrama, *Ich werde dich auf Händen tragen* (*I'll Carry You On My Hands*). Starring Kristina Söderbaum once again, the film moves in exactly the opposite direction as *Opfergang*: from a beach to a bourgeois interior. The 1958 film thus reversed the Third Reich melodrama's effort to flee the domestic sphere in favor of the fantasized spaces of overseas empires. In the postwar melodrama, Söderbaum plays a single woman who has been disappointed by her past temporary lovers and the lies born of male passion and consents to marry a Tyrolean widower and antiques dealer (thus a man who represents exactly the sort of tradition-bound lifestyle that so many Third Reich films denounced as "philistine"). The heroine then leaves the north German coast (the scene of *Opfergang*'s finale) and spends most of the rest of the film indoors, very much unlike Söderbaum's militaristically horse-riding character in her 1944 melodrama. When she arrives in her new home, the heroine finds her new husband's daughter, a boyish child with an angry spirit, and a portrait of the child's dead mother above the fireplace. The ensuing family tensions are subsequently resolved by the husband in a different manner than in most Third Reich melodramas: instead of smashing the antiques, slashing the maternal portrait, and divorcing the child like the industrial dictator hero of Harlan's 1937 (anti-)family melodrama, *Der Herrscher,* the male protagonist of this postwar Harlan melodrama works on pacifying and unifying the family. Characteristically, however, the reconstitution of the nuclear family is achieved with the help of a Catholic priest who preaches a repressive ethic of female masochism. After the widower's daughter runs away from home, the priest escorts the masculine girl back to the house and tells her (as if conveying a programmatic message to all German women in the audience): "With every blow, guilt will be removed from you . . . If you get beaten now, then you just clench your teeth and you take it." By the end of the film, the daughter has finally been chastised and the wife entirely de-eroticized.

The stylistic excesses of the Nazi melodrama *Opfergang* give way here to a more domesticated sentimentality. In the final scene of *Ich werde dich auf Händen tragen,* Söderbaum's character is once again shown lying in bed with the same weak pallor as at the end of her 1944 melodrama, but instead of an orgasmic death, a shot of two newborn babies in a crib follows the close-up of the heroine in bed. Her now conventionally feminine stepdaughter then begs for forgiveness, trumpets on the sound track proclaim the restoration of a peaceful order, and a gate opens to reveal an exterior shot of a carefully tended garden outside the secure home—in direct opposition to the ocean of *eros* and *thanatos* onto which *Opfergang*'s final gates opened. The bourgeois domesticity and nuclear family conventions that had been assaulted twenty years earlier by the Nazi melodrama *Der Herrscher* were now reborn in the Adenauer-era cinema, reproduced by the very same fascist filmmaker.

The conservative restoration characteristic of the West German melodrama of the 1950s applied to some extent to the cinema of East Germany as well, in accordance with a similar return to conventional sexual morality in the German Democratic Republic (GDR). As Dagmar Herzog has argued, there was a "turn toward a socialist variant of sexual conservatism" in the 1950s and 1960s in East Germany, with repressive tendencies that had "part Stalinist, part ex-Nazi, part petty bourgeois" origins.[12] However, the prudish culture of the first fifteen to twenty years of the GDR did not accompany the same overvaluation of traditional nuclear family domesticity in East German cinema as in West German cinema of the same era. In many respects, East German filmmakers responded to the legacy of Nazi cinema in a different manner than West German filmmakers, most obviously through the overt antifascist rhetoric of East German films. In opposition to the popularity of the *Heimatfilm* and other melodramatic genres in the West in the 1950s, the East German state-owned film industry Deutsche Film AG (DEFA) did not find melodrama to be as amenable to the socialist project. Although nationalistic pathos was certainly a characteristic feature of Stalinist cinema, the socialist master narrative of rational progress through the historical dialectic did not conform easily with melodrama's fatalism and circularity, and the positive hero mandated by socialist realism was most often embodied by male characters.[13] Melodramatic women's pictures were not common among DEFA films of the 1940s to 1950s,[14] and the few melodramas approximating this genre showed that the tension between the public and private spheres was reconciled differently in the East German cinema than in both Third Reich and Adenauer-era melodramas.

The first DEFA production, *Die Mörder sind unter uns* (*The Murderers Are Among Us,* 1946), could be considered a domestic melodrama, though the main question posed by the film concerns the postwar treatment of Nazi war criminals. Directed by another former employee of the Nazi film industry, Wolfgang Staudte, *Die Mörder sind unter uns* did suggest—somewhat like Harlan's *Ich werde dich auf Händen tragen*—that German guilt could be redeemed through feminine nurturance, and it also reveals the initial postwar longing for a return to a harmonious domestic sphere. Starring Hildegard Knef as a former concentration camp inmate who returns to Berlin in 1945, falls in love with a former Wehrmacht soldier, and heals him of his posttraumatic stress disorder by reestablishing an orderly domesticity, Staudte's film hints at a restoration of traditional gender roles. Ultimately, however, this film does not endorse the same reprivatization as West German melodramas. Rather than ending in an idealized image of a reconstituted nuclear family, the final sequence of the film calls on spectators to recognize the victims of war crimes and to bring the guilty to justice. As Hester Baer has argued, the gender politics in *Die Mörder sind unter uns* are not entirely conventional, since the film posits an active and productive female gaze, even while demonstrating in conservative fashion how nurturing women could help restore the damaged postwar male subjectivity. At the end of the film the female protagonist does not surrender entirely to domesticity, but retains her work as a graphic designer of political posters, and thus the film, in Baer's estimation, "fails to attain the kind of closure that would ensure the restoration of traditional gender ideology."[15] In its optimistic (though admittedly problematic) vision of a realigned gender dynamic in the Soviet sector, *Die Mörder sind unter uns* appears to be a response to Nazi melodramas like *Die vier Gesellen* (see chapter 2), which cynically demonstrated the necessary capitulation of women to marriage as a primarily economic institution. Bearing a strong resemblance to Ingrid Bergman's graphic designer character in *Die vier Gesellen,* Hildegard Knef's character seems to overcome (or repress) the Third Reich woman's forced subjection to gender inequality as she speaks with glowing eyes about returning to the socially useful work of reconstruction. *Die Mörder sind unter uns* thus corresponds to the utopian, future-directed orientation of socialism and its stress on female participation in the labor force.

A few other DEFA melodramas of the immediate postwar period demonstrate the difficulty in reconciling the private realm of emotion with the project of building a postwar public sphere in a Marxist country. Joshua Feinstein has noted that the topics of love and sexuality presented continual challenges for film directors of the East German film industry; at the same time that DEFA films were often faulted by critics and officials for lacking in emotion, the leaders of the regime discouraged scenes that might arouse erotic feelings. As Feinstein asserts in reference to the censoring of nude bathing and carnival scenes in Slatan Dudow's 1959 film *Verwirrung der Liebe* (*Love's Confusion*), "Above all, officials objected to the film's sensuality, which they perceived to be a threat to socialist morality."[16] The fear of sensuality among the GDR leadership, as Dagmar Herzog has argued, arose from the suspicion that indulgence in private pleasures might depoliticize the populace and turn it away from socialism.[17] Even marriages were often depicted as relatively chaste in DEFA films of the 1950s, and romantic relations sometimes appear as an impediment to the construction of a collectivist society. In *Roman einer jungen Ehe* (*Story of a Young Couple,* 1952), a troubled

marriage serves as a metaphor for Cold War ideological divisions, with the
female partner representing socialist virtue and the male partner the moral
decay of the West (also embodied by the character of an ex-Nazi West German film director, a thinly veiled representation of Veit Harlan). Dudow's
Frauenschicksale (*Destinies of Women,* 1952), in which a West Berlin playboy
seduces a series of young women and drives one to commit murder, equates
erotic desire to capitalistic materialism and aggression, and all of these are
coded as manifestations of Western degeneracy. By the end of the film each
of the female protagonists has managed to extricate herself from her affective
snare by relocating to the more "rational" East and by becoming a productive worker in the new, forward-looking socialist society.[18] In such films the
East German cinema's rhetoric of reconstruction and progress echoes some
aspects of the fascist modernization project, and its problematization of the
private sphere may also recall some aspects of Nazi melodrama. But DEFA
differed fundamentally from Nazi cinema in its refusal to eroticize violence,
and it differed from Adenauer-era cinema in its refusal to relegate women
to a subordinate and predominantly familial role.

Conclusion

Film melodramas of the Third Reich, as I have argued throughout this book,
reflect the generally embattled status of domesticity under German fascism.
Unlike classical Hollywood melodramas, which aimed to bolster the ideological norms of the middle-class nuclear family and Christian sexual morality,
Nazi melodramas appealed to viewers with deceptive discourses of liberation
from conventional sexual morals and familial structures. Instead of engaging
the rhetoric of a return to tradition, Nazi cinema promoted images of a fascist
cultural modernity, a nonetheless reactionary modernization that aimed to
advance the militarist and genocidal goals of the Third Reich rather than
the emancipation of its citizens. Repeatedly invoking images of a repressive
nineteenth- and early twentieth-century past, Third Reich melodramas not
only described bourgeois morality as antithetical to a wartime fascist order
and to Germany's planned colonialist future but also presented Nazism as a
youthful rebellion against philistinism. Film melodrama thus constituted a
key battleground in German fascism's multiple projects of modernization,
militarization, and the dissolution of the private sphere.

As an imperialist regime, the leaders of the Nazi state intended to push
beyond the walls of the home, to expand the borders of the Reich abroad,
and to induct German citizens into a greater servitude to the fascist nation.
Romance melodramas, as we have seen, supported this goal by training

audiences in lifestyle choices and character traits that corresponded to Nazism's colonialist aspirations. These included seemingly modernized gender roles, even extending to heroines who strive for higher education and work in traditionally male-dominated professions. Yet the goal of such narratives was not to achieve greater gender equality and genuinely liberatory modernization, but to serve the pragmatic needs of an imperialist economy by increasing the wartime labor pool and redefining the feminine role as a subordinate and self-sacrificial one within the workplace, as much as it had been previously in the home. Similarly, Nazi cinema's ostensibly progressive defense of single motherhood disguised a much more regressive goal: to shift the responsibility for reproduction to women alone. Since familial demands stood in conflict with industrial productivity in the fascist imagination and women were viewed as holding too much authority in the bourgeois home, many Third Reich domestic melodramas called the legitimacy of monogamous marriage into question and argued for a departure from conventional family structures. Breaking with genre conventions as well, the stability of the family was not equated with the stability of the nation in most Nazi melodramas. In contrast to the claim of Hollywood's wartime melodramas that the war was being fought in defense of middle-class domesticity, Christianity, and nuclear family values, Nazi home front films suggested that greater pleasures were to be found in a more risk-filled life beyond quotidian, civilian existence.

Outside the home and in conquered territories, Nazi films promised, lay the possibility of intensified erotic experience. With conscious calculation, Goebbels's Propaganda Ministry planned for eroticized imagery and narratives to fulfill a political function, both by inciting spectators to militarist action and by distracting them from the destructive consequences of fascist rule. Film melodrama, as a mode concerned primarily with the realm of emotion and sexual relations, played a key role in this incitement by affectively binding spectators to the Reich. Since Nazi films offered sexual content that exceeded the more restrictive codes of Hollywood films, spectators were invited to view German fascism as a system that allowed for the expression of elemental drives. Violent feelings in particular were elicited from viewers, as Nazi melodramas were structured to appeal to a more intense form of sadistic voyeurism than comparable Hollywood melodramas. Lacking a firm concept of genres as gendered, Third Reich filmmakers oriented melodramas, conventionally considered "women's pictures" within Hollywood cinema, toward male spectators as well. Nazism's perverse imagination, as it was reflected in the melodramas of the Third Reich, thus centered on male-oriented fantasies of polygamy, incest, and sexual power over colonized peoples and coerced partners.

Although Nazi melodramas were highly popular with both foreign and domestic audiences, the evidence of spectator response presented in this book proves that some viewers reacted negatively to such appeals. As much as Goebbels endeavored to engineer uniform spectatorship through vigilant control over each film's relative dosage of melodramatic affect while attempting to contain the threat inherent in stylistic excess, absolute control over spectator response was never entirely achieved, and the goals of the Ministry of Propaganda often stood in conflict with the interests of female, rural, and Catholic viewers in particular. Security Service reports demonstrate that the domestic realm proved to be a continual source of problems for a regime fixated on homogeneity: the disinclination of many German women to support the war in the expected manner or to conform to the Third Reich's population policies, the resistance of conservative and rural populations to cultural products that reflected urban and secular attitudes, and the bitterness of the lower classes about their own exploitation in wartime work and military service all gave the Nazi authorities cause for concern. The pseudo-emancipatory appeals of Nazi culture, which promised liberation from the strictures of (petit) bourgeois morality, were intended primarily for the upper strata of male members of the Reich; all others in the supposedly unified *Volksgemeinschaft* were to serve the interests of the political, military, and corporate leadership. But the desires of many segments of the population did not entirely conform to the regime's narratives of liberation through servitude outside of the home.

After the defeat of the Third Reich many Germans wished to retreat to a more orderly private sphere. In the East this desire was quickly subsumed under the ideological imperative to focus on the building of a socialist society, and private pleasures were generally neglected in the DEFA cinema until the 1970s. In the West, Nazi cinema's incitements to colonialist fantasies gave way to the more domesticated consumerist and touristic attractions of Adenauer-era cinema. A decade later the reprivatization of the immediate postwar period in West Germany was in turn viewed as problematic by many members of the younger generation. The restitution of domesticity in the West German culture of the 1950s was followed by a renewed rejection of bourgeois morality in the critical theory and protest movements of the late 1960s, as the sexual revolution in West Germany gave rise to a process of liberalization or "sexual evolution" in the East as well.[19] Younger West Germans who had grown up in the repressive environment of the Adenauer era and later began to excavate the guilt of their parents' generation for the crimes of the Third Reich often misrecognized the connection between bourgeois morality and Nazism, aided by Freudian interpretations of the fascist persona. Assuming that the 1950s obsession with sexual propriety was simply an unbroken continuation of Nazi culture and that petty bourgeois family values underpinned Nazi convictions, many leftist West Germans of the 1960s and '70s equated an anti-puritanical stance with an antifascist position.[20] Yet, as this investigation of film melodrama under German fascism has demonstrated, the attack on puritanical sexual morality was very much at the core of Nazi culture's appeals. Genuine sexual equality within both the private and public spheres and the decolonization of the erotic imagination, on the other hand, may legitimately be considered antifascist values.

Notes

Introduction. Melodrama in the Nazi Cinema

1. Mulvey, *Fetishism and Curiosity,* 29.

2. Marcuse, *Technology, War, and Fascism,* 161.

3. Brooks, *Melodramatic Imagination,* 5.

4. Cook, "Melodrama and the Woman's Picture," 249.

5. Cawelti, "Evolution of the Social Melodrama," 33.

6. Ibid., 34.

7. Boberach, *Meldungen aus dem Reich,* 6:1812.

8. The Security Service reported in January 1941 that *Die ewige Jude* was being badly received by audiences, and that both male and female spectators had fainted during the butcher scene. Ibid., 6:1918–1919.

9. Schulte-Sasse, *Entertaining the Third Reich,* 4.

10. Ibid.

11. See, for example, Lang, *American Film Melodrama,* 3–13; and Elsaesser, "Tales of Sound and Fury," 182–88.

12. Landy, *Imitations of Life,* 20. See also Landy, *Fascism in Film,* 276–329.

13. Cook, "Melodrama and the Woman's Picture," 251.

14. On the issue of excess and subversion, see Christine Gledhill, "The Melodramatic Field," in Gledhill, *Home Is Where the Heart Is,* 6–12; and Thompson, "The Concept of Cinematic Excess." For research suggesting that female spectators identify with the transgressive moments of woman's films more than their patriarchal narrative resolutions, see Jackie Stacey, *Star Gazing.*

15. See, for example, Landy, *Imitations of Life,* 16.

16. Brooks, *Melodramatic Imagination.*

17. On the melodrama and the woman's film, see Gledhill, "Melodramatic Field," 10–11.

18. See Mulvey, *Visual and Other Pleasures,* 41–47.

19. My definition of melodrama is partially adapted from Astrid Pohl's usefully concise definition in *TränenReiche BürgerTräume,* 39–40.

20. Griffin, *Modernism and Fascism*; and Griffin, *A Fascist Century*. For related accounts of fascism and modernity, see Ben-Ghiat, *Fascist Modernities*; Herf, *Reactionary Modernism*; and Payne, "Fascism as 'Generic' Concept."

21. On the hegemonic aims of Nazi cinema and the response to Nazi films abroad, see Welch, *Cinema and the Swastika*.

22. Herzog, *Sexuality and German Fascism*; and Herzog, *Sex after Fascism*.

23. See Welch, *Propaganda and the German Cinema, 1933–1945*; and Leiser, *Nazi Cinema*.

24. In addition to Schulte-Sasse's *Entertaining the Third Reich*, see Rentschler, *Ministry of Illusion*; Koepnick, *Dark Mirror*; Hake, *Popular Cinema of the Third Reich*; and Petro, "Nazi Cinema at the Intersection of the Classical and the Popular."

25. See Ascheid, *Hitler's Heroines*; Carter, *Dietrich's Ghosts*; and Bruns, *Nazi Cinema's New Women*.

26. For shorter studies that do offer comparative analyses, see Eder, "Das Populäre Kino im Krieg," 379–416; Rentschler, "Hollywood Made in Germany: *Lucky Kids*," in *Ministry of Illusion*, 99–122; and Witte, "Visual Pleasure Inhibited."

27. Sontag, "Fascinating Fascism," 91.

28. Sabine Hake describes the style of Third Reich genre films similarly: "they might be described as an impoverished, derivative version of the Hollywood original." Hake, *Popular Cinema of the Third Reich*, 12.

29. In contrast to my argument, Astrid Pohl asserts in her study on Nazi melodramas that they fall into the two categories of "affirmation and subversion," but that the vast majority were affirmative of bourgeois culture. Pohl, *TränenReiche BürgerTräume*, 283.

30. Rentschler, *Ministry of Illusion*, 218; and Witte, "Ästhetische Opposition?"

31. See, particularly, Rentschler, *Ministry of Illusion*, 125–45; Lowry, *Pathos und Politik*; and Jameson, *Political Unconscious*, 286–87.

32. Barthes, *Mythologies*, 84.

33. O'Brien, *Nazi Cinema as Enchantment*.

34. Schulte-Sasse, *Entertaining the Third Reich*, 9.

35. See, particularly, Schulte-Sasse, *Entertaining the Third Reich*; Rentschler, *Ministry of Illusion*; and O'Brien, *Nazi Cinema as Enchantment*, for their focus on pleasure and the utopian appeals of Nazi cinema.

36. Sontag, "Fascinating Fascism," 93.

37. See, for example, Davidson, "Cleavage: Sex in the Total Cinema of the Third Reich"; and Gordon, "Fascism and the Female Form."

38. Herzog, "Hubris and Hypocrisy, Incitement and Disavowal: Sexuality and German Fascism," in *Sexuality and German Fascism*, 3.

39. Foucault, *History of Sexuality*, 1:150. My argument also departs from George Mosse's understanding of Nazi aesthetics as "beauty without sensuality" and Nazi culture as upholding bourgeois notions of "respectability." Mosse, *Fascist Revolution*, 183–97; and Mosse, *Nationalism and Sexuality*, 153–80.

40. On the relationship between contemporary American right-wing politics and sexualized images of the Third Reich, see Slane, *Not So Foreign Affair*.

Chapter 1. Fascist Melodrama

1. Williams, "Melodrama Revised," 42.

2. One such response was to *Das Mädchen von Fanö* (*The Girl from Fanö*, 1941): "An overly complicated story about fishermen with a psychological backdrop . . . Dreadful literature!" Goebbels, *Die Tagebücher von Joseph Goebbels*, 440.

3. Schatz, "Family Melodrama," 154.

4. A more differentiated classification follows: 40 percent comedies, 30 percent melodramas, 7 percent action/adventure, 7 percent crime, 6 percent musicals, 3 percent war or military films, 0.06 percent feature documentaries, 0.05 percent explicit propaganda/ political films, 0.02 percent fantasy, and 6 percent drama or other. My assessment of the number of melodramas produced in the Third Reich is higher than that of Astrid Pohl, who counts 220 films with "dominant" or "significant" melodramatic elements, thus about 20 percent of the total production in the Third Reich. Pohl, *TränenReiche BürgerTräume*, 35. My calculations are based upon the genre categories given in Ulrich J. Klaus, *Deutsche Tonfilme, 1929–1945*. The following genre categories were counted as melodramas: *Artistenfilm, Arztroman, Eheroman, Eifersuchtsdrama, Familienroman, Frauenroman, Frauen- und Liebesroman, Frauenromanze, Frauentragödie, Heimatfilm, Heimatroman, Jugendroman, Jungmädchengeschichte, Jungmädchenroman, Kleinstadtroman, Künstlerroman, Liebesfilm, Liebesgeschichte, Liebesroman, Liebesromanze, Liebestragödie, Melodrama, Musikerroman, Psychologischer Film, Romanze, Russische Ballade, Sängerfilm, Schauspielerroman, Schicksalsroman, Sittenroman, Studentenroman, Traumspiel*, and *Volksstück*.

5. Klaus's categorization of genre admits only a very small number of explicit propaganda films, while in Gerd Albrecht's estimation, about 14 percent of Third Reich features were propaganda films. Albrecht, *Nationalsozialistische Filmpolitik*, 110.

6. Ibid., 102. One Third Reich work that offers vague genre categories (but also does not use the term "melodrama") is Koch and Braune, *Von deutscher Filmkunst*.

7. For genre taxonomies, see Bauer, *Deutscher Spielfilm Almanach, 1929–1950*; Klaus, *Deutsche Tonfilme, 1929–1945*; and Hobsch, *Film im "Dritten Reich."*

8. There were about 170 romance melodramas produced between 1933 and 1945; this number is based upon Klaus's genre classification and includes films listed as *Liebesroman, Romanze, Liebesgeschichte, Liebesfilm, Liebesdrama, Liebestragödie*, or *Liebesromanze*. About 25 productions are listed by Klaus as maternal or family melodramas (*Mutterroman/ Familienroman*).

9. Klaus lists about twenty-one films as *Heimat* films (*Deutsche Tonfilme*), while Pohl lists thirty-six (thus about 2–3 percent of total Third Reich production). Pohl, *TränenReiche BürgerTräume*, 373–74. In contrast, 20 percent of films produced in West Germany in the 1950s were *Heimat* films. Von Moltke, *No Place Like Home*, 22.

10. Doane, *Desire to Desire*, 38.

11. The Third Reich film closest to the Hollywood gothic melodrama would likely be *Verwehte Spuren* (*Covered Tracks*, 1938); however, here the suspicion of murder falls not on a family member, but on the police.

12. Modleski, *Loving with a Vengeance*. On the Hollywood gothic melodrama, see Doane, *Desire to Desire*, and Cavell, *Contesting Tears*.

13. Very few films of the Third Reich feature ghosts or other supernatural occurrences. Exceptions are *Das Schloß in Flandern* (*The Castle in Flanders*, 1936) and *Das Spuk im Schloß* (*The Ghost in the Castle*, 1945), the latter of which was never premiered.

14. Goebbels, diary entry of April 8, 1941, *Tagebücher, 1924–1945*, 4:1557.

15. On the centrality of melodrama for film theory since the late 1960s, see Laura Mulvey, "'It Will Be a Magnificent Obsession': The Melodrama's Role in the Development of Contemporary Film Theory," in Bratton, Cook, and Gledhill, *Melodrama: Stage, Picture, Screen,* 121–33.

16. Neale, *Genre and Hollywood,* 187. For more on the shifting definitions of melodrama, see Singer, *Melodrama and Modernity.*

17. Ibid., 194.

18. Moeller, *Der Filmminister,* 75.

19. See, for example, Goebbels's comments on the Hollywood film *The Good Earth* in his diary entry of January 15, 1941. Goebbels, *Die Tagebücher von Joseph Goebbels,* 4:468.

20. A characteristic review of *Mutterliebe* praised the melodrama for being more distressing than sentimental. It is a film, wrote the reviewer, "which distresses more than touches." Maraun, "Meisterklasse aus Wien. Der beste Film des Monats: 'Mutterliebe,'" 141.

21. Goebbels, "Dr. Goebbels's Speech at the Kaiserhof on March 28, 1933," 154.

22. Söderbaum, *Nichts bleibt immer so,* 183.

23. Pohl, *TränenReiche BürgerTräume,* 313–35.

24. Compulsory film screenings began at age ten for both genders. In a 1944 survey, A. U. Sander listed among the ten favorite films of BDM and HJ leaders *Der große König, Ohm Krüger, Stukas,* and *Kadetten.* Since almost twice as many girls responded to the survey as boys, this suggests that all of these war-related films were shown to the BDM as well as the HJ. Sander, *Jugend und Film,* 118. Elizabeth Prommer's postwar study also confirms that girls were shown war films in the compulsory screenings. Prommer, *Kinobesuch im Lebenslauf,* 209.

25. Quoted in Albrecht, *Nationalsozialistische Filmpolitik,* 80.

26. Ibid., 71.

27. Stahr, *Volksgemeinschaft vor der Leinwand?* 39–52.

28. Sander, *Jugend und Film,* 55.

29. Altenloh, *Zur Soziologie des Kinos,* 78–79.

30. Kracauer, "Little Shopgirls Go to the Movies," in *Mass Ornament,* 291–304.

31. Stahr, *Volksgemeinschaft vor der Leinwand?* 78–83.

32. Panofsky, "Was will das Publikum auf der Leinwand sehen?" n.p.

33. Thorp, *America at the Movies,* 5–8.

34. Hake, *Popular Cinema of the Third Reich,* 83.

35. "Sie weint im Kino," n.p.

36. On Mussolini and the "feminine" multitude, see Falasca-Zamponi, *Fascist Spectacle,* 23–25.

37. Adolph Hitler, *Mein Kampf* (Munich: Zentralverlag der NSDAP, 1939), 201.

38. Quoted in Lowry, *Pathos und Politik,* 204.

39. Schatz, "Family Melodrama," 149.

40. Witte, *Lachende Erben, Toller Tag,* 46.

41. Ibid., 48.

42. Cook, "Melodrama and the Woman's Picture," 256.

43. Hake, *Popular Cinema of the Third Reich,* 74.

44. Goebbels, diary entry of August 21, 1940, *Die Tagebücher von Joseph Goebbels,* 4:290.

45. Diary entry of February 16, 1940, ibid., 4:45.

46. Diary entry of October 10, 1940, ibid., 4:359.

47. Diary entry of March 12, 1940, ibid., 4:70.

48. Rentschler, *Ministry of Illusion*, 255.

49. One example was *Wir tanzen um die Welt* (*We're Dancing across the World*), which spectators reportedly found "kitschy." SD report of April 19, 1940, in Boberach, *Meldungen aus dem Reich*, 4:1024.

50. Goebbels, *Tagebücher, 1924–1945*, 4:1752.

51. Ibid., 4:1631.

52. SD report of June 8, 1942, in Boberach, *Meldungen aus dem Reich*, 10:3912. The original Italian title was *Ridi pagliaccio!* (1941).

53. Ibid.

54. Goebbels, diary entry of July 30, 1940, *Die Tagebücher von Joseph Goebbels*, 4:259.

55. BArch R 55 / 20001e, 41–42.

56. Werder, *Trugbild und Wirklichkeit*, 9.

57. Hake, *Popular Cinema of the Third Reich*, 172–88.

58. Rentschler, *Ministry of Illusion*, 216–17.

59. Bordwell, Staiger, and Thompson, *Classical Hollywood Cinema*, 3–7.

60. "Das Herz der Königin–ein Film ohne Schwenkaufnahmen," 175.

61. Carter, *Dietrich's Ghosts*, 73.

62. Brooks, *Melodramatic Imagination*, 56.

63. Films with full or partial female nudity that exceeded Hollywood Production Code standards included the following: *Olympia* (1938), *Verwehte Spuren* (*Covered Tracks*, 1938), *Das Unsterbliche Herz* (*The Immortal Heart*, 1939), *Umwege zum Glück* (*Detours to Happiness*, 1939), *Der Postmeister* (*The Postmaster*, 1940), *Kleider machen Leute* (*Clothes Make the Man*, 1940), *Jud Süss* (1940), *Die Kellnerin Anna* (*The Waitress Anna*, 1941), *Kitty und die Weltkonferenz* (*Kitty and the World Conference*, 1940), *Zwei in einer großen Stadt* (*Two in a Big City*, 1942), *Das Bad auf der Tenne* (*The Bath on the Threshing Floor*, 1943), *Liebespremiere* (*Premiere of Love*, 1943), *Opfergang* (*Sacrifice*, 1944), *Münchhausen* (1944), and *Es lebe die Liebe* (*Long Live Love*, 1944).

64. Oertel, *Filmspiegel*, 124.

65. Mulvey, "Visual Pleasure and Narrative Cinema," in *Visual and Other Pleasures*, 14–30.

66. Herzberg, "*Das Mädchen Irene*," n.p.

67. Goebbels, *Tagebücher, 1924–1945*, 3:992.

68. See the SD report of December 3, 1942, in Boberach, *Meldungen aus dem Reich*, 12:4528; and the report of April 1, 1943, in Boberach, *Meldungen aus dem Reich*, 13:5040.

69. Carter, *Dietrich's Ghosts*, 74.

70. Witte, *Lachende Erben, Toller Tag*, 42.

71. Sontag, "Fascinating Fascism," 91.

72. *Der Postmeister* was the third most popular film of 1940, after *Wunschkonzert* and *Jud Süss*. Rentschler, *Ministry of Illusion*, 250.

73. Betz, "*Der Postmeister*," n.p.

74. Goebbels, diary entry of March 24, 1940, *Die Tagebücher von Joseph Goebbels*, 4:86.

75. In his review of *Der Postmeister*, Hans-Walther Betz commented, "Many elements reference the individual style of Cukor's interpretation of *Camille*."

76. Goebbels, "Dr. Goebbels's Speech at the Kaiserhof on March 28, 1933," 154.

77. Cawelti, "Evolution of the Social Melodrama," 33.

78. *Anna Karenina* cost $1,152,000, equivalent to about 2,800,000 Reichsmark (RM). Martin Quigley, ed., *1935–1936 International Motion Picture Almanac* (New York: Quigley Publishing, 1935), 1015. The budget of *Anna Karenina* was thus about 250 percent higher than the budget of *Der Postmeister. Der Postmeister* cost 1,025,000 RM and earned 4,286,000 RM. Klaus, *Deutsche Tonfilme,* 11:120–21.

79. Schlüpmann, "Faschistische Trugbilder weiblicher Autonomie," 44.

80. Heinzlmeier, Menningen, and Schulz, *Die großen Stars des deutschen Kinos,* 43.

81. Klaus, *Deutsche Tonfilme,* 11:121.

82. Boberach, *Meldungen aus dem Reich,* 4:1169.

83. Ibid.

84. *Wunschkonzert* had about 8.4 million more viewers than *Der Postmeister.* Rentschler, *Ministry of Illusion,* 250.

85. Schwark, "*Der Postmeister,*" n.p.

86. Betz, "*Der Postmeister.*"

87. Studlar, *In the Realm of Pleasure.*

88. Betz, "*Der Postmeister.*"

89. Volz, "Der beste Film des Monats: *Der Postmeister,*" 241.

90. Mulvey, "Visual Pleasure and Narrative Cinema," in *Visual and Other Pleasures,* 14–30.

91. Rodowick, "Madness, Authority, and Ideology in the Domestic Melodrama of the 1950s," 241.

Chapter 2. Romance Melodrama

1. Albrecht, *Nationalsozialistische Filmpolitik,* 139.

2. Doane, *Desire to Desire,* 96.

3. Albrecht, *Nationalsozialistische Filmpolitik,* 136.

4. As Sabine Hake has pointed out, race is the "absent marker" of Third Reich popular cinema and is usually visible only as a subtext but not as an explicit element of film narratives. Hake, *Popular Cinema of the Third Reich,* 14.

5. Goebbels, diary entry of April 10, 1937, *Tagebücher, 1924–1945,* 3:1064.

6. My argument differs from Karsten Witte's account in particular. In his study of Third Reich comedy, Witte claimed that the Nazis attempted to remove all eroticism from the cinema, which, he argued, led to the general ineffectiveness of Nazi propaganda films. Witte, *Lachende Erben, Toller Tag,* 123.

7. Haskell, *From Reverence to Rape,* 163–64. Haskell introduces a fourth category, "affliction films." This subgenre, which Mary Ann Doane takes up in her categorization as "medical discourse films," was generally missing in Nazi cinema. Doane, *Desire to Desire,* 35.

8. Quoted in Albrecht, *Nationalsozialistische Filmpolitik,* 186.

9. As Antje Ascheid has noted: "Capitalizing on actresses' foreign allure and exotic looks simply was the rule rather than the exception." Ascheid, *Hitler's Heroines,* 40.

10. Peter von Werder is one writer who criticized this discrepancy. His 1941 *Trugbild und Wirklichkeit* is an attack on Third Reich cinema's interest in "sex and luxury," its urban

milieus, and its responsiveness to audience tastes at the expense of blood-and-soil race consciousness. Werder, *Trugbild und Wirklichkeit*, 15.

11. See, for example, Petro, *Joyless Streets*, 221.

12. Heinzlmeier, Menningen, and Schulz, *Die großen Stars des deutschen Kinos*, 126.

13. Quoted in Moeller, *Der Filmminister*, 102.

14. "Schluß mit 'Gretchen'!" n.p.

15. Ibid.

16. Modleski, *Loving with a Vengeance*, 18.

17. Herzog, "Hubris and Hypocrisy, Incitement and Disavowal," in Herzog, *Sexuality and German Fascism*, 4.

18. Quoted in Katharina Sykora, "Heroische Seelenrevue: Die zehn Ufa-Filme mit Zarah Leander," in Töteberg, *Die große Liebe*, 4.

19. Drag dance numbers appeared in the following films: *Heißes Blut* (*Hot Blood*, 1936), *Und du, mein Schatz, fährst mit* (*And You, My Dear, Will Come Along*, 1937), *Die göttliche Jette* (*The Divine Jette*, 1937), and *Wir machen Musik* (*We Make Music*, 1942). More horse-riding and athletic tomboys could be found in *Ein ganzer Kerl* (*A Regular Fellow*, 1935), *Die Geierwally* (*Wally of the Vultures*, 1940), and *Opfergang* (*Sacrifice*, 1944).

20. Films in which women pass as men, either in a suit or in a military uniform, include the following: *Viktor und Viktoria* (*Viktor and Viktoria*, 1933), *Abschiedswalzer* (*Farewell Waltz*, 1934), *Schwarzer Jäger Johanna* (*Black Fighter Johanna*, 1934), *Das Mädchen Johanna* (*Joan of Arc*, 1935), *Capriccio* (1938), and *Trenck, der Pandur* (*Trenck, the Pandur*, 1940).

21. There is evidence that the gender styling of the Third Reich was too modern for some citizens. In 1940 anonymous protests against the masculinization of women were posted in Berlin streets. Goebbels ordered action against these protests in the following command: "The regional propaganda bureau will immediately have the notices removed which were posted in parts of Berlin and speak out in preposterous terms against the fashion of women's pants." RMVP minutes of June 22, 1940, BArch R 55 / 20001c.

22. Cited in Reich, "What Is Class Consciousness?" (1934), *Sex-Pol: Essays, 1929–1934*, 288.

23. Marcuse, *Technology, War, and Fascism*, 85–86.

24. Goebbels, diary entry of December 11, 1937, *Tagebücher, 1924–1945*, 3:1167.

25. Goebbels, diary entry of October 24, 1939, ibid., 3:1338.

26. October 12, 1942, letter from the Reichsfilmdramaturg Frank Maraun to the Reichsfilmintendant, BArch R 109 II/16.

27. The SD repeatedly recorded the comments of rural spectators who objected to the plentitude of urban high-society films, such as the following report in July 1940: "According to numerous reports, more and more people are objecting to the social milieu, the environment and lifestyle of many film narratives. It is said that the milieu of the 'C.E.O.' and the 'idle rich' is still too prominent." SD report of July 22, 1940, in Boberach, *Meldungen aus dem Reich*, 5:1405.

28. Offermanns, *Internationalität und europäischer Hegemonialanspruch des Spielfilms der NS-Zeit*, 94–95.

29. Memo from F. Maraun to Reichsfilmintendant, June 25, 1942, BArch R 109 II/18.

30. Memo from F. Maraun to Reichsfilmintendant, April 13, 1942, ibid.

31. "Erste Prüfaufnahmen der Bavaria," memo from F. Maraun, May 4, 1942, ibid.

32. Goebbels acknowledged this in a 1942 diary entry: "In the long run, we won't be able to avoid setting up a brothel quarter in the capital, just like in Hamburg, Nuremberg and other big cities. One cannot organize and govern a city of four million according to bourgeois-moralistic points of view." Bleuel, *Das saubere Reich,* 262. On the strategic use of prostitution by military authorities, see Annette F. Timm, "Sex with a Purpose: Prostitution, Venereal Disease, and Militarized Masculinity in the Third Reich," in Herzog, *Sexuality and German Fascism,* 223–55.

33. Werder, *Trugbild und Wirklichkeit,* 30.

34. Ibid.

35. See Sabine Hake, "Mapping the Native Body: on Africa and the Colonial Film in the Third Reich," in *The Imperialist Imagination,* edited by Friedrichsmeyer, Lennox and Zantop, 163–88.

36. As one indication of this double standard, a Third Reich draft of a law regulating relations between colonizer and colonized in future German territories in Africa mandated that sexual relations between a German woman and an African man should be punished by death, but not relations between a German man and an African woman. Schmokel, *Dream of Empire,* 171.

37. The Security Service reported on multiple occasions that non-Germanic men enjoyed continuing popularity with German women, and particularly that non-"Aryan" exchange students were considered highly attractive. On July 16, 1942, the SD reported, for example: "Now, as before, it is particularly conspicuous that foreign students in Hanover are very often seen in the company of German women, and in most cases, it is the German girls who are the more active party. They often positively chase the foreigners and show themselves to be easily accessible to particularly exotic types." Boberach, *Meldungen aus dem Reich,* 10:3960.

38. Volz, *Hans Söhnker: Zwischen Bühne und Film,* 28.

39. As Stephen Lowry points out in regard to "men's genres" in Nazi cinema, male characters in Nazi films rarely change over the course of the film and do not learn from experience: "Whether the hero wins or goes under in a grandiose manner does not seem to be so important; the main thing is that he believes firmly in his goal." Lowry, *Pathos und Politik,* 224.

40. Memo of April 13, 1942, BArch R 109 II/18.

41. The SPD suggested that Nazism was a gay movement in a 1931 press campaign. Schilling, *Schwule und Faschismus,*13. Wilhelm Reich also suggested an intrinsic connection between Nazism and homosexuality in his essay "What Is Class Consciousness?" *Sex-Pol: Essays, 1929–1934,* 275–332. Andrea Slane has perceptively detailed how this false logic persists among contemporary American conservatives who use homophobic rhetoric to suggest a link between progressivism and Nazism, and thus to style themselves in a irrational manner as antifascists. Slane, *Not So Foreign Affair,* 71–108.

42. See, for example, Maraun, "Der Held: die Gemeinschaft," 49.

43. According to the conventional pattern of both Victorian-era theatrical melodrama and the male-centered mythic literary romances of the pre-bourgeois era, the hero and heroine are located on one side of a dualistic moral structure and the villain on other, and the heroine becomes the reward for the hero's successful quest. On the romance, see Frye, *Anatomy of Criticism,*186–206.

44. Cook, "Melodrama and the Woman's Picture," 254.

45. Haskell, *From Reverence to Rape*, 150.

46. Marcuse, *Technology, War, and Fascism*, 142–43.

47. Haskell, *From Reverence to Rape*, 151.

48. Indeed, there is evidence that some female spectators actually responded negatively to images of successful career women in Nazi films because such lifestyles were essentially unattainable. In her study of young peoples' opinions about films they had seen, A. U. Sander recorded the response of a BDM girl who expressed discontent over the unrealistic career successes of female protagonists. Nazi girls lacked figures with whom they could identify, said the respondent: "It doesn't always have to be the film girls with their impossible luxury apartments in the city, with their fantastic careers, on elegant aristocratic estates, or in their love for dance, circus, cabaret or operetta." Sander, *Jugend und Film*, 133–34.

49. Koonz, *Mothers in the Fatherland*, 46.

50. Ibid., 209.

51. As Sabine Hake has pointed out, in Nazi cinema "unmarried women were primarily defined through their professional status." Hake, *Popular Cinema of the Third Reich*, 192.

52. For another example of the caricature of housewives, see the discussion of *Die göttliche Jette* in Bechdolf, *Wunsch-Bilder?* 56–68.

53. "Hofball in Leinigen: Von der Filmarbeit zu 'Heimat,'" n.p.

54. Quoted in Moeller, *Der Filmminister*, 191.

55. Usually these are glamorous positions in "feminine" industries such as fashion or the arts. Occasionally, female protagonists manage more masculine industries: *Die unmögliche Frau* (*The Impossible Woman*, 1936) features a female head of an oil company, and *Alles für Gloria* (*Everything for Gloria*, 1941) has a female director of a record company.

56. To cite a few examples: *Unser Fräulein Doktor*'s heroine is a professor of mathematics, and in *Ein Mann mit Grundsätzen* (*A Man with Principles*, 1943), the female protagonist is a doctoral candidate in chemistry. *Die Frau am Scheidewege* (*The Woman at the Crossroads*, 1938), *Parkstraße 13* (*Park Street Nr. 13*, 1939), *Damals* (*Back Then*, 1943), *Der gebieterische Ruf* (*The Higher Call*, 1944), and *Das Herz muss schweigen* (*The Heart Must Be Still*, 1944) feature female physicians or medical researchers as central protagonists. *Die schwarze Robe* (*The Black Robe*, 1944) concerns a female attorney, and *Ein Mädchen mit Prokura* (*A Girl with Power of Attorney*, 1934) also thematizes the legal profession. *Rivalen der Luft* (*Rivals in the Sky*, 1934) and *Capriolen* (1937) feature female pilots.

57. Female physicians were barred from receiving public health insurance payments in 1935. Koonz, *Mothers in the Fatherland*, 145.

58. Ibid., 206.

59. In addition to the above-cited medical doctors and law school graduates, a few other films feature women with or studying for advanced degrees. A supporting role in *Angelika* (1940) presents a female law student, and in *Die Frau ohne Bedeutung* (*A Woman of No Importance*), Marianne Hoppe plays a medical student specializing in sports medicine. A Fräulein Doktor appears in the 1935 melodrama *Liebe geht wohin sie will* (*Love Goes Where It Wants*), as well as in *Eine Frau wie Du* (see the discussion of this film later in the chapter).

60. Boberach, *Meldungen aus dem Reich*, 10:3957.

61. SD report of July 16, 1942, in ibid.

62. As many scholars of the Hollywood cinema have noted, the film noir functioned as a particular repository for such American anxieties. See Krutnik, *In a Lonely Street*, 57–72.

63. Hake, *Popular Cinema of the Third Reich*, 196.

64. "Frauenberufe auf der Leinwand," n.p.

65. Ibid.

66. "Frauenberufe, die der Film schuf," n.p. A further article called for films that would help both young men and women choose a profession: "Films should offer lively excerpts from the professional world. Since the borders between male and female professions are fluid, documentary films about careers should as a matter of principle show both men and women at work." Huth, "Filme für die Berufsauswahl," n.p. See also "Frauenarbeit im Filmspiegel," n.p.

67. "Schluß mit 'Gretchen'!" n.p.

68. Ibid. Emphasis in the original version.

69. In her obedience to the male lead doctor and willingness to experiment on human subjects, Hanna's character shows some of the same traits as the real Dr. Herta Oberheuser, convicted in 1947 at the Nuremberg trials for having tortured and conducted deadly experiments on at least sixty Polish girls. As Iris-Maria Nix has pointed out, Oberheuser's discipline and willingness to disregard moral concerns for the advancement of Nazi "science" ultimately benefited the careers of her male superiors. Nix, "Von der 'Fortpflanzungs'-zur 'Vernichtungsauslese,'" in Kuhn, *Frauenleben im NS-Alltag*, 276.

70. Spielhofer, "Filme des Monats," 75.

71. SD report of August 22, 1940, in Boberach, *Meldungen aus dem Reich*, 5:1493.

72. Herzog, *Sex after Fascism*, 9.

73. Timm, *Politics of Fertility in Twentieth-Century Berlin*, 162.

74. Ossowska, *Bourgeois Morality*, 17.

75. Ibid., 2.

76. Adorno, *Problems of Moral Philosophy*, 86.

77. Aschheim, *Nietzsche Legacy in Germany, 1890–1990*, 238.

78. Ibid.

79. Nietzsche, *Beyond Good and Evil*, 153–56.

80. The "Decree for the Fight against the Nudist Culture Movement" was passed on March 3, 1933. Bleuel, *Das saubere Reich*, 11.

81. Ibid., 281.

82. Goebbels, diary entry of February 3, 1939, *Tagebücher, 1924–1945*, 4:1305.

83. Diary entry of January 30, 1939, ibid., 4:1306.

84. Diary entry of November 21, 1935, ibid., 3:911.

85. Diary entry of November 23, 1935, ibid., 3:912. Goebbels also fought to loosen censorship standards for popular literature. In his diary entry of December 10, 1937, he noted: "Also sharply debated the issue of indecent literature that could 'overexcite' the youth. Easing up there too. No chastity commissions. The Führer speaks out strongly against moral hypocrisy." *Tagebücher, 1924–1945*, 3:1166.

86. See Kreimeier, *Ufa Story*, 158–72.

87. Bleuel, *Das saubere Reich*, 28–29.

88. Ibid.

89. Beyer, *Die Gesichter der Ufa*, 13.

90. Oertel, *Filmspiegel*, 123.

91. "Die Tänzerin im Atelier," 120.

92. Boberach, *Meldungen aus dem Reich*, 16:6463. Emphases in the original text.

93. *Die goldene Stadt, Münchhausen,* and *Das Bad auf der Tenne* were listed by the Reichsfilmintendant in 1944 as some of the most financially successful productions of the war years. *Die goldene Stadt* topped the list of the highest-grossing films from 1941 to 1944 with receipts totaling 12.5 million Reichsmark, *Münchhausen* was in tenth place at 8 million RM earnings, and *Das Bad auf der Tenne* tied for number seventeen at about 6 million RM. Memo Reichsfilmintendant Bacmeister to Reichsminister Goebbels, December 6, 1944, BArch R 109 II/14.

94. Lowry, *Pathos und Politik*, 95.

95. See SD report of July 17, 1941, in Boberach, *Meldungen aus dem Reich*, 7:2526. The report states that police actions were initiated against the writers of a church pamphlet advocating the *Josefsehe,* or celibate marriage.

96. Werder, *Trugbild und Wirklichkeit*, 28.

97. Doane, *Desire to Desire*, 104.

98. Ibid., 118.

99. Cook, "Melodrama and the Woman's Picture," 256.

100. Goebbels objected strongly to Wysbar's style in his 1936 film *Fährmann Maria,* and the director subsequently left for the United States. Goebbels, *Tagebücher, 1924–1945,* 3:921.

101. Sander, *Jugend und Film*, 134.

Chapter 3. Domestic Melodrama

1. The original German text of the joke was in the form of a rhyming poem: "Der nach russischer Art regiert, / Sein Haar nach französischer Mode frisiert, / Sein Schnurrbart nach englischer Art geschoren, / Und selbst [nicht] in Deutschland geboren, / Der uns den römischen Gruß gelehrt, / Von unseren Frauen viele Kinder begehrt, / Und selbst keine erzeugen kann, / Das ist in Deutschland der führende Mann." SD report of August 2, 1943, in Boberach, *Meldungen aus dem Reich*, 15:6098.

2. Koonz, *Mothers in the Fatherland*, 67.

3. Cited in Pine, *Nazi Family Policy, 1933–1945*, 15.

4. Bleuel, *Das saubere Reich*, 84.

5. Robert C. Reimer, "Turning Inward: An Analysis of Helmut Käutner's *Auf Wiedersehen, Franziska; Romanze in Moll; and Unter den Brücken,*" in Reimer, *Cultural History through a National Socialist Lens,* 218. See also Drewniak, *Der deutsche Film,* 239–49.

6. Barthes, *Mythologies*, 84–87.

7. Marcuse, *Technology, War, and Fascism*, 84–85.

8. Theweleit, *Male Fantasies*, 2:252.

9. Code text reprinted in Walsh, *Women's Film and Female Experience, 1940–1950,* 207.

10. Ibid., 215.

11. Basinger, *Woman's View*, 328.

12. Schulte-Sasse, *Entertaining the Third Reich*, 283.

13. Ibid., 285.

14. Walsh, *Women's Film and Female Experience, 1940–1950*, 215.

15. Panofsky, "Was will das Publikum auf der Leinwand sehen?" n.p.

16. Picker, *Hitlers Tischgespräche im Führerhauptquartier, 1941–1942*, 293.

17. Rentschler, *Ministry of Illusion*, 218. See also Marc Silberman's reading of the film in *German Cinema: Texts in Context*, 81–96.

18. David Bathrick, "Modern Writ German: State of the Art as Art of the Nazi State," in Reimer, *Cultural History through a National Socialist Lens*, 6.

19. Frank Maraun memo to Reichsfilmintendant on June 3, 1942, regarding "Liste der deutschen Filmspielleiter," BArch R 109 II/18.

20. Quoted in Fox, *Filming Women in the Third Reich*, 201. Fox suggests that Goebbels condemned the film, a conclusion that is not supported by this citation or any other available evidence.

21. "*Romanze in Moll* Bild- und Text-Information" (Berlin: Vertriebs-Presse-Referat der Deutschen Filmvertriebs-Gesellschaft, n.d.), Bundesarchiv-Filmarchiv file 13986.

22. Ibid.

23. Ibid.

24. Ibid.

25. Ilse Urbach, *Das Reich*, July 18, 1943. Review included in Bundesarchiv-Filmarchiv file on *Romanze in Moll*, file 13986.

26. Ibid.

27. Felix Henseleit, review of *Romanze in Moll, Film-Kurier*, June 28, 1943, n.p.

28. Mary-Elizabeth O'Brien, for example, claims that the entire genre of films to which *Es war eine rauschende Ballnacht* belonged, a genre she terms "the historical musical," served to "emphasize marriage as the fulfillment of individual desire and the means to social harmony." O'Brien, *Nazi Cinema as Enchantment*, 47–48.

29. Quoted in SD report of July 17, 1941, in Boberach, *Meldungen aus dem Reich*, 7:2526.

30. Ibid.

31. "Warum nicht mal ein Ehescheidungsfilm?" *Film-Kurier*, January 23, 1939, n.p.

32. In one recorded instance, Hitler intervened when the Navy Supreme Command refused to grant permission to an officer to marry his pregnant girlfriend, based upon the German navy's traditional "unwritten rules" against premarital sexuality. Henry Picker recorded Hitler's response thus: "National Socialism . . . rejects the 'unwritten laws' passionately because they are based on a completely false morality; they are the views of an outdated, past world." Picker, *Hitlers Tischgespräche im Führerhauptquartier*, 341.

33. Goebbels, diary entry for June 9, 1936, *Tagebücher, 1924–1945*, 3:958.

34. Diary entry for December 10, 1937, ibid., 3:1166.

35. On the new divorce law, see Stephenson, *Women in Nazi Society*, 42–44.

36. Ibid., 43.

37. Song text transcribed from the program to *Umwege zum Glück* (*Das Programm von heute* 402), Bundesarchiv-Filmarchiv file 17516.

38. Herzberg, "Umwege zum Glück," n.p.

39. Ibid.

40. Ibid.

41. Betz, "Lil Dagover sah wieder wunderschön aus," n.p.

42. Picker, *Hitlers Tischgespräche im Führerhauptquartier,* 341.

43. Ibid., 164.

44. In December 1930 Heydrich pulled a woman out of the water after a boating accident, and a relationship ensued, although Heydrich was already engaged to someone else. The adultery case was taken to military court, and Heydrich was dismissed as chief lieutenant of the marines, but he later transferred to the SS. Bleuel, *Das saubere Reich,* 8.

45. At the time of filming, Harlan was still married to his second wife, Hilde Körber, with whom he had two children. Noack, *Veit Harlan: Des Teufels Regisseur,* 133.

46. Ibid., 23.

47. Goebbels had been planning to divorce his wife, Magda, and leave for Japan with Lida Baarova until Hitler intervened and had Baarova deported in order to avoid any public relations damage. On Magda and Joseph Goebbels's responses to *Die Reise nach Tilsit,* see Söderbaum, *Nichts bleibt immer so,* 134.

48. Boberach, *Meldungen aus dem Reich,* 4:1024.

49. Koonz, *Mothers in the Fatherland,* 399.

50. Reprinted in Pine, *Nazi Family Policy, 1933–1945,* 39.

51. Ibid., 180.

52. Zantop, "*Kolonie and Heimat,*" 4.

53. Ibid, 8.

54. Žižek, *Fright of Real Tears,* 44.

55. See, for example, Fox, *Filming Women in the Third Reich,* 205.

56. Kappelhoff, "Politik der Gefühle," 247–65.

57. Žižek, *Fright of Real Tears,* 48–49.

58. Susan Sontag, *Illness as a Metaphor,* 20–25.

59. Doane, *Desire to Desire,* 119.

60. Harlan, *Im Schatten meiner Filme,* 164.

61. Quoted in Burghardt, *Die deutsche Frau,* 8.

62. Bleuel, *Das saubere Reich,* 203. See also Grunberger, *12-Year Reich,* 249.

63. Marcuse, *Technology, War, and Fascism,* 163.

64. Noël Carroll, "The Moral Ecology of Melodrama: The Family Plot and *Magnificent Obsession,*" in Landy, *Imitations of Life,* 186.

65. Rentschler, *Ministry of Illusion,* 58.

66. Horkheimer, "Authoritarianism and the Family," 388.

67. See Welch, *Propaganda and the German Cinema,* 134–38; and Witte, "Der barocke Faschist," 155–58.

68. See Schatz, "The Family Melodrama," in *Imitations of Life,* 148–167; and Laura Mulvey, "Social Hieroglyphics: Reflections on Two Films by Douglas Sirk," in *Fetishism and Curiosity,* 29–39.

69. Carroll, "Moral Ecology of Melodrama," in Landy, *Imitations of Life,* 189.

70. Ibid.

71. Harlan, *Im Schatten meiner Filme,* 35.

72. Reprinted in Mertens, *Die großen deutschen Filme,* n.p.

73. Hans Spielhofer, "Filme des Monats: *Der Herrscher,*" *Der deutsche Film* 1, no.10 (1937): 301.

74. Schatz, "Family Melodrama," 161.

75. *Der Herrscher*'s dialogue echoed Hitler's own pronouncements in his table talk when he commented: "[Man] is the slave of his thoughts: his work and his duties dominate him, and there may come moments in which he really has to say to himself: to hell with my wife, to hell with my child! . . . If I had a wife, she would always come to me with the reproach: 'And me?' . . . I don't believe that a man like me will ever marry . . . There is nothing better in the world than to train a young thing: a girl 18, 20 years old is as bendable as wax." Picker, *Hitlers Tischgespräche*, 164.

76. Mulvey, "Melodrama In and Out of the Home," 82.

77. Ibid., 89.

78. H. N., "Höhen und Tiefen," n.p.

79. BArch R 55 / 20210a, 537–39.

80. On the mother-son oedipal obsessions of Hollywood melodrama, see Mulvey, *Fetishism and Curiosity*, 29–39.

81. Lowry, *Pathos und Politik*, 102. For an analysis of *Die goldene Stadt* in English, see Lowry, "Ideology and Excess in Nazi Melodrama."

82. See, for example, Ascheid, *Hitler's Heroines*, 3; and Fox, *Filming Women in the Third Reich*, 46.

83. "Die Frau um Vierzig," n.p.

84. Schatz, "Family Melodrama," 158.

85. *Liebe geht seltsame Wege* (*The Ways of Love Are Strange*, 1937) is another of these narratives, although the rival is the protagonist's niece rather than her daughter.

86. Osten, "Film-Kinder/Kinder im Film," 5–7.

87. Goebbels, diary entry of February 16, 1940, *Die Tagebücher von Joseph Goebbels*, 4:44.

88. Memo from Reichsfilmintendant to Reichsminister, December 6, 1944, BArch R 109 II/14.

89. Memo from Frowein to Reichsminister regarding script to *Schwester Jette*, November 24, 1944, BArch R 109 II/14.

90. Doane, *Desire to Desire*, 83.

91. On classical Hollywood and single mothering, see Christian Viviani, "Who Is Without Sin? The Maternal Melodrama in American Film, 1930–39," in Gledhill, *Home Is Where the Heart Is*, 83–99.

92. Third Reich films that feature incidences of premarital or extramarital pregnancy include the following: *Was wissen denn Männer* (*What Do Men Know*, 1933), *Das Recht auf Liebe* (*The Right to Love*, 1934), *Mutter und Kind* (*Mother and Child*, 1934), *Das Mädchen vom Moorhof* (*The Girl of the Moors*, 1935), *Der grüne Domino* (*The Green Domino*, 1935), *Junges Blut* (*Young Blood*, 1936), *Straßenmusik* (*Street Music*, 1936), *Eine Frau ohne Bedeutung* (*A Woman of No Importance*, 1936), *Nachtwache im Paradies* (*Night Watch in Paradise*, 1937), *Die vier Gesellen* (*The Four Companions*, 1938), *Heimat* (*Homeland*, 1938), *Liebelei und Liebe* (*Flirtation and Love*, 1938), *Jugend* (*Youth*, 1938), *Die Frau am Scheidewege* (*The Woman at the Crossroads*, 1938), *Drei Väter um Anna* (*Three Fathers for Anna*, 1939), *Hurra, ich bin Papa* (*Hurrah, I'm a Papa!* 1939), *Eine Frau wie Du* (*A Woman Like You*, 1939), *Die barmherzige Lüge* (*The Merciful Lie*, 1939), *Anton der Letzte* (*Anthony the Last*, 1939), *Befreite Hände* (*Freed Hands*, 1939), *Mutterliebe* (*Mother Love*,

1939), *Zwischen Hamburg und Haiti* (*Between Hamburg and Haiti*, 1940), *Herzensfreud-Herzensleid* (*Heart's Joy and Heart's Pain*, 1940), *Kora Terry* (1940), *Ein Leben lang* (*A Life Long*, 1940), *Aufruhr im Damenstift* (*Revolt in the Old Ladies' Home*, 1941), *Auf Wiedersehen, Franziska* (*Farewell, Franziska*, 1941), *Unser kleiner Junge* (*Our Little Boy*, 1941), *Die goldene Stadt* (*The Golden City*, 1942), *Altes Herz wird wieder jung* (*Old Heart Becomes Young Again*, 1943), *Liebe, Leidenschaft und Leid* (*Love, Passion, and Pain*, 1943), and *Opfergang* (*Sacrifice*, 1944).

93. Oertel, *Filmspiegel*, 125.

94. Bleuel, *Das saubere Reich*, 199.

95. Quoted in Pine, *Nazi Family Policy*, 38.

96. Bleuel, *Das saubere Reich*, 63.

97. On the conformity of Sierck/Sirk's early films with Nazi ideology, see Hake, *Popular Cinema of the Third Reich*, 107–27; Koch, "From Detlef Sierck to Douglas Sirk"; and Trumpener, "Puerto Rico Fever."

98. RMVP minutes of December 29, 1939, BArch R 55 / 20001a.

99. Riegler, "Schöne Mädchen–kluge Frauen," n.p.

100. Maraun, "Besuch bei Ucicky," 150.

101. Žižek, *Sublime Object of Ideology*, 82.

102. "Rund um die Produktion 1939/40," 42.

103. Fox, *Filming Women in the Third Reich*, 51.

104. As Lisa Pine notes, Nazi propaganda in favor of large families was not supported by material benefits. The housing situation for families with many children was often disastrous, a situation the regime did little to alleviate. Pine, *Nazi Family Policy*, 112–16.

105. In 1933 there were 1.9 children per married couple; in 1939 there were 1.3. In 1939, 20.6 percent of married couples were childless. Statistics cited in Ulrike Eichborn, "Ehestanddarlehen. Dem Mann den Arbeitsplatz, der Frau Heim, Herd und Kinder," in Kuhn, *Frauenleben im NS-Alltag*, 61.

106. Koonz, *Mothers in the Fatherland*, 186–87.

107. Pine, *Nazi Family Policy*, 46.

108. SD report of July 22, 1940, in Boberach, *Meldungen aus dem Reich*, 5:1411.

109. Marcuse, *Technology, War and Fascism*, 162.

110. SD report of April 20, 1942, in Boberach, *Meldungen aus dem Reich*, 10:3648.

111. SD report of May 13, 1943, in ibid., 13:5239–40.

112. SD report of September 9, 1940, in ibid., 4:1554. For a further example of the rural populace's resistance to eroticism in Nazi entertainment, see SD report of December 2, 1940, in ibid., 6:1825.

113. Goebbels, diary entry of November 27, 1935, *Tagebücher, 1924–1945*, 3:914.

114. RMVP minutes from April 1, 1940, BArch R 55 / 20001c.

115. The Propaganda Ministry minutes added that the new policy did not reflect any prudery on the part of the regime: "The Minister points out that this regulation has nothing to do with 'hypocritical moralizing' [*Moralin*]." RMVP minutes from December 5, 1940, BArch R 55 / 20001c.

116. Moeller, *Filmminister*, 231.

117. Letter to Frauenschaftsleiterin Elsa Muhr-Jordan, BArch R 55 / 20210. (Name of letter writer withheld due to privacy regulations.)

118. Letter to Reichsminister Goebbels, October 26, 1942, BArch R 55 / 20210. The film to which the letter writer refers was a short film that showed excerpts from an operetta titled *Die blaue Maske* (*The Blue Mask*).

119. Memo from K. Frowein to Reichsminister, October 1944, BArch R 109 II/13.

120. Ibid.

Chapter 4. Home Front Melodrama

1. *Mrs. Miniver* was shown in closed screenings to German military personnel and filmmakers and was called an "exemplary model for the treatment of contemporary subjects" by an RMVP official. Memo to Reichsminister, December 2, 1944, BArch R 109 II/14.

2. Memo from Dr. Bacmeister to Goebbels regarding "Auslandspresseecho zu dem Film *Opfergang*," January 13, 1945, BArch R 109 II/15.

3. I quote the name "Müller" from Heinrich Himmler's comments on the subject of Germany's polygamous future, in which he emphasized that women's feelings should not be considered if the Germans were to maximize reproduction: "Who will ask in 300 or 500 years if a Miss Müller or Schulze was unhappy?" Bleuel, *Das saubere Reich,* 203.

4. Of the 50 million worldwide deaths caused by World War II, fewer than a half million were Americans, or less than 1percent. O'Brien and Parson, *Home Front War,* 3.

5. Reprinted in Walsh, *Women's Film and Female Experience,* 206–16.

6. Combs and Combs, *Film Propaganda and American Politics,* 53.

7. One overview of Hollywood film propaganda counts 278 World War II–related films released in the United States between December 1941 and August 1945, with almost all set during the war itself and referencing contemporary events. Fyne, *Hollywood Propaganda of World War II,* 220–27. According to my own count of Nazi World War II films, there were approximately 19 feature films released between September 1939 and May 1945 that directly referenced the war; of these, 9 are action or battle films and 10 could be considered home front films.

8. Quoted in Koppes and Black, "What to Show the World," 280.

9. According to opinion polls, as late as December 1942 more than 35percent of Americans still felt that they did not understand the reasons for the war and their nation's goals in fighting it. Winkler, *Politics of Propaganda,* 54.

10. Handel, *Hollywood Looks at Its Audience,* 99–101. Handel himself was skeptical about these conclusions, but there is little doubt that American producers viewed women as the majority of their audiences.

11. The interview was conducted during the war by the Institute of Psychoanalysis in Chicago and is quoted by Handel in *Hollywood Looks at Its Audience,* 123. Handel came to similar conclusions in his own research, which was supplied to producers during the war.

12. Ibid., 122–23.

13. Ibid., 149.

14. Ibid., 121–22.

15. Ibid., 121.

16. Quoted in Bird and Rubenstein, *Design for Victory,* 32.

17. Quoted in Maureen Honey, "Remembering Rosie: Advertising Images of Women in World War II," in O'Brien and Parson, *Home Front War,* 87.

18. Polan, *Power and Paranoia*, 6.

19. Rupp also underlines the fact that the financial and status benefits of factory work were much higher in the United States, whereas the pay in German munitions factories remained low and the status barrier that separated workers from the middle classes was not overcome through German propaganda appeals to the *Volksgemeinschaft*. Rupp, *Mobilizing Women for War*, 174.

20. The number of women working in Germany increased only 1 percent during World War II, but the increase in the United States was 32 percent. Rupp, *Mobilizing Women for War*, 75. In 1939, 36 percent of German women worked outside the home, while in the United States in 1940, the figure was 27.9 percent. Ibid., 185–86.

21. Renov, *Hollywood's Wartime Woman*, 100.

22. A 1944 War Manpower Commission poster, for example, featured the image of a woman in overalls with a man standing behind her and the caption: "I'm Proud . . . my husband *wants* me to do my part." Bird and Rubenstein, *Design for Victory*, 87.

23. For example, an advertisement for the Monsanto corporation that connected the war effort with promises of postwar domesticity read: "'There'll come a day . . . when a lot of the good new things of peacetime will become important to Rosie the Housewife.'" Cited in Honey, "Remembering Rosie," 98.

24. Advertisement from the Sheldon-Claire company. Bird and Rubenstein, *Design for Victory*, 85.

25. Blum, *V Was for Victory*, 67.

26. Maureen Honey has also argued that the family was presented in wartime advertising as "the key element of endangered American beliefs" and housewives became "symbolic of the besieged nation." Honey, "Remembering Rosie," 99.

27. Emphasis in the original text. Cited by Blum, *V Was for Victory*, 28.

28. Polan, *Power and Paranoia*, 83.

29. Ibid., 155.

30. Code reprinted in Walsh, *Women's Film and Female Experience*, 215.

31. Mulvey, "Melodrama In and Out of the Home," 82.

32. Noël Carroll, "The Moral Ecology of Melodrama: The Family Plot and *Magnificent Obsession*," in Landy, *Imitations of Life*, 190.

33. Sontag, "Fascinating Fascism," 87.

34. Thorp, *America at the Movies*, 5–8.

35. Quoted in Glancy, *When Hollywood Loved Britain*, 155.

36. Rudy Behlmer, ed., *Memo from David O. Selznick* (New York: Viking Press, 1972), 334–35.

37. Clayton R. Koppes, "Hollywood and the Politics of Representation: Women, Workers, and African Americans in World War II Movies," in O'Brien and Parson, *Home Front War*, 28.

38. Doane, *Desire to Desire*, 80.

39. Koppes, "Hollywood and the Politics of Representation," 30.

40. As Michael Renov has noted, *Since You Went Away* must be viewed in the context of the race riots of 1943 and the paranoid response to the new wartime social mobility of African Americans, including many black domestics who left household service to take higher-paying jobs in war industries. Renov, *Hollywood's Wartime Women*, 25.

41. Doane, *Desire to Desire*, 79.

42. O'Brien, *Nazi Cinema as Enchantment*, 130.

43. Witte, *Lachende Erben*, 177.

44. Goebbels added with a note of frustration, "We could never show that in Berlin." This is misleading, since Berlin revue shows did regularly feature nude dances, but persistent complaints from more conservative and rural spectators prevented Goebbels from taking advantage of the weapon of female nudity to the full extent that he desired. Diary entry of October 19, 1940, *Tagebücher, 1924–1945,* 4:1488.

45. Bleuel, *Das saubere Reich*, 143.

46. RMVP minutes of April 22, 1940, BArch R 55 / 20001c.

47. Letter to Goebbels dated October 26, 1942, BArch R 55 / 20210.

48. Ibid.

49. The SD report for May 5, 1941, for example, registers discontent among rural women: "Above all it is from farming women, who are heavily burdened by the absence of their husbands, the drafting of male laborers, the bad weather and so forth, that one can often hear: 'If only it was over!,' 'If only the damn war were finally over!' etc." Boberach, *Meldungen aus dem Reich,* 7:2260–61. See also the report for June 23, 1941, regarding reactions to the outbreak of war on the Soviet front. Ibid., 7:2428.

50. This term is used often in the reports, such as in the following report regarding the newsreels of early June, 1940: "Characteristically, multiple reports . . . have determined that these newsreels have not entirely satisfied the average audience's lust for the sensational." Boberach, *Meldungen aus dem Reich,* 4:1266.

51. Ibid.

52. Ibid., 4:1180.

53. Ibid., 4:1122.

54. Ibid., 8:3389.

55. Ibid., 8:3386–89.

56. Bleuel, *Das saubere Reich*, 96.

57. Bundesarchiv-Filmarchiv file 1048.

58. Quoted in Stephenson, *Women in Nazi Society*, 67.

59. Hake, *Popular Cinema of the Third Reich*, 62.

60. See chapter 2 for a discussion of Peter von Werder's objections to the Nazi cinema in his 1941 book, *Trugbild und Wirklichkeit*.

61. This sequence is described in Robert C. Reimer, "Turning Inward: An Analysis of Helmut Käutner's *Auf Wiedersehen, Franziska; Romanze in Moll;* and *Unter den Brücken,*" in Reimer, *Cultural History through a National Socialist Lens,* 220–21.

62. Beyer, *Die Gesichter der Ufa,* 260.

63. Schlüpmann, "Faschistische Trugbilder weiblicher Autonomie," 63–64.

64. Goebbels noted in his diary on June 16, 1941, in regard to the upcoming offensive: "The Führer estimates the campaign [will last] for 4 months, I estimate fewer. Bolshevism will collapse like a house of cards." Goebbels, *Tagebücher, 1924–1945,* 4:1601.

65. The SD reported on January 22, 1942: "Many soldiers report home, with no inhibitions, virtually hair-raising stories about the strains they have to endure, such as cold, bad food, clothing, etc. . . . Because of this situation, the effectiveness of the press and

broadcasting, particularly the film newsreels, is seriously reduced." Boberach, *Meldungen aus dem Reich*, 9:3196–97.

66. Food shortages were serious enough to cause a perilous decline in worker productivity and class tensions in 1942. While the wealthy could easily obtain scarce foodstuffs on the black market, factory workers with ten-hour shifts complained of constant feelings of hunger, and the SD reported that workers regularly fainted on the job. The same week that *Die große Liebe* opened, on June 18, 1942, the SD noted a growing apathy about the war caused by the more pressing concerns about nutrition. Boberach, *Meldungen aus dem Reich*, 10:3837–38.

67. On the trivialization of war in Nazi films, see Siegfried Kracauer, "Propaganda and the Nazi War Film," in *From Caligari to Hitler*, 274–331.

68. Hippler, "Der Tod in Kunst und Film," 7–8. In an earlier issue of the same journal, a reviewer criticized *Auf Wiedersehen, Franziska* for not keeping its distance from death and allowing Buck to die in close-up. Spielhofer, "Filme des Monats," *Der deutsche Film* 5, no. 11/12 (1941): 236.

69. Boberach, *Meldungen aus dem Reich*, 10:3759.

70. Ibid.

71. The RMVP estimated that *Die große Liebe* was the fourth most successful film produced between 1941 and 1944, while *Der große König* ranked twenty-first. Memo from Bacmeister to Reichsminister of December 6, 1944, BArch R 109 II/14.

72. Lowry, *Pathos und Politik*, 176.

73. Mulvey, "Melodrama In and Out of the Home," 82.

74. See Mary-Elizabeth O'Brien on the self-reflexive treatment of cinema spectatorship in the film in *Nazi Cinema as Enchantment*, 140–44.

75. The fact that war is presented in *Die große Liebe* as stimulating for private passions has also been noted by Mary-Elizabeth O'Brien. Ibid., 136.

76. Quoted in Michael Töteberg, "Dann werden tausend Märchen wahr," in Töteberg, *Die große Liebe*, 14.

77. Sontag, "Fascinating Fascism," 73–105. See also Friedländer, *Reflections of Nazism*, 74–78; and Peucker, "The Fascist Choreography," 280.

78. Foucault, *History of Sexuality*, 1:156.

79. Lowry, *Pathos und Politik*, 154. See also Brockmann, "*Die große Liebe*," 176–79.

80. Schulte-Sasse, *Entertaining the Third Reich*, 299.

81. Mulvey, *Fetishism and Curiosity*, 29.

82. Schulte-Sasse, *Entertaining the Third Reich*, 293–94.

83. Fox, *Filming Women in the Third Reich*, 94.

84. Quoted in Albrecht, *Nationalsozialistische Filmpolitik*, 258.

85. Boberach, *Meldungen aus dem Reich*, 10:3900–3901.

86. SD report for February 20, 1941, ibid., 6:2029.

87. Ibid., 9:3202.

88. Although the lower classes had a higher birthrate, they were viewed with suspicion by the regime and were not considered as "racially valuable" as the middle classes; in fact, lower-class families with a large number of children were sometimes labeled as "asocials." Pine, *Nazi Family Policy*, 117–46.

89. Boberach, *Meldungen aus dem Reich,* 9:3200.

90. Ibid., 14:5339–40. Emphasis in the original text.

91. Ibid., 4:1024. The last film listed was actually titled *Männer müssen so sein* (1939).

92. Minutes of meeting on February 17, 1940, BArch R 55 / 20001b.

93. In the RMVP's list of the most successful films of 1941 to 1944, *Immensee* ranked third after *Die goldene Stadt* and *Der weisse Traum*. BArch R 109 II/14.

94. Söderbaum, *Nichts bleibt immer so,* 183.

95. "Die Frau um Vierzig," n.p. See chapter 3 for a further discussion of this topic.

96. O'Brien, *Nazi Cinema as Enchantment,* 150.

97. SD report of July 22, 1944, in Boberach, *Meldungen aus dem Reich,* 17:6653.

98. SD report of March 23, 1944, in ibid., 16:6439.

99. Ibid., 16:6439–40.

100. Ibid., 16:6443.

Epilogue. Postwar Melodrama

1. Boberach, *Meldungen aus dem Reich,* 16:6488.

2. Ibid., 16:6481–82.

3. Ibid., 16:6488.

4. Memo from Reichsfilmintendant Bacmeister to Reichsminister Goebbels dated January 13, 1945, re: "Auslandspresseecho zu dem Film *Opfergang,*" BArch R 109 II/15.

5. Ibid.

6. A further Swiss reviewer cited in the same document criticized *Opfergang*'s ambiguities and excesses and compared it unfavorably to the film's more orderly literary source: "The characteristic elements of Binding's work, of his people, figures, moods and actions—namely the measured quality, the clarity and unambiguousness—have been turned into the opposite, into a bombast of feelings." BArch R 109 II/15.

7. Herzog, *Sex after Fascism,* 103.

8. I have borrowed the term "reprivatization" from Herzog. See ibid., 104.

9. Von Moltke, *No Place Like Home,* 118.

10. Ibid., 128.

11. Söderbaum, *Nichts bleibt immer so,* 247.

12. Herzog, *Sex after Fascism,* 185.

13. Joshua Feinstein argues that the type of the "resolute male comrade" typifies the DEFA film of the 1950s, when female protagonists were more marginal. Feinstein, *Triumph of the Ordinary,* 132.

14. According to Marc Silberman's historiography, the first true DEFA "woman's film," *Lots Weib* (*Lot's Woman*), was not released until 1965. Silberman, *German Cinema: Texts in Context,* 164.

15. Baer, *Dismantling the Dream Factory,* 42.

16. Feinstein, *Triumph of the Ordinary,* 87.

17. Herzog, *Sex after Fascism,* 196.

18. For a more extended discussion of *Roman einer jungen Ehe* and *Frauenschicksale,* see Pinkert, *Film and Memory in East Germany,* 106–27.

19. Herzog, *Sex after Fascism,* 202.

20. Ibid., 156–60.

Bibliography

Bundesarchiv (German Federal Archives) Files

BArch R 55 / 20001a
BArch R 55 / 20001b
BArch R 55 / 20001c
BArch R 55 / 20001e
BArch R 55 / 20210
BArch R 55 / 20210a
BArch R 109 II/13
BArch R 109 II/14
BArch R 109 II/15
BArch R 109 II/16
BArch R 109 II/18

Bundesarchiv-Filmarchiv (German Federal Film Archive) Files

Auf Wiedersehen, Franziska, File 1048
Romanze in Moll, File 13986
Umwege zum Glück, File 17516

Books and Articles

Adorno, Theodor. *Problems of Moral Philosophy.* Stanford, CA: Stanford University Press, 2000.

Albrecht, Gerd. *Nationalsozialistische Filmpolitik: Eine soziologische Untersuchung über die Spielfilme des Dritten Reiches.* Stuttgart: Ferdinand Enke, 1969.

Altenloh, Emilie. *Zur Soziologie des Kino: Die Kino-Unternehmung und die sozialen Schichten ihrer Besucher.* Leipzig: Spamersche Buchdruckerei, 1914.

Ascheid, Antje. *Hitler's Heroines: Stardom and Womanhood in Nazi Cinema.* Philadelphia: Temple University Press, 2003.

Aschheim, Steven. *The Nietzsche Legacy in Germany, 1890–1990.* Berkeley: University of California Press, 1992.

Baer, Hester. *Dismantling the Dream Factory: Gender, German Cinema, and the Postwar Quest for a New Film Language.* New York: Berghahn, 2009.

Barthes, Roland. *Mythologies.* Translated by Annette Lavers. New York: Hill and Wang, 1972.

Basinger, Jeanine. *A Woman's View: How Hollywood Spoke to Women, 1930–1960.* London: Chatto and Windus, 1993.

Bauer, Alfred. *Deutscher Spielfilm-Almanach, 1929–1950.* Munich: C. Winterberg, 1976.

Bechdolf, Ute. *Wunsch-Bilder? Frauen im nationalsozialistischen Unterhaltungsfilm.* Tübingen: Tübinger Vereinigung für Volkskunde, 1992.

Ben-Ghiat, Ruth. *Fascist Modernities: Italy, 1922–1945.* Berkeley: University of California Press, 2001.

Betz, Hans-Walther. "*Der Postmeister.*" *Der Film: die illustrierte Wochenschrift.* May 11, 1940, n.p.

———. "Lil Dagover sah wieder wunderschön aus: *Umwege zum Glück.*" *Der Film: die illustrierte Wochenschrift.* May 27, 1939. n.p.

Beyer, Friedemann. *Die Gesichter der Ufa: Starportraits einer Epoche.* Munich: Wilhelm Heyne Verlag, 1992.

Bird, William L., and Harry R. Rubenstein. *Design for Victory: World War II Posters on the American Home Front.* New York: Princeton Architectural Press, 1998.

Bleuel, Hans Peter. *Das saubere Reich: Theorie und Praxis des sittlichen Lebens im Dritten Reich.* Bern/Munich: Scherz Verlag, 1972.

Blum, John Morton. *V Was for Victory: Politics and American Culture during World War II.* New York: Harcourt Brace Jovanovich, 1976.

Boberach, Heinz, ed. *Meldungen aus dem Reich: Die geheimen Lageberichte des Sicherheitsdienstes der SS, 1938–1945.* 17 vols. Herrsching: Pawlak Verlag, 1984.

Bordwell, David, Janet Staiger, and Kristin Thompson. *The Classical Hollywood Cinema: Film Style and Mode of Production to 1960.* New York: Columbia University Press, 1985.

Bratton, Jacky, Jim Cook, and Christine Gledhill, eds. *Melodrama: Stage, Picture, Screen.* London: British Film Institute, 1994.

Brockmann, Stephen. "*Die große Liebe* (1942) or Love and War." In *A Critical History of German Film.* 167–79. Rochester, NY: Camden House, 2010.

Brooks, Peter. *The Melodramatic Imagination: Balzac, Henry James, Melodrama, and the Mode of Excess.* New Haven, CT: Yale University Press, 1995.

Bruns, Jana F. *Nazi Cinema's New Women.* New York: Cambridge University Press, 2009.

Burghardt, Christina. *Die deutsche Frau: Küchenmagd–Zuchtsau–Leibeigene im III. Reich: Geschichte oder Gegenwart?* Münster: Verlag Frauenpolitik, 1978.

Carter, Erica. *Dietrich's Ghosts: The Sublime and the Beautiful in Third Reich Film.* London: British Film Institute, 2004.

Cavell, Stanley. *Contesting Tears: The Hollywood Melodrama of the Unknown Woman.* Chicago: University of Chicago Press, 1996.

Cawelti, John G. "The Evolution of the Social Melodrama." In Landy, *Imitations of Life,* 33–49.

Combs, James E., and Sara T. Combs. *Film Propaganda and American Politics.* New York: Garland, 1994.

Cook, Pam. "Melodrama and the Woman's Picture." In Landy, *Imitations of Life,* 248–62.

Davidson, John E. "Cleavage: Sex in the Total Cinema of the Third Reich." *New German Critique* 98 (Summer 2006): 101–33.

Doane, Mary Ann. *The Desire to Desire: The Woman's Film of the 1940s.* Bloomington: Indiana University Press, 1987.

Drewniak, Boguslaw. *Der deutsche Film, 1938–1945: Ein Gesamtüberblick.* Düsseldorf: Droste, 1987.

Eder, Jens. "Das Populäre Kino im Krieg. NS-Film und Hollywoodkino—Massenunterhaltung und Mobilmachung." In *Mediale Mobilmachung I: Das Dritte Reich und der Film,* edited by Harro Segeberg. 379–416. Munich: Wilhelm Fink Verlag, 2004.

Elsaesser, Thomas. "Tales of Sound and Fury: Observations on the Family Melodrama." In *Movies and Methods.* Vol. 2. 165–89, edited by Bill Nichols. Berkeley: University of California Press, 1985.

Falasca-Zamponi, Simonetta. *Fascist Spectacle: The Aesthetics of Power in Mussolini's Italy.* Berkeley: University of California Press, 1997.

Feinstein, Joshua. *The Triumph of the Ordinary: Depictions of Daily Life in the East German Cinema, 1949–1989.* Chapel Hill: University of North Carolina Press, 2002.

Foucault, Michel. *The History of Sexuality.* 2 vols. Translated by Robert Hurley. New York: Vintage, 1990. ·

Fox, Jo. *Filming Women in the Third Reich.* New York: Berg, 2000.

"Frauenarbeit im Filmspiegel." *Film-Kurier.* August 7, 1942. n.p.

"Frauenberufe auf der Leinwand." *Film-Kurier.* July 11, 1944. n.p.

"Frauenberufe, die der Film schuf." *Film-Kurier.* January 8, 1937. n.p.

"Die Frau um Vierzig: Anmerkungen zur Thematik einiger neuer Filme." *Film-Kurier.* April 15, 1943. n.p.

Friedländer, Saul. *Reflections of Nazism: An Essay on Kitsch and Death.* Translated by. Thomas Weyr. New York: Harper and Row, 1984.

Friedrichsmeyer, Sara, Sara Lennox, and Susanne Zantop, eds. *The Imperialist Imagination: German Colonialism and Its Legacy.* Ann Arbor: University of Michigan Press, 1998.

Frye, Northrop. *Anatomy of Criticism: Four Essays.* Princeton, NJ: Princeton University Press, 2000.

Fyne, Robert. *The Hollywood Propaganda of World War II.* Metuchen, NJ: Scarecrow Press, 1994.

Glancy, H. Mark. *When Hollywood Loved Britain: The Hollywood "British" Film, 1939–45.* Manchester, UK: Manchester University Press, 1999.

Gledhill, Christine. *Home Is Where the Heart Is: Studies in Melodrama and the Woman's Film.* London: British Film Institute, 1987.

Goebbels, Joseph. "Dr. Goebbels's Speech at the Kaiserhof on March 28, 1933." Translated by Lance W. Garmer. In *German Essays on Film,* edited by Richard McCormick and Alison Guenther-Pal. 153–58. New York: Continuum, 2004.

———. *Tagebücher, 1924–1945.* Edited by Ralf Georg Reuth. 5 vols. Munich: Piper, 1992.

———. *Die Tagebücher von Joseph Goebbels: Sämtliche Fragmente.* 15 vols. Edited by Elke Fröhlich. München: KG Saur, 1987.

Gordon, Terri. "Fascism and the Female Form: Performance Art in the Third Reich." *Journal of the History of Sexuality* 11, no. 1/2 (2002): 164–200.

Griffin, Roger. *A Fascist Century.* Edited by Matthew Feldman. New York: Palgrave Macmillan, 2008.

———. *Modernism and Fascism: The Sense of a Beginning under Mussolini and Hitler.*
Basingstoke: Palgrave Macmillan, 2007.

Grunberger, Richard. *The 12-Year Reich: A Social History of Nazi Germany, 1933–1945.*
New York: Da Capo, 1995.

Hake, Sabine. *Popular Cinema of the Third Reich.* Austin: University of Texas Press, 2001.

———. "The Melodramatic Imagination of Detlef Sierck: *Final Chord* and Its Resonances."
Screen 38, no. 2 (1997): 129–48.

Handel, Leo. *Hollywood Looks at Its Audience.* Urbana: University of Illinois Press, 1950.

Harlan, Veit. *Im Schatten meiner Filme.* Gütersloh: Sigbert Mohn, 1966.

Haskell, Molly. *From Reverence to Rape: The Treatment of Women in the Movies.* Chicago:
University of Chicago, 1987.

Heinzlmeier, Adolf, Jürgen Menningen, and Berndt Schulz. *Die großen Stars des deutschen
Kinos.* Herford: Busse + Seewald, 1985.

Herf, Jeffrey. *Reactionary Modernism: Technology, Culture, and Politics in Weimar and the
Third Reich.* Cambridge: Cambridge University Press, 1984.

Herzberg, Georg. "*Das Mädchen Irene.*" *Film-Kurier.* October 10, 1936. n.p.

———. "*Umwege zum Glück.*" *Film-Kurier.* May 25, 1939. n.p.

"Das Herz der Königin—ein Film ohne Schwenkaufnahmen." *Der deutsche Film* 4, no.
9 (1940): 175.

Herzog, Dagmar. *Sex after Fascism: Memory and Morality in Twentieth-Century Germany.*
Princeton, NJ: Princeton University Press, 2005.

———. *Sexuality in Europe: A Twentieth-Century History.* New York: Cambridge University Press, 2011.

———, ed. *Sexuality and German Fascism.* New York: Berghahn, 2005.

Hippler, Fritz. "Der Tod in Kunst und Film." *Der deutsche Film* 6, no. 6/7 (1941/1942): 6–8.

Hobsch, Manfred. *Film im "Dritten Reich": Alle Deutsche Spielfilme von 1933 bis 1945.* 6 vols.
Berlin: Schwarzkopf and Schwarzkopf, 2010.

"Hofball in Leinigen: Von der Filmarbeit zu 'Heimat.'" *Filmwelt.* March 25, 1938. n.p.

Horkheimer, Max. "Authoritarianism and the Family." In *The Family: Its Function and
Destiny,* edited by Ruth Nanda Anshen. 359–74. New York: Harper and Brothers, 1959.

Huth, Albert. "Filme für die Berufsauswahl." *Film-Kurier.* July 11, 1940. n.p.

Jameson, Fredric. *The Political Unconscious: Narrative as a Socially Symbolic Act.* Ithaca,
NY: Cornell University Press, 1981.

Kappelhoff, Hermann. "Politik der Gefühle: Veit Harlan, Detlef Sierck und das Melodrama
des NS-Kinos." *Mediale Mobilmachung I: Das Dritte Reich und der Film,* edited by Harro
Segeberg. 247–65. Munich: Wilhelm Fink Verlag, 2004.

Klaus, Ulrich J. *Deutsche Tonfilme: Filmlexikon der abendfüllenden deutschen und
deutschsprachigen Tonfilme nach ihren deutschen Uraufführungen.* 14 vols. Berlin: Klaus
Verlag, 1988–2004.

Koch, Gertrud. "From Detlef Sierck to Douglas Sirk." Translated by Gerd Gemünden.
Film Criticism 3, no. 2/3 (1999):14–32.

Koch, Heinrich, and Heinrich Braune. *Von deutscher Filmkunst: Gehalt und Gestalt.* Berlin:
Scherping, 1943.

Koepnick, Lutz. *The Dark Mirror: German Cinema between Hitler and Hollywood.* Berkeley: University of California Press, 2002.

Koonz, Claudia. *Mothers in the Fatherland: Women, the Family and Nazi Politics.* New York: St. Martin's, 1995.

Koppes, Clayton R., and Gregory D. Black. *Hollywood Goes to War: How Politics, Profits, and Propaganda Shaped World War II Movies.* Berkeley: University of California Press, 1990.

———. "What to Show the World: The Office of War Information and Hollywood, 1942–1945." In *The Studio System,* edited by Janet Staiger. 279–97. New Brunswick, NJ: Rutgers University Press, 1995.

Kracauer, Siegfried. *From Caligari to Hitler: A Psychological History of the German Film.* Princeton, NJ: Princeton University Press, 1947.

———. *The Mass Ornament: Weimar Essays.* Translated by Thomas Y. Levin. Cambridge: Harvard University Press, 2005.

Kreimeier, Klaus. *The Ufa Story: A History of Germany's Greatest Film Company, 1918–1945.* New York: Hill and Wang, 1996.

Krutnik, Frank. *In a Lonely Street: Film Noir, Genre, Masculinity.* New York: Routledge, 1991.

Kuhn, Annette, ed. *Frauenleben im NS-Alltag.* Pfaffenweiler: Centaurus-Verlagsgesellschaft, 1994.

Landy, Marcia. *Fascism in Film: The Italian Commercial Cinema, 1931–1943.* Princeton, NJ: Princeton University Press, 1986.

———, ed. *Imitations of Life: A Reader on Film and Television Melodrama.* Detroit: Wayne State University Press, 1981.

Lang, Robert. *American Film Melodrama: Griffith, Vidor, Minnelli.* Princeton, NJ: Princeton University Press, 1989.

Leiser, Erwin. *Nazi Cinema.* Translated by Gertrud Mander and David Wilson. New York: Collier, 1975.

Lowry, Stephen. "Ideology and Excess in Nazi Melodrama: *The Golden City.*" *New German Critique* 74 (Spring-Summer 1998): 125–49.

———. *Pathos und Politik: Ideologie in Spielfilmen des Nationalsozialismus.* Tübingen: Niemeyer, 1991.

Maraun, Frank. "Besuch bei Ucicky, Der Regisseur von *Mutterliebe.*" *Der deutsche Film* 4, no. 8 (1940): 148–151.

———. "Der Held: Die Gemeinschaft." *Der deutsche Film* 4, no. 2 (1939): 49–52.

———. "Meisterklasse aus Wien. Der beste Film des Monats: '*Mutterliebe.*'" *Der deutsche Film* 4 no. 7 (1940): 141–42.

Marcuse, Herbert. *Technology, War and Fascism: Collected Papers of Herbert Marcuse.* Vol. 1. Edited by Douglas Kellner. New York: Routledge, 1998.

Mertens, Eberhard, ed. *Die großen deutschen Filme: Ausgewählte Filmprogramme, 1930–1945.* Hildesheim: Olms Presse, 1995.

Modleski, Tania. *Loving with a Vengeance: Mass-Produced Fantasies for Women.* London: Methuen, 1985.

Moeller, Felix. *Der Filmminister: Goebbels und der Film im Dritten Reich.* Berlin: Henschel, 1998.

Mosse, George. *The Fascist Revolution: Toward a General Theory of Fascism.* New York: Howard Fertig, 2000.

———. *Nationalism and Sexuality: Middle-Class Morality and Sexual Norms in Modern Europe*. Madison: University of Wisconsin Press, 1985.

Mulvey, Laura. *Fetishism and Curiosity*. Bloomington: Indiana University Press, 1996.

———. "Melodrama In and Out of the Home." In *High Theory/Low Culture: Analysing Popular Television and Film*, edited by Colin MacCabe. 80–100. Manchester, UK: Manchester University Press, 1986.

———. *Visual and Other Pleasures*. New York: Palgrave Macmillan, 2009.

N., H. "Höhen und Tiefen: Anmerkungen zu dem Film *Der Herrscher.*" *Filmwelt*. January 3, 1937. n.p.

Neale, Stephen. *Genre and Hollywood*. New York: Routledge, 2000.

Nietzsche, Friedrich. *Beyond Good and Evil*. Edited by Rolf-Peter Horstmann and Judity Norman. Cambridge: Cambridge University Press, 2002.

Noack, Frank. *Veit Harlan: Des Teufels Regisseur*. Munich: Belleville, 2000.

O'Brien, Kenneth Paul, and Lynn Hudson Parsons, eds. *The Home Front War: World War II and American Society*. Westport, CT: Greenwood Press, 1995.

O'Brien, Mary-Elizabeth. *Nazi Cinema as Enchantment: The Politics of Entertainment in the Third Reich*. Rochester, NY: Camden House, 2004.

Oertel, Rudolf. *Filmspiegel: Ein Brevier aus der Welt des Films*. Vienna: Wilhelm Frick Verlag, 1941.

Offermanns, Ernst. *Internationalität und europäischer Hegemonialanspruch des Spielfilms der NS-Zeit*. Hamburg: Dr. Kovac, 2001.

Ossowska, Maria. *Bourgeois Morality*. New York: Routledge and Kegan Paul, 1986.

Osten, Peter. "Film-Kinder/Kinder im Film." *Der deutsche Film* 6, no. 10 (1942): 5–7.

Panofsky, Walter. "Was will das Publikum auf der Leinwand sehen? Die einen wünschen lebenswahre Stoffe, die anderen den Sprung aus der Alltäglichkeit." *Film-Kurier*. September 24, 1938. n.p.

Payne, Stanley G. "Fascism as 'Generic' Concept." In *The Fascism Reader*, edited by Aristotle Kallis. 82–88. New York: Routledge, 2003.

Petro, Patrice. *Joyless Streets: Women and Melodramatic Representation in Weimar Germany*. Princeton, NJ: Princeton University Press, 1989.

———. "Nazi Cinema at the Intersection of the Classical and the Popular." *New German Critique* 74 (Spring/Summer 1998): 41–55.

Peucker, Brigitte. "The Fascist Choreography: Riefenstahl's Tableaux." *Modernism/Modernity* 11, no. 2 (2004): 279–97.

Picker, Henry. *Hitlers Tischgespräche im Führerhauptquartier, 1941–1942*. Edited by Percy Ernst Schramm. Stuttgart: Seewald, 1965.

Pine, Lisa. *Nazi Family Policy, 1933–1945*. New York: Berg, 1997.

Pinkert, Anke. *Film and Memory in East Germany*. Bloomington: Indiana University Press, 2008.

Pohl, Astrid. *TränenReiche BürgerTräume: Wunsch und Wirklichkeit in deutschsprachigen Filmmelodramen, 1933–1945*. Munich: Edition Text + Kritik, 2010.

Polan, Dana. *Power and Paranoia: History, Narrative, and the American Cinema, 1940–1950*. New York: Columbia University Press, 1986.

Prommer, Elizabeth. *Kinobesuch im Lebenslauf: eine historische und medienbiographische Studie*. Konstanz: UVK Medien, 1999.

Reich, Wilhelm. *The Mass Psychology of Fascism.* Translated by Vincent R. Carfagno. New York: Farrar, Straus, and Giroux, 1970.

———. *Sex-Pol: Essays, 1929–1934.* Edited by Lee Baxandall. New York: Random House, 1972.

Reimer, Robert C., ed. *Cultural History through a National Socialist Lens: Essays on the Cinema of the Third Reich.* Rochester, NY: Camden House, 2000.

Renov, Michael. *Hollywood's Wartime Woman: Representation and Ideology.* Ann Arbor: UMI Research Press, 1988.

Rentschler, Eric. *The Ministry of Illusion: Nazi Cinema and Its Afterlife.* Cambridge, MA: Harvard University Press, 1996.

Riegler, Th. "Schöne Mädchen–kluge Frauen." *Filmwelt.* January 19, 1940. n.p.

Rodowick, David N. "Madness, Authority, and Ideology in the Domestic Melodrama of the 1950s." In Landy, *Imitations of Life,* 237–47.

"Rund um die Produktion 1939/40." *Der deutsche Film* 4, no. 2 (1939): 38–49.

Rupp, Leila. *Mobilizing Women for War: German and American Propaganda, 1939–1945.* Princeton, NJ: Princeton University Press, 1978.

Sander, A. U. *Jugend und Film.* Berlin: Zentralverlag der NSDAP, 1944.

Schatz, Thomas. "The Family Melodrama." In Landy, *Imitations of Life,* 148–67.

Schilling, Heinz-Dieter. *Schwule und Faschismus.* Berlin: Elefanten Press, 1983.

Schlüpmann, Heide. "Faschistische Trugbilder weiblicher Autonomie." *Frauen und Film* 44/45 (October 1988): 44–66.

"Schluß mit 'Gretchen'!" *Film-Kurier.* October 13, 1937. n.p.

Schmokel, Wolfe W. *Dream of Empire: German Colonialism, 1919–1945.* Westport, CT: Greenwood Press, 1980.

Schulte-Sasse, Linda. *Entertaining the Third Reich: Illusions of Wholeness in Nazi Cinema.* Durham, NC: Duke University Press, 1996.

Schwark, Günther. *"Der Postmeister."* *Film-Kurier.* May 11, 1940. n.p.

"Sie weint im Kino." *Der Film: die illustrierte Wochenschrift.* June 17, 1933. n.p.

Silberman, Marc. *German Cinema: Texts in Context.* Detroit: Wayne State University Press, 1995.

Singer, Ben. *Melodrama and Modernity: Early Sensational Cinema and Its Contexts.* New York: Columbia University Press, 2001.

Slane, Andrea. *A Not So Foreign Affair: Fascism, Sexuality, and the Cultural Rhetoric of American Democracy.* Durham, NC: Duke University Press, 2001.

Söderbaum, Kristina. *Nichts bleibt immer so: Rückblenden auf ein Leben vor und hinter der Kamera.* Bayreuth: Hestia, 1983.

Sontag, Susan. "Fascinating Fascism." In *Under the Sign of Saturn.* 73–105. New York: Farrar, Straus and Giroux, 1980.

———. *Illness as a Metaphor.* New York: Farrar, Straus and Giroux, 1977.

Spielhofer, Hans. "Filme des Monats." *Der deutsche Film* 1, no.10 (1937): 301–2.

———. "Filme des Monats." *Der deutsche Film* 5, no. 4 (1940): 74–75.

———. "Filme des Monats." *Der deutsche Film* 5, no. 11/12 (1941): 235–237.

Stacey, Jackie. *Star Gazing: Hollywood Cinema and Female Spectatorship.* London: Routledge, 1994.

Stahr, Gerhard. *Volksgemeinschaft vor der Leinwand? Der Nationalsozialistische Film und sein Publikum.* Berlin: Verlag Hans Theissen, 2001.

Stephenson, Jill. *Women in Nazi Society*. New York: Harper and Row, 1975.

Studlar, Gaylyn. *In the Realm of Pleasure: Von Sternberg, Dietrich, and the Masochistic Aesthetic*. Urbana: University of Illinois Press, 1988.

"Die Tänzerin im Atelier." *Der deutsche Film* 1, no. 4 (1936): 120–121.

Theweleit, Klaus. *Male Fantasies*. 2 vols. Translated by Stephen Conway, Erica Carter, and Chris Turner. Minneapolis: University of Minnesota Press, 1987 and 1989.

Thompson, Kristin. "The Concept of Cinematic Excess." In *Narrative, Apparatus, Ideology*, edited by Philip Rosen. 130–42. New York: Columbia University Press, 1986.

Thorp, Margaret Farrand. *America at the Movies*. New Haven, CT: Yale University Press, 1939.

Timm, Annette F. *The Politics of Fertility in Twentieth-Century Berlin*. Cambridge: Cambridge University Press, 2010.

Töteberg, Michael, ed. *Die große Liebe*. Ufa-Magazin no. 18. Berlin: Deutsches Historisches Museum, 1992.

Trumpener, Katie. "Puerto Rico Fever: Douglas Sirk, *La Habanera*, and the Epistemology of Exoticism." In *"Neue Welt"/"Dritte Welt": Interkulturelle Beziehungen Deutschlands zu Lateinamerika und der Karibik*, edited by Sigrid Bauschinger and Susan Cocalis. 115–40. Tübingen: Francke Verlag, 1994.

Volz, Robert. "Der beste Film des Monats: *Der Postmeister*." *Der deutsche Film* 4, no. 12 (1940): 240–41.

———. *Hans Söhnker: Zwischen Bühne und Film*. Berlin: Hermann Wendt, 1938.

Von Moltke, Johannes. *No Place Like Home: Locations of Heimat in German Cinema*. Berkeley: University of California Press, 2005.

Walsh, Andrea S. *Women's Film and Female Experience, 1940–1950*. New York: Praeger, 1984.

"Warum nicht mal ein Ehescheidungsfilm?" *Film-Kurier*. January 23, 1939. n.p.

Welch, David. *Propaganda and the German Cinema, 1933–1945*. London: I. B. Tauris, 2001.

Welch, David, and Roel Vande Winkel. *Cinema and the Swastika: The International Expansion of Third Reich Cinema*. New York: Palgrave Macmillan, 2007.

Werder, Peter von. *Trugbild und Wirklichkeit: Aufgaben des Films im Umbruch der Zeit*. Leipzig: Schwarzhäupter, 1943.

Williams, Linda. "Melodrama Revised." *Refiguring American Film Genres*, edited by Nick Browne. 42–88. Berkeley: University of California Press, 1998.

Winkler, Allan M. *The Politics of Propaganda: The Office of War Information*. New Haven, CT: Yale University Press, 1978.

Witte, Karsten. "Ästhetische Opposition? Käutners Filme im Faschismus." *Sammlung Jahrbuch für antifaschistische Literatur und Kunst* 2 (1979): 113–23.

———. "Der barocke Faschist: Veit Harlan und seine Filme." In *Intellektuelle im Bann des Nationalsozialismus*, edited by Karl Corino. Hamburg: Hoffmann und Campe, 1980.

———. *Lachende Erben, Toller Tag: Filmkomödie im Dritten Reich*. Berlin: Vorwerk, 1995.

———. "Visual Pleasure Inhibited: Aspects of the German Revue Film." *New German Critique* 24–25 (Fall/Winter 1981–82): 238–63.

Zantop, Susanne. "*Kolonie* and *Heimat*: Race, Gender, and Postcolonial Amnesia in Veit Harlan's *Opfergang* (1944)." *Women in German Yearbook* 17 (January 2002): 1–13

Žižek, Slavoj. *The Fright of Real Tears: Krzysztof Kieślowski between Theory and Post-Theory*. London: BFI, 1999.

———. *The Sublime Object of Ideology*. New York: Verso, 1989.

Index

LAURA HEINS is an assistant professor of media studies and Germanic languages and literatures at the University of Virginia.

The University of Illinois Press
is a founding member of the
Association of American University Presses.

Composed in 10.5/13 Minion Pro
by Lisa Connery
at the University of Illinois Press
Manufactured by Thomson-Shore, Inc.

University of Illinois Press
1325 South Oak Street
Champaign, IL 61820-6903
www.press.uillinois.edu